PROJECT
MANAGEMENT
ESSENTIALS

PROJECT MANAGEMENT
ESSENTIALS

DEEPAK PANDEY

A QUINTESSENTIAL GUIDE TO A
SUCCESSFUL PROJECT

TATE PUBLISHING & *Enterprises*

Published by Tate Publishing & Enterprises, LLC
127 E. Trade Center Terrace | Mustang, Oklahoma 73064 USA
1.888.361.9473 | www.tatepublishing.com

Tate Publishing is committed to excellence in the publishing industry. The company reflects the philosophy established by the founders, based on Psalm 68:11,
"The Lord gave the word and great was the company of those who published it."

Book design copyright © 2011 by Tate Publishing, LLC. All rights reserved.
Cover design by Kellie Southerland
Interior design by Lindsay B. Behrens

Published in the United States of America
ISBN: 978-1-61777-786-8
1. Business & Economics / Project Managemen
2. Business & Economics / General
11.06.08

TABLE OF CONTENTS

SECTION 5: PROJECT MONITORING AND CONTROL

INTRODUCTION

Project management is an integral and essential part of any project, irrespective of the size of it or the domain or industry it belongs to.

I have substantial experience in software development and project management, and my perception about the project management role has changed significantly as I gained experience in managing various medium to large-scale projects and programs. Before I started my career as a project manager, I always had this impression that a project manager's job is very easy. He gets all the privileges and power and does not have much work to do. When I handled my first project as a project manager, I realized it is not such an easy role after all. As I gained more experience in this role, I faced so many complex situations and scenarios, and it made me realize how complex this role can get. There are so many factors that can impact the success of a project and unless a project manager is equipped with all the necessary skills and resources to handle the project, chances of project success are very less. Every project I handled gave me a new experience, something new to learn from.

As I was going through my project management experience and learning from it, I was documenting the necessary articles and topics which would help any project manager in managing a project. This collection over a period of time has helped me in handling and executing new projects that came along. I wanted to share this information with all those professionals who would like to take up project management as their career option. It would also help the professionals who are already in this field and learning from their day-to-day experiences. I hope that the information available in this book will be of use to all those who are interested in this field of project management.

Since most of my projects have been software development and maintenance projects, the topics covered in this book specifically address the needs of managing such projects but can be referred to for any kind of project management activities as some of the project management concepts are generic, irrespective of which field the project belongs to.

Below, I have provided an overview of how the book has been structured and the key topics covered in this book. This book has five major sections, namely Project Management Overview, Project Scope and Risk Management, Approach to Project Execution Methodology, Estimation Process, and Project Monitoring and Control.

The project management[1] overview section provides an overview on what project management is all about and what kind of skills a project manager should be equipped with to be able to manage the project successfully. The topics include discussions on the technical side of the project management and the necessity of soft skills that a project manager should have. Soft skills refer to personality traits, social graces, facility with language, personal habits, friendliness, and optimism that mark people to varying degrees. Soft skills complement hard skills, which are the technical requirements of a job. From project management perspective some of these soft skills are the ability to visualize the big picture, the ability to sense the potential risks in project, the ability to communicate effectively with the team and stakeholders, and so on. Generally, the soft skills are neglected by the managers, and these become the major bottleneck in the success of the project. This section also discusses the importance and need of leadership qualities and how these qualities can help in building an effective team for the purpose.

Project Scope and Risk Management section focuses more on the technical aspect of the project management. One of the chapters in this section talks about the importance of scope definition and how it is neglected in general by most of the managers. If there is clarity in the scope of the project requirement, it can solve various other issues that may arise otherwise. Risk management is another area of discussion as part of this section. Managing risks is another important aspect of project management that is generally ignored by project managers. The chapter on risk management discusses what risk management all about is and how it can aid in the success of a project if done diligently. This chapter also discusses tools such as FMEA that can be used for effective risk management in a project.

The section named Approach to Project Execution Methodology is dedicated to general project execution methodology that can be used for executing a software project. This section has chapters that discuss different life cycle models, execution methodology, and details of each of the life cycle steps. The V-process model is described in detail for providing better understanding on the life cycle model, with each life cycle step having an entry and exit criteria and the expected deliverables. It is understood that a generalized life cycle model cannot be used for all kinds of projects. Sometimes, the life cycle model has to be modified or changed, depending on the nature of the project being handled. But, in general, there are certain common features that all the project life cycle models have. These are discussed in various chapters under this section.

The fourth section is on Estimation Processes and covers topics such as estimation process and estimation methods. Estimation has always been a difficult task for any project manager and providing a good estimate for a project takes good understanding of project management processes, experience in managing different types of project, ability to assess the complexity involved, risks associated with the project, and many other factors. There are various tools and techniques that may help a project manager to achieve proper estimates for a given project or task. Beyond tools and techniques, I feel that the project manager should also have soft skills to manage this task effectively. Estimation is a combination of the scientific concepts and the soft skills put together, or rather can be called as a combination of art and science.

The last section is project monitoring and control. This section has discussions on various topics covered under different chapters. The chapters stress key project management areas, such as project timetable, meeting management, status reporting and project tracking, change management, quality management, communication plan, and so on. These are the essential elements of project management, and a project manager should be aware of these concepts to be able to manage a project and program successfully.

The appendix covers details on certain key concepts, such as Work Breakdown Structure (WBS), the difference between a project and a product life cycle, and the concept of a stakeholder. It also describes samples of WBS, project activities based on Capability Maturity Model (CMM) standards, and project management plan which could be referred by the reader.

In this book, I have used my experiences from one of the projects that I managed as examples. This project was about developing a workflow management system for retail pharmacies. The customer for which this product was developed is one of the leading healthcare service providers in the Healthcare market. Let's call this project as "Project X-1". Customer had an existing product and they wanted to redevelop it using the latest technology. There was a need to add new features to the product as well. My company was chosen as a vendor to work on this project along with customer team. I was designated as the project manager from my company to handle this project. It was estimated that the project will need around 10,000 person days of effort to get completed. The project was done in two locations, first one being at customer site in the USA, called "onsite" and the second one at vendor location (India), called "offshore". For me to manage this project, I had to look at the big picture and divide the whole project in multiple phases so that I could manage the project well and as per customer expectations. I followed a basic V-process model for the overall project. In some places, we used iterative process model as well. For the convenience, the project was divided into 2 major phases. The "Phase-I" comprised of high level tasks such as process definition, project planning, estimation, requirement gathering and reverse engineering. The "Phase-II" consisted of Design, Development, Testing, Implementation, and Documentation. I am hopeful that these examples will give a better perspective on the concepts that are being discussed.

In the end, I would like to thank my friends and colleagues who have encouraged me and helped me in coming out with this book. Last but not the least, my family has been very supportive of me in taking this endeavor, and I am very grateful to them. I am hoping that this book will be good help to all those who aspire to become successful project managers.

A PERSPECTIVE—PROJECT MANAGEMENT
IS ART AS WELL AS SCIENCE

The Key to Project Management Success

Change is inevitable. Organizations are changing at a swift pace in order to satisfy their customers and stay competitive. It is in this environment that project managers must learn to thrive, delivering products and services that meet the needs of the organization and assist businesses in delivering value to their customers. It is not surprising that project management has become a profession in its own right. Project managers who can be successful in this environment are sought after.

An important question is: "What makes a project successful?" Some would define a successful project simply as satisfying the client's requirements within a schedule and budget limitations and without putting additional burden on the project team. But the focus should be on adding value to the business. Therefore, simply meeting requirements does not define project success. Delivering business value does.

So, a project manager should be able to deliver business value. Project management is art as well as science. Understanding processes, tools, and techniques—the science of project management—and knowing when and how to apply them is only part of the answer. Another important ingredient for successful project delivery is soft skills, the art of project management, and the timeless principles of working within an organization. Soft skills help to define the business value, clarify the vision, determine requirements, provide direction, build teams, resolve issues, and mitigate risk. Without the appropriate soft skills, the likelihood of project success diminishes.

The Technical Skills

Project managers must have the appropriate processes, tools, and techniques at their fingertips to deliver projects. A key resource for many project managers today is the Project Management Institute's Project Management Body of Knowledge (PMBOK), which provides the manager with generally accepted processes, tools, and techniques of project management. It groups the processes into nine knowledge areas, detailing what is required by the process (the inputs), what occurs during the process, and the deliverables of the process (the outputs). This document provides the project manager with a guide; however, the appropriate implementation of these processes, tools, and techniques on a given project is a challenge. Understanding the best way to do this comes with experience.

Of course, there are many other project management practices available in today's market. For example, the Unified Software Development Process outlines a process that is use-case driven, architecture-centric, iterative, and incremental. It requires a different approach to project management in order to be successful, while still using some of the PMBOK practices. The same holds true for Critical Chain Project Management. While this form of managing projects has a different focus than the Critical Path—the Critical Chain—it does not replace all of the processes and tools of the PMBOK.

It is true that the technical skills associated with these project management practices can be learned from a textbook and can be further developed through experience. But if a project manager focuses on these practices and lacks the broader soft skills, success will be very difficult. Consider the following scenarios: Managing scope without being able to clearly communicate its meaning can cause unclear deliverables and requirements and an unsatisfied client. Developing a project plan without engaging the team appropriately can lead team members to ignore the plan and create mistrust within the team. Managing communications without the ability to develop an open and honest exchange of ideas within the project team can result in issues not being raised until they reach a critical point. Making use of all these processes and procedures without displaying leadership in delivering the end product or service will result in failure.

Even with a mastery of technical skills and a keen sense of when to use them, a project will rarely be completely successful without the appropriate application of soft skills.

The Important Aspect—Soft Skills

A clear understanding of the soft skills[2] of project management and the ability to apply these skills effectively throughout the life cycle of a project will enhance the success of a project exponentially. Few projects fail because the Gantt chart/PERT is wrong, the roles and responsibilities are not mapped out in a matrix, or the cost charts were off. More often, they fail because of a project manager's inability to communicate effectively, work within the organization's culture, motivate the project team, manage stakeholder expectations, understand the business objectives, solve problems effectively, and make clear and knowledgeable decisions. These are the skills that take time to acquire through experience, coaching, and mentoring. The following soft skills are crucial for successful project management:

Communication—This is, quite simply, the most important soft skill for all project managers. They must have the ability to convey complex ideas easily, clearly articulate what must be accomplished, keep the team moving toward a common goal, provide an environment that allows team members to communicate openly and honestly, admit their own mistakes without losing respect, negotiate, listen, facilitate, and so on.

Organizational effectiveness—Project managers must understand the corporate culture, the organizational dynamics, and the individuals they are dealing with. With this understanding, they will be able to obtain resources more effectively, gain support, and build a stronger foundation for the effort.

Leadership—Project managers must lead. They frequently do not have direct authority, yet they do have direct responsibility. They must build authority through appropriate leadership and provide direction to the team to achieve the common goal. They should lead by example.

Problem solving and decision making—Resolving issues or solving problems is a large portion of what a project manager does every day. Each phase of a project has its own unique set of problems. Without strong problem-solving skills, the sheer volume of issues that are a normal part of every project will soon overwhelm the project manager.

Team building—Building a team in the business environment is a challenge. Frequently, a project team is made up of borrowed resources from other functional areas within the organization and usually also has vendors and suppliers. Creating a team atmosphere where the team believes that they are all in this together is a critical component to project success.

Flexibility and creativity—Having a proven framework to guide a project manager is not enough. The project manager must also adapt to the needs of the project. Since every project is unique, each may require different components, templates, tools, and techniques.

Trustworthiness—The project manager must have the trust of all of the stakeholders involved in the project. Simply meeting deadlines is just one facet of this. A project manager must also be able to convey that he can be trusted day-to-day to do what is right at the right time to keep the project successful and the client satisfied.

The list above does not include everything. Time management, stress management, customer relationship management, expectation management, coaching, mentoring, and sound business judgment are other soft skills that a project manager needs to be successful.

KNOWING THE BIG PICTURE

A project manager operates within the context of the enterprise itself, and so a full understanding of the organization and how it works is essential. The figure below represents the "big picture" of an enterprise, the system in which daily activity takes place. The outer box represents the unwritten and written rules by which the organization operates. The middle box is where the leadership of the organization puts into practice these rules of operation. The core is where project management and other capabilities within the organization are developed and supported.

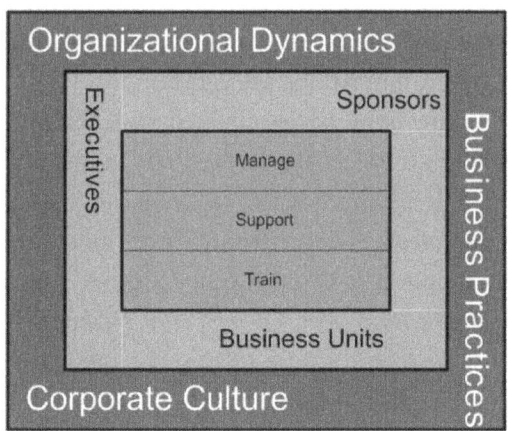

Rules To Know

When undertaking a project, it is necessary to understand both the business's corporate culture and its organizational dynamics. A project manager must work within these unwritten guidelines to be successful. An understanding of culture and organizational dynamics will state who to work with and how to work with them. It is also clear that both culture and organizational dynamics change over time. These changes come about through the restructuring, downsizing, or flattening of the organization itself or by changes in key players, all of which could impact a project. These two aspects, corporate culture and organizational dynamics, influence the business practices within the enterprise.

Understanding business practices, the written guidelines, is the third key element. Each business unit within an organization may run projects differently. In some cases, business practices might be missing, the participants expecting magic to deliver successful projects or in other situations, a clearly defined project management methodology might already be in place. If a project manager is not prepared to deal with this diversity and insists on sticking to a given method, no matter how strong the method is, the project could suffer. If a client, sponsor, user, or project team is expecting some information in a particular format and receives it in a different, less familiar form, confusion will be the end result.

When an organization has no defined business practice around project delivery, the project manager is not only challenged with managing the project effort but also must educate the various stakeholders in their roles and responsibilities of project management. This is a tall order and can be a roadblock to success. Skillful and constant communication with all involved is critical. The project manager may use processes, tools, and techniques that they know are successful—but must remain flexible.

Building Relationships at the Executive Level

One would think that with the many volumes written about project management, executives, sponsors, and business units involved in a project would understand their roles and responsibilities. But instead, there is often a gap between what is required from these audiences and what actually occurs. Working within the organization to educate these groups of people is a key responsibility of the project manager. It is essential to guide the sponsor in building the relationships necessary for project success and to identify key individuals and groups within the organization that must be appropriately engaged. Without these relationships, a project can get stuck in political bogs; it can be difficult to have changes approved and get sign-off on key phases, slowing the progress of a project to a crawl. On the other hand, strong relationships can help a project move forward. Building these relationships before the project gets started will ensure appropriate involvement, maintaining these relationships during the project will ensure successful implementation, and closing out the project on good terms with all involved will ensure that future efforts will have a greater likelihood of success. Communication and organizational effectiveness are critical skills to apply where the support for the project at the organizational level exists.

Sustain for Continued Success

The core of the organization is where project managers actually manage the work that produces the end product or service for which the project was chartered in the first place. This is where the technical or hard skills come into play. This is also where you will find the actual management and support of the project itself, including any training required for team members. The project manager who believes they have all of the answers is doomed to fail. Understanding the natural laws of growth and development makes for successful project managers. The continued development of both the art and the science of project management will serve to strengthen the individual project manager. The organization itself must support the continued development of individuals within the organization to sustain their ability to provide themselves with skilled individuals in the art and science of project management.

Business Is Complex—Grow With It

Today's work environment is inherently complex, constantly changing, and focused on customer satisfaction. Today's project manager must be able to apply the processes, tools, and techniques of the trade efficiently and effectively to be successful. However, without mastering the timeless soft skills to supplement the hard skills, few project managers will succeed. This combination of art and science[3], while taking into consideration the broader organizational context, will lead to successful projects.

As an example, in "Project X-1", most of the "Phase-I" activities were done onsite. Since, this was the first time we were working for this customer, it was very important for me to decide on a team of resources who were matured enough to work along with the customer team, had the business knowledge as well as technical knowledge, had the ability to understand customer processes and make it adaptable with our internal processes, could get to know all the stakeholders and their expectations, could establish good first impressions with the customer, and most importantly of all, could decide on the feasibility of the project and our ability as a vendor to complete the project as per the stakeholder's expectations. I chose a team which consisted of Architect, Business Analyst, Quality Analyst, and Project Lead. This team was successfully able to understand the goal of the project and stakeholder's expectations, established a good relationship with the executives and stakeholder's from customer side and accordingly developed the project execution strategy for the project.

We were able to understand different groups from the customer side that were involved in this project. The Product Management Group was responsible for understanding their customer needs and providing a product roadmap and requirements accordingly. The Research & Development Group was responsible for the construction and testing of the product and took inputs from the Product Management Group. Infrastructure Group was responsible for taking care of hardware and software needs of the project. The Implementation Group was responsible for implementing the developed product at end customer site. The Customer Operations Group was involved in providing support to the end customer once the product was deployed at their site. All these different groups were managed by a Senior Management Group that was responsible for providing budget for the project, management of various teams, tracking the progress of the project, and approvals. The Senior Management Group members along with the leads from all other group along with the vendor team were the Stakeholders in this project.

CHAPTER 2
KEY STEPS TO PROJECT MANAGEMENT

This chapter focuses on the key steps that are involved in project management[4]. As the project starts, following are the key steps that a project manager should start working on.

THE SPECIFICATION

A specification is the definition of the project: a statement of the problem, not the solution. Normally, the specification contains errors, ambiguities, misunderstandings, and insufficient details, which could lead to a project failure eventually. There should be a written definition of what is required and by when, and this must be agreed upon by all involved. There are no shortcuts to this. If project manager fails to spend the time initially, it will cost him far more later on.

The agreement upon a written specification has several benefits as mentioned below:

- The clarity will reveal misunderstandings.

- The completeness will remove contradictory assumptions.

- The rigor of the analysis will expose technical and practical details.
- The agreement forces all concerned to actually read and think about the details.

The work on the specification can be seen as the first stage of quality assurance since the problems are being looked for and countered in the very foundation of the project. From this perspective, the creation of the specification clearly promotes a large investment of time. From a purely defensive point of view, the agreed specification also provides protection against any second thoughts, or new ideas, halfway through the project. Once the project is underway, changes cost time and money. The existence of a clearly agreed upon specification enables resistance to change or gives provision to charge for such changes. Further, there is also a tendency to forget what was originally thought, and the agreed upon specifications act as proof of work being done as instructed.

The places to look for errors in a specification are:
- The global context: Don't focus too narrowly on the work of one team, and fail to consider how it fits into the larger picture.

- The interfaces: Between your team and both its customers and suppliers, there are interfaces. At these points, something gets transferred. Exactly what, how, and when should be discussed and agreed upon from the very beginning. Never assume a common understanding, because you will be wrong. Define and agree on your interfaces, and maintain a friendly contact throughout the project.

- Timescales: Don't underestimate the time involved for work. Realistic dates must be added. The detail should include a precise understanding of the extent of any intermediate stages of the task, particularly those that have to be delivered.

- External dependencies: Your work may depend upon that of others. Make this very clear so that these people, too, will receive warning of your needs. Highlight the impact that these problems would have upon your project, so that everyone is quite clear about their importance.

- Resources: The specification should identify the materials, equipment, and manpower needed for the project. The agreement should include a commitment by the managers to allocate or to fund them.

This seems to make the specification sound like a long document. It should not be. Each of the above could be a simple subheading, followed by either bullet points or a table. The intent is not to write a brochure; it is simply to state the definition of the project in a clear, concise, and unambiguous manner.

Of course, the specification may change. If circumstances or simply the understanding changes, the specification will be out of date. The specifications should not be considered as cast in stone but rather as a display board where everyone involved can see the current, common understanding of the project. If the contents are changed, everyone must know about the change.

PROVIDING STRUCTURE

Having decided what the specification intends, the project manager's next problem is to decide what he and his team actually need to do and how to do it. A manager has to provide some form of framework both to plan and to communicate what needs to be done. Without a structure, the work is a series of unrelated tasks that provide little sense of achievement and no feeling of advancement. If the team has no grasp of how individual tasks fit together toward an understood goal, then the work will seem pointless, and they will feel only frustration. To take the planning forward, therefore, the manager needs to turn the specification into a complete set of tasks with a linking structure. Fortunately, these two requirements are met at the same time, since the derivation of such a structure is the simplest method of arriving at a list of tasks.

Work Breakdown Structure

Once the manager has a clear understanding of the project, it is then described as a set of simpler separate *activities*. If any of these are still too complex to be easily organized, it has to be broken down into another level of simpler descriptions, and so on, until everything can be managed. Thus, one complex project is organized as a set of simple tasks that together achieve the desired result. Each level of the project can be understood as the amalgamation of a few simply described smaller units.

For example, as part of "Phase-I" of "Project X-1", the project management activities consisted of major activities such as preparation of project charter and project plan, scope and requirement definition of the project, strategies and process definitions for architecture and design, development, testing, configuration management, communication and so on, and project estimation. Each of these high level activities was further broken down into smaller activities which were easily manageable. For example, "the scope and requirement of the project" activity had sub activities such as creating a "wish-list" of product features; surveying to get views of the end customer on the product feature; creating a navigable user interface prototype; prioritizing requirements; and detailing requirements, reverse-engineering exercises, reviews, and sign-offs. Hence, a major activity was broken down into simpler ones, which made estimation, task allocation, and tracking of these activities easy.

In planning any project, some simple steps should be followed: if an item is too complicated to manage, it becomes a list of simpler items. People call this producing a work breakdown structure to make it sound more formal and impressive. Without following this formal approach, it is difficult to remember all the niggling little details. With this procedure, the details are simply displayed on the final lists. One common fault is to produce too much detail at the initial planning stage. The level of detail should be such that there is a clear instruction for the person who will actually do the work and to have a reasonable estimate for the total time/effort involved. The former is needed to allocate the task, and the latter is required to finish the planning.

Task Allocation

The next stage is a little complicated. The tasks have to be allocated to different team members in the team and, at the same time, these tasks need to be ordered so that they are performed in a sensible sequence. Task allocation is not simply a case of handing out the various tasks on the final lists to the team members available; it is far subtler than that. The allocation of tasks should thus be seen as a means of increasing the skills and experience of the team involved—when the project is done, the team should have gained. In simple terms, it should be considered what each member of the team is capable of, and sufficient complexity of tasks should be allocated to match that. The tasks allocated are not the ones on the final lists, but they are adapted to better suit the needs of team's development. Tasks are molded to fit people, which is far more effective than the other way around. Sometimes tasks can be grouped and allocated together. For instance, some tasks that are seemingly independent may benefit from being done together since they use common ideas, information, and talents.

As in "Project X-1", once the major activity, "the scope and requirement of the project", was broken down into simpler tasks, it was easy to allocate the tasks to the team members. For example, the business analysts at onsite were allocated the task of creating the "wish-list", developing the detailed requirements, and reviews. The offshore team developed the user interface prototype and reverse engineering document.

The ordering of the tasks is really quite simple, although sketching a sequence diagram helps to think it through. PERT charts are the accepted outcome, but sketches will suffice. Getting the details exactly right, however, can be a long and painful process, and often, it may not fetch desired results. The degree to which the future can be predicted is limited, so, too, should be the detail of the planning. Broad outlines should be drawn by which the progress can be monitored, and sufficient details should be available to assign each task when it needs to be started.

Estimation

At the initial planning stage, the main objective is to get a realistic estimate of the time involved in the project. This must be established not only to assist higher management with their planning, but also to protect the team from being expected to do the impossible. The most important technique for achieving this is known as *estimation*.

Estimating schedules is extremely difficult, but it is helped by two approaches: Make estimates of the simple tasks at the bottom of the work breakdown structure and look for the longest path through the sequence diagram and use the experience from previous projects to improve estimating skills. The corollary to this is that the records of all projects should be kept in an easily accessible form as they are done. Managing this planning phase is vital to the success of the manager and the project.

There are two practical problems in estimation. The first is being too optimistic. It is human nature to ignore the difficulties and assume the best-case scenario at the beginning of a new project—estimates should be realistic. In practice, there should be a little slack built in the estimates to allow for some tolerance against mistakes. This is known as defensive scheduling. Second is the pressure from senior management to deliver quickly, especially if the project is being sold competitively. The temptation to rely upon speed as the only selling point should be resisted. Other factors, such as good quality, history of adherence to initial schedules, previous customer satisfaction, historical data, and facts should be taken into account.

ESTABLISHING CONTROLS

When the planning phase is over and agreed upon, the execution phase begins. Once it is in motion, a project acquires a direction and momentum that is totally independent of anything that was predicted. If this is understood from the start, the roller coaster that follows could be enjoyed. To gain some hope, however, the means to monitor and to influence the project's progress need to be established at the start (within the plan). There are two key elements to the control of a project:

- Milestones (clear, unambiguous targets of what, by when)
- Established means of communication

For a project manager, the milestones are a mechanism to monitor progress and for the team, they are short-term goals that are far more tangible than the hazy, distant completion of the entire project. The milestones maintain the momentum and encourage effort. They allow the team to judge their own progress and to celebrate achievement throughout the project rather than just at its end. The simplest way to construct milestones is to take the timing information from the work breakdown structure and sequence diagram. When it has been estimated how long each sub-task will take, it can be identified by when each of these sub-tasks will actually be completed. This is simple and effective; however, it lacks creativity.

A second method is to construct more significant milestones. These can be found by identifying stages in the development of a project that are recognizable as steps toward the final product. Sometimes, these are simply the higher levels of your structure. For instance, the completion of a market-evaluation phase could be a milestone. Sometimes, they cut across many parallel activities, for instance, a prototype of the eventual product or a mockup of the new brochure format. If you are running parallel activities, this type of milestone is particularly useful since it provides a means of pulling together the people on different activities, and so:

- They all have a shared goal, that is, the common milestone.

- Their responsibility to and dependency upon each other is emphasized.

- Each can provide a new viewpoint on the others' work.

- The problems to do with combining the different activities are highlighted and discussed early in the implementation phase.

- The project manager has something tangible which senior management can recognize as progress.

- The project manager has something tangible that his team can celebrate and which constitutes a short-term goal in a possibly long-term project.

- It provides an excellent opportunity for quality checking and for review.

Communication is very important. To monitor progress, to receive early warning of danger, to promote cooperation, to motivate through team involvement; all of these rely upon communication. Regular reports are invaluable—if the project manager clearly defines what information is needed and he teaches his team how to provide it in a rapidly accessible form. Often, these reports merely say, "Progressing according to schedule." This may not be enough as the message is there but the evidence is missing. The progress should be monitored with concrete, tangible measurements, and if this is done, the data should be included in the report. The real value of this practice comes when progress is not according to schedule.

THE ARTISTRY IN PLANNING

At the planning stage, the project manager can deal with far more than the mere project at hand as long has he understands the big picture. The project manager can also shape the overall model of team's working using the division and type of activities to be assigned.

Team's Involvement

The team, too, must be involved in the planning of projects, especially in the lower levels of the work breakdown structure. Not only will they provide information and ideas, but also, they will feel ownership in the final plan. This does not mean that the project should be planned by the committee; rather, the manager should plan the project based upon all the available experience and creative ideas. As an initial approach, the manager could attempt the first level of the work breakdown structure, which would help him to communicate the project to the team and then ask for comments. Then, using these, the final levels could be refined by the people to whom the tasks will be allocated. However, since the specification is so vital, all of the team should inspect it in detail.

Dangers In Review

There are two pitfalls to avoid in project reviews: they can be too frequent, and they can be too drastic. The constant trickle of new information can lead to a vicious cycle of planning and revising that shakes the team's confidence in any particular version of the plan and that destroys the very stability that the structure was designed to provide. The project manager must decide the balance. It should be decided objectively and explained beforehand when the review phases will occur and should be made as scheduled milestone in itself. Even though the situation may have changed since the last review, it is important to recognize the work that has been accomplished during the interim. Firstly, it should not be abandoned since the team will be discouraged feeling that they have achieved nothing. Secondly, this work itself is part of the new situation: it has been done; it should provide a foundation for the next step, or at least the basis of a lesson well learnt. A project manager should always try to build upon the existing achievements of the team.

Testing and Quality

No plan is complete without explicit provision for testing and quality. A wise manager will know that this should be part of each individual phase of the project. This means that no activity is completed until it has passes the defined criteria that establish its quality, and these are best defined at the beginning as part of the planning. When devising the schedule, allocated time for this part of each activity must be included. This should be established philosophy for the team by including testing as a justified cost.

Optimization

Optimization refers to the process or procedures used to make a system as effective or functional as possible. The project manager should be able to provide direction to the team on what the project goals are and how to achieve them most effectively. For instance, stating the testing criteria at the beginning will provide direction to the team on what and how much has to be done. If the team is motivated well, they will take pride in their work and want to do the best job possible. If it is clear at the onset exactly what is needed, then they are more likely to stop when that has been achieved. Generalities should be avoided, and stipulated boundaries should be defined. The same is also true when choosing the tools or building blocks of the project. While it might be nice to have use of the most modern versions or to develop an exact match to your needs, often there is an old/existing version that will serve almost as well, and the difference is not worth the time to invest in obtaining or developing the new one. Whenever possible, what is available should be used, unless the difference in the new version is worth the time, money, and the initial pains.

Another important aspect to consider is reusability. Too much effort on aspects of the project that are particular to that one job should be discouraged. In the specification phase, these should be eliminated as much as possible through negotiation with the customer. If it is unavoidable, then in the implementation phase, these parts should be left until the last. The reason being that a general piece of work can be tailored to many specific instances; thus, if the work is in a general form, it can be rapidly reused for other projects. On the other hand, if something is produced that is cut to fit exactly one specific case, that piece of work may have to be repeated entirely, even though the next project is fairly similar. At the planning phase, a manager should bear in mind the future and the long-term development of the team, as well as the requirements of the current project.

Time Constraints

A project manager has to regulate the pressure and workload that is imposed upon his team. The project manager must protect them from the unreasonable demands of the rest of the company. Once a realistic schedule has been arrived at, it should be finalized against all the resistance that is faced. If an unrealistic deadline is imposed on the project, it should be discussed and opposed by giving valid reasons. There could be some compromise and mutual agreements before the final schedule is arrived at. The schedule and timeline should be finalized by keeping both the organization's and project team's interests in mind.

In case of compromising situations, alternate options could be looked at. A prototype service or product could be offered at an earlier date. This might, in some cases, be sufficient for the customer to start the next stage of his/her own project with the understanding that the project would be completed at a later date and the final version would then replace the prototype.

The complexity of the product, or the total number of work items, might be reduced. This might, in some cases, be sufficient for the customer's immediate needs. Future enhancements or additional work items would then be the subject of a subsequent negotiation.

An alternative schedule could be arrived at by asking for specific set of resources, having better skills or prior knowledge on the product domain. Thus, a project manager has to provide a clear picture of the situation and a possible solution.

Consider the example of "Project X-1"; a "wish-list" of the features required in the product was prepared. Depending on the budget and time to market, some of the list items with low priority were eliminated. Similarly, the construction phase was done following the iterative model so that independent set of requirements could be coded and tested in parallel.

Planning for Error

The most common error in planning is to assume that there will be no errors in the implementation: in effect, the schedule is derived on the basis of, "If nothing goes wrong, this will take …" Of course, recognizing that errors will occur is the reason for implementing a monitoring strategy on the project. Thus, when the inevitable does happen, the manager can react and adapt the plan to compensate. However, by carefully considering errors in advance, changes could be made to the original plan to enhance its tolerance. The planning should consider and incorporate the impact of potential roadblocks and risks before it is finalized.

A manager should be able to predict where the errors will occur. By examining the activities list, it can usually be pinpointed which activities are risky (for instance, those involving new equipment) and which are quite secure (for instance, those your team has done often before). The risky areas might then be given a less stringent timescale. Another possibility is to apply a different strategy, or more resources, to such activities to minimize the disruption. For instance, training or consultancy could be included for new equipment, or the activity might be done in parallel with some other activity to gain time.

For example, in "Project X-1", one such activity was to set up a test lab (replicating a retail pharmacy) at offshore location so that the team could develop and test the product. While doing the WBS for the project requirements, this activity was seen as a risky item and to mitigate the risk, customer approved the budget and provided support to set up the lab at offshore.

Post-Project Analysis

At the end of any project, time should be allocated to review the lessons and information on both the work itself and the management of that work. It can be an open meeting, with open discussion, with the whole team and all customers and suppliers. This will be helpful for the future projects and communications with your customers and suppliers.

Planning for the Future

With all these considerations in merely the planning[5] stage of a project, it is perhaps surprising that projects get done at all. In fact projects do get done, but seldom in the predicted manner and often as much by force as by careful planning. The point, however, is that this method is non-optimal. Customers feel let down by late delivery, staff is demoralized by constant pressure for impossible goals, corners get cut, which harms the manager's reputation, and each project has to overcome the same problems as the last.

With planning, projects can run on time and interact effectively with both customers and suppliers. Everyone involved understands what is wanted, and emerging problems are seen and dealt with long before they cause damage. If projects need to run this way—then quality time must be invested in planning.

CHAPTER 3
LEADERSHIP AND TEAM BUILDING

What Is Leadership?

Many people believe that leadership is simply being the first, biggest, or most powerful. Leadership in organizations has a different and more meaningful definition. Very simply put, a leader is someone who sets direction in an effort and influences people to follow that direction. How they set that direction and influence people depends on a variety of factors.

There are also numerous theories about leadership or about carrying out the role of a leader, such as servant leader, democratic leader, principle-centered leader, group-man theory, great-man theory, visionary leader, situational leader, etc. Leaders carry out their roles in a wide variety of styles, such as autocratic, democratic, participatory, hands off, etc. Often, the leadership style depends on the situation, including the life cycle of the organization.

Leading and Managing—Are They Different?

Traditional views of management associate it with four major functions: planning, organizing, leading, and controlling/coordinating.

However, many educators, practitioners, and writers disagree with this traditional view. One view is that separating *leading* from *managing* can be destructive. Another view is that to be a very effective member of an organization, you need skills in the functions of planning, organizing, leading, and coordinating activities. The key is that one need to be able to emphasize different skills at different times.

Leading is different than planning, organizing, and coordinating because leading is focused on influencing people, while the other functions are focused on resources in addition to people. But that difference is not enough to claim that leading is different than managing. The assertion that "leading is different than managing" and the ways in which these assertions are made can suggest the view that the activities of planning, organizing, and coordinating are somehow less important than leading. The assertion can also convince others that they are grand and gifted leaders who can ignore the mere activities of planning, organizing, and coordinating. They can leave these lesser activities to others with less important things to do in the organization.

The Challenge of Suggesting Which Methods to Use

The particular competencies that a person needs in order to lead at a particular time in an organization depend on a variety of factors, such as:

- Whether that person is leading one other individual, a group, or a large organization.

- The extent of the leadership skills that person already has.

- That person's basic nature and values.

- Whether the group or organization is for-profit or non-profit, new or long established, and large or small.

- The particular culture (or values and associated behaviors) of whomever is being led.

The above considerations can make it very challenging when trying to determine what competencies someone should have in order to be a better leader. For the same reason the leadership-training programs in institutions typically assert a set of standard competencies, for example, decision making, problem solving, managing power and influence, and building trust.

TEAM BUILDING AND GROUP LEADERSHIP

Team building is the process of improving collective performance. A simple but effective methodology involves:

- Establishing ownership of shared goals

- Removing inhibitors to achievement of those goals

- Introducing enablers such as awareness, resources, information, processes, etc., to help achieve those goals

- Using team building processes in the correct sequence to gradually raise performance, akin to climbing a ladder one step at a time

A Structured Process

If a manager wants to build a team rather than just bond the individuals closer, a structured process[6] is needed. Before starting, it should be decided what improvements are required and if they are realistic for the team to achieve. The next step would be to decide how long it will take to achieve those results. Often, fun remains a key objective for such a session. If it is the only one or is only combined with a desire to get the team to become closer, organizing a team bonding session is an ideal solution. If, however, the expectations are set higher than that—then something more structured need to be planned.

Key Characteristics of Team Building

The following steps should be considered for team building success:

- Have definite session and longer-term goals, and know how the session goals lead to the longer term ones.

- Use an engaging and varied base activity that involves each participant in something that he or she enjoys doing.

- Use an activity that achieves that engagement while having genuine parallels to the workplace and has relevance with the session goals.

- Select an activity that requires the same kind of skill sets and team approaches that are needed at work—albeit one that is removed from the work itself.

- Consider using an independent facilitator to allow all levels to join in as equals.

- Debrief using a predefined process that highlights the workplace parallels and allows the participants to extract their own learning.

- Use a proven mechanism to transfer the learning back to the workplace, ideally integrated within the debriefing process itself.

Reason for Ineffective Team Building

In many cases, advanced techniques are used, even as there is a lack of buy in to the shared objectives. Commitment to team building activities is predicated on commitment to the overall direction. In the forming stage, individuals are committed, at most, to their own objectives. Members will only invest time in storming activities if they think it is worth it, that is, if the collective objectives are seen as important as their own. A common mistake is for individuals to think that being committed to their own objectives means they are committed to the team. As in the age-old saying that a house needs to be built on rock, the foundation of all team building is commitment to the shared goal.

If team building is viewed as a commodity, as a product to be purchased from a supplier, then it is unlikely to have any lasting value. Having an away day, playing games or doing fun things will generally lead to lasting and improved collective performance only in the context of a good plan, where events are designed to meet specific objectives and outcomes. Any offsite event should be designed to meet specific goals and outcomes.

The choice of intervention strategy depends not only on the current state of teamwork, but also on the nature of the people. For highly motivated individuals, it can be enough to set a high level direction and then allow individuals to contribute to the detailed development of the goals. For others, whose natural motivations are more individual, there may need to be objective-based rewards that require teamwork. In some instances, where high levels of teamwork cannot be achieved, they may only be effective in the forming stage, which is highly dependent on leadership. Interventions fall into four main areas:

- Individual—Development of individual skills, establishing familiarity with shared processes

- Relational—Improvement of unconscious dynamics, creating a sense of common purpose and commitment

- In/Out Groups—Tackling the barriers between different organizational units

- Cultural—Building a teamwork ethos in larger organizations

The foundation of good teamwork is having a shared commitment to common objectives. Without this, all other forms of team building will have a limited impact. Therefore, before using any team building exercises and activities or looking at relationships in the team or embarking on other forms of team building, a foundation of shared commitment needs to be put in place by:

- Clarifying the team goals and building ownership/commitment to those goals across the team
- Identifying any issues which inhibit the team from reaching their goals, and removing the inhibitors
- Putting in place enablers to help the goals be achieved to higher standards
- Using team processes in the correct sequence to help the team climb one rung at a time up the ladder of performance

Team building is therefore not just a single event, nor is it something that can be done by someone outside the team. It is a task primarily for the team manager and the team members themselves. Team building with a group can be counterproductive, detracting from individual performance without any compensatory collective benefit. There is often a lack of understanding of the difference between a group and a team. A group is a set of people with individual objectives who happen to share the same boss, or the same workplace, or be part of the same organizational unit. In a group, individuals might even have the same objectives. For example, in a sales force, everyone might have the same sales target to meet, but they may also compete against each other rather than cooperate. A team is a group that works toward a single, common objective. In fact, they might have different individual objectives, but those objectives contribute to the higher, collective one.

For example, in "Project X-1", some resources worked on the requirements, some did the design, some developed the code, and others did the testing. But they were all accountable together for the product development and were not judged solely on individual objectives.

TYPES OF TEAM BUILDING

Once the basic foundation of shared commitment has been established, the approach then taken to team building depends on the size of the team and the types of issues that may be inhibiting good teamwork.

Individuals

In a project environment, where team composition is continually changing, the emphasis must be on selecting people who are self-starters and developing the skills in individuals to become effective team members very quickly. The "scale" involved is one person, and the manager is endeavoring to change the skills and abilities of the individual at operating within a team or within multiple teams.

Small Teams

In teams where membership is static, typically in management teams, the motivational challenge is to align the drive of the disparate individuals around the same goals. There can be many inhibitors to performance, such as personality, dynamics, processes etc., and how the individuals within the team relate to each other can have a big bearing on team performance. So, if a member leaves, or another joins, the dynamics of the team can be changed greatly, and the task of team building has to start again. Here, the scale is small—say, two to about twelve—and the main priorities are to build the foundation of collective ownership of team objectives and then overcome inhibitors through team bonding, facilitation, processes, etc.

Team Islands

A larger scale operates between teams. Where the teams do not relate well, they are called "team islands." The motivational challenge is to overcome the problem of "in/out groups" so that people have positive attitudes toward those in other teams. There are often many barriers between teams that inhibit team performance, but not all of them can be removed. The main task, therefore, is bridging, or forming a relationship, between the teams.

Large Teams

The largest scale is organizational culture change. With the exception of the senior management team, any changes to personnel have limited impact on the corporate culture. The key aim of company-wide team building is to change the behaviors and attitudes prevalent in the organization, which are almost independent of who actually works there—new recruits who are "different" often start behaving in accord with the existing culture.

BUILDING A WINNING TEAM

Approach

Ability to relate—Every possibility, from landing the contract to having a romantic evening, hinges on one's ability to relate. But neither profit nor pleasures are the primary motivation for teamwork. Productive teamwork helps in handling challenges and adapting through change with more confidence. Working well on any team generates energy and enthusiasm for life.

Some are more skilled than others—This ability is learned. One can be effective with people using common sense and a few fundamental principles.

Vision means being able to excite the team with large, desired outcomes. The first step in vision is to project such a goal. It must contain challenge, appeal to personal pride, and provide an opportunity to make a difference and know it. Then the goal can become a powerful vision. When a large, missionary-friendly goal has been pictured and clearly communicated, the vision is complete.

Commitment can be a dangerous concept because of its attendant assumptions. Some may assume, for example, that commitment means long hours, while to others it may mean productivity. When expectations are defined, success rates soar. When leaders assume that everyone should be committed, as a matter of course, we overlook the difficulties many have with certain commitments. If people cannot initially commit, it doesn't mean they don't care. More often, it means they do care and they are caught up in a process of doubt. This process precedes every meaningful commitment. Effective leaders catalyze this process so that the critical mass of people can pass through this stage efficiently on their way to genuine commitment and innovative strategies. This pre-commitment process is the same for team leaders and members. Commitments contain unknowns, and some warn of possible failure. When leaders do not understand the commitment process, they tend to seek accountability without providing support. Without a means to process doubts and fears, people often feel pressured to commit but can't. One option, often unconscious, is to pretend to commit, to say *yes* and mean *maybe* at best. The solution to this set of problems is twofold: establish an atmosphere of trust, and within that atmosphere, encourage inclusion.

Trust[7] is the remedy to the fears and risks attendant to meaningful commitment. Trust means confidence in team leadership and vision. When trust prevails, team members are more willing to go through a difficult process, supported through ups, downs, risk, and potential loss. Trust is most efficiently established when leadership commits to vision first, and everyone knows those commitments are genuine. The process for leaders to commit is the same as for everyone else: assess pre-commitment doubts, questions, unknowns, and fears. This involves three simple steps: list the unknowns, assess worst-case scenarios and their survivability, and research the unknowns. The list of unknowns reveals some answers and further questions. Some of these questions lend themselves to research, and some have no apparent answers from our pre-commitment position. These latter comprise the bottom line or irreducible risk. Leadership now understands the potential loss and gain involved in the new vision. At this point, leadership can commit itself and prepare to include other team members. That preparation must include a plan for leadership to share visibly both risk and reward with the other team members who will be coming on board. With leadership's commitment to a clear vision and a genuine plan to share risks and rewards, the atmosphere for trust is in place.

Inclusion means getting others to commit to the team effort. Since leaders now understand this process firsthand, they need only to communicate with the potential team members to complete inclusion. The basic tasks are to communicate the vision, make sure it is understood, communicate leadership's commitment, and elicit and address peoples' doubts. Leaders will need three communication skills to achieve inclusion. These are the non-assumptive question, good listening, and directed response.

- Non-assumptive questions ("What do you think?" "Can you tell me what is happening with this report?") invite real answers because they are inclusive, not intrusive. Questions containing assumptions ("Why are you skeptical?" "Why is this report so incomplete?") invite defensiveness. When converting an atmosphere of change and possibly skepticism to trust, added defensiveness is counterproductive.

- Listening means separating the process of taking in information from the process of judging it. Kept separate, both processes are valuable. When they are mixed, especially when the receiver is a designated leader, the sender is tempted to stop communicating or to change the message midstream.

- Directed response—Effective team leaders demonstrate responsiveness. Since leaders have already processed their own pre-commitment doubts, many questions can be answered on the spot. Some require research and a timeline for response.

Help Exchange is the final step in creating the team is to establish a corroborative, balanced strategy for reaching the committed vision. This plan will consist of all of the tasks and help exchange necessary to realize the overall vision. At this point, the leadership role is to catalyze consensus, not to issue orders. Consensus occurs easily when most feel their ideas were heard and considered, whether or not the team ultimately chooses those ideas. Obtaining consensus again requires use of leadership communication skills: non-assumptive questions, good listening, and directed response. Effective teams often produce lively discussions of divergent viewpoints before reaching consensus.

Characteristics of Well-Functioning Teams

- Purpose—Members proudly share a sense of why the team exists and are invested in accomplishing its mission and goals.

- Priorities—Members know what needs to be done next, by whom, and by when to achieve team goals.

- Roles—Members know their roles in getting tasks done and when to allow a more skillful member to do a certain task.

- Decisions—Authority and decision-making lines are clearly understood.

- Conflict—Conflict is dealt with openly and is considered important to decision-making and personal growth.

- Personal traits—members feel their unique personalities are appreciated and well utilized.

- Norms—Group norms for working together are set and seen as standards for every one in the groups.

- Effectiveness—Members find team meetings efficient and productive and look forward to this time together.

- Success—Members know clearly when the team has met with success and share in this equally and proudly.

- Training—Opportunities for feedback and updating skills are provided and taken advantage of by team members.

Characteristics of a High-Performance Team

- Participative leadership—creating interdependence by empowering, freeing up, and serving others

- Shared responsibility—establishing an environment in which all team members feel responsibility as the manager for the performance team

- Aligned on purpose—having a sense of common purpose about why the team exists and the function it serves

- High communication—creating a climate of trust and open, honest communication

- Future-focused—seeing change as an opportunity for growth.

- Focused on task—keeping meetings and interactions focused on results

- Creative talents—applying individual talents and creativity

- Rapid response—identifying and acting on opportunities

Guidelines for Effective Team Membership

- Contribute ideas and solutions

- Recognize and respect differences in others

- Value the ideas and contributions of others

- Listen and share information

- Ask questions and get clarification

- Participate fully and keep your commitments

- Be flexible and respect the partnership created by a team—strive for the "win-win"

- Have fun, and care about the team and the outcomes

SECTION 2
PROJECT SCOPE AND RISK MANAGEMENT

CHAPTER 1
PROJECT SCOPE MANAGEMENT

Project scope management includes the processes required to ensure that the project includes all the work required, and only the work required, to complete the project successfully. Project scope management is primarily concerned with defining and controlling what is and is not included in the project. The fundamental steps involved in project scope management that a project manager needs to look at are:

- Scope Planning—creating a project scope management plan that documents how the project scope will be defined, verified, controlled, and how the work breakdown structure (WBS) will be created and defined.

- Scope Definition—developing a detailed project scope statement as the basis for future project decisions.

- Create WBS—subdividing the major project deliverables and project work into smaller, more manageable components.

- Scope Verification—formalizing acceptance of the completed project deliverables.

- Scope Control—controlling changes to the project scope.

These processes interact with each other and with processes in the other knowledge areas as well. Each process can involve effort from one or more persons or groups of persons, based on the needs of the project. Each process occurs at least once in every project and occurs in one or more project phases, if the project is divided into phases. Although the processes are presented here as discrete components with well-defined interfaces, in practice they can overlap and interact in ways not detailed here. In the project context, the term scope can refer to:

- Product scope—The features and functions that characterize a product, service, or result.

- Project scope—The work that needs to be accomplished to deliver a product, service, or result with the specified features and functions.

This chapter focuses on the processes used to manage the project scope. These project scope management processes, and their associated tools and techniques, vary by application area, are usually defined as part of the project life cycle, and are documented in the project scope management plan. The approved detailed project scope statement and its associated WBS and WBS dictionary are the scope baseline for the project. A project generally results in a single product, but that product can include subsidiary components, each with its own separate, but interdependent, product scope. Completion of the project scope is measured against the project management plan, the project scope statement, and it's associated WBS and WBS dictionary, but completion of the product scope is measured against the product requirements. Project scope management needs to be well integrated with the other knowledge area processes so that the work of the project will result in delivery of the specified product scope.

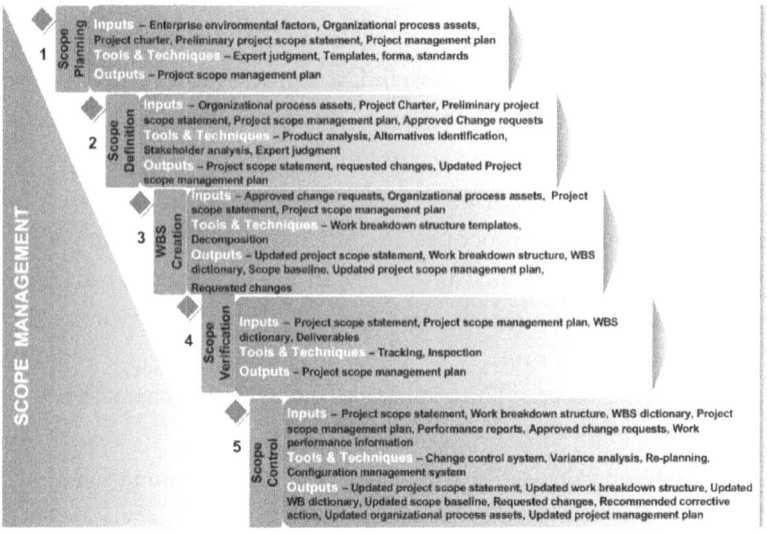

Getting the right result is the principal aim of project sponsors and project managers. Projects, once initiated, typically are not left incomplete or unworkable. The failure to manage scope is reflected in the consequent cost overruns and schedule delays. Poor scope management is manifested as runaway changes that are attributed to indecisive owners and incompetent designers. Project managers excuse themselves from an aggressive role in controlling the evolution of the design configuration because it is classed as a technical issue, not a management concern.

THE DEFINITION OF PROJECT SCOPE

Project scope can be defined as the primary measure of project performance that deals with the client's requirements for function, capacity, and content. In other words, it is the bounded set of verifiable end products, deliverables, or outputs that the project team undertakes to provide to the client of the project. This proposed definition uses the word *scope* to designate the required products or results of the project. The word derives from the Greek *skopos,* meaning aim or object. Thus, the specialized meaning proposed here is faithful to the original in its reference to the physical items and capabilities the team aims to create through the project and which are the objective of the project.

The Broad Description of a Project

The undertaking by a project team to carry out a project for a client is comprehensively described in three categories:

- Scope: The required set of end results or products with specified physical and functional characteristics; the outputs

- Deadlines: Dates by which the results are due

- Budget: Upper limits on the inputs, i.e. money or other resources that may be consumed in creating the results.

The project success is meaningful only if the scope objective was obtained on time and within budget, and provided that it made a contribution to the strategic mission of the enterprise. In other words, the project performance can be measured against an integrated baseline that incorporates criteria that cover "all three dimensions of a project, i.e. cost, scope and schedule." Bringing a project to completion within the cost, schedule, and scope objectives contained in the project charter satisfies the general criteria for success. However, how well risks were assessed and how the form of contract with sellers was chosen are also evaluation criteria.

The achievement of the goals and objectives is a measure of project success, but there may be stakeholders, other than the client or customer, with different criteria for success. Identifying the measures of successful performance that should be agreed upon between the client and the project team, and which are objectively verifiable, is very important. The project manager, the team members, and the project manager's employer all may have their own explicit or hidden objectives, which may or may not be compatible with the client's requirements as reflected in the project charter.

Work Done by the Project Management Institute

In the work by the Project Management Institute (PMI) to define the Project Management Body of Knowledge (PMBOK)[8], several definitions of project scope have been offered.

As per one definition, scope management is defined as the process of controlling the scope of the project in terms of the aims, goals, and objectives of the sponsor. However, "scope of the project" is left undefined in the section of the report dealing with scope management. The glossary of terms in the section of the report dealing with cost management does offer a definition of project scope: "to define in general the product to be manufactured, purchased, or constructed." The subtopics under this definition suggest there should be a client approval of the scope statement. In this statement, the scope is suitably broken down into work packages, and an engineering report clarifies the project at the detailed level.

The scope objective of a project is a distinct and separately verifiable measure of project performance. Putting it together with the cost and schedule measures tends to obscure the need for developing strategies, methods, and controls aimed at ensuring success in this dimension. The failure to make the distinction may lead to the incorrect perception that managing the scope is the same as managing the cost plus managing the schedule. Scope is an objective for a project and should be specified in terms of the results to be achieved. It is wrong to include in the specification the means chosen to achieve the desired end. The confusion of ends and means appears to be a common failing among project management practitioners. Some of the prominent faults in understanding the scope are stating activities rather than end items, exceeding the scope, failing to be specific, and omitting important deliverables.

IMPORTANCE OF SCOPE MANAGEMENT

Achieving the right results, or in other words, fulfilling the scope objective is the primary test of effective performance by project management. It takes precedence over the constraints of deadlines and budgets. The failure to manage and control this aspect of the objectives is a principal reason why projects fail. In spite of its importance and its perceived bearing on project success, the management of scope is neglected in the practice of project management.

Planning problems can be cited as the most frequent obstacle to success. Within this category, an unclear definition of goals, objectives, scope, plans, or design is the predominant planning problem. The failure to manage scope could be a probable cause for why cost and schedule overruns are experienced on software development projects. An insufficient definition of the nature and configuration of the desired end product, lack of knowledge of the expected project output, and failure to manage changes in product configuration are described as management errors that drive up the originally estimated volume of work and consequently cause cost overruns.

Scope objectives should take priority over time and cost objectives. After all, the very reason for initiating a project is to meet a need for a specified end product or capability.

The following explanations are possible reasons for the neglect of scope management:

- The concept is inadequately or erroneously defined.

- Scope is not easily quantified.

- Scope management problems are manifested as other kinds of problems.

- Scope is regarded as a technical issue, not a management concern.

Inadequate or erroneous definitions of the concept of scope take two forms: Either they divert management attention onto the time and cost objectives, or they confound ends with means by equating scope with work effort. Generally, scope is defined to include work content and resources; scope reporting is defined to include cost and schedule status and the integrated cost/schedule performance baseline. With such an understanding, it is no wonder that the concept of legitimate propositions regarding the management of scope are combined with descriptions of techniques, reports, and controls for activity planning, schedule compliance, and budget adherence.

There is a need to document project requirements and parameters as a basis for future design decisions, for accomplishing verification measures, and for evaluating design changes, and the need to subsequently report on "technical performance status." This resort to obtuse generalization stems largely from the failure to define the proper concern of scope management clearly as achieving an end product that conforms to the client's requirements of function, capacity, or performance capability.

Scope control has been neglected as a management topic because it cannot be readily quantified in the same way as can schedule and cost. It is difficult to summarize the degree to which the anticipated results of a project conform to or deviate from the agreed requirements, unless one presents all the complex information that underlies the assessment. There is no convenient single indicator of performance when it comes to scope. Scope is a multidimensional variable, and there are mutual inconsistencies among the dimensions.

Attempts to measure scope accomplishment in units of time or cost may, in part, explain the tendency to misdiagnose problems in scope management.

Why Is It Generally Neglected?

Scope management may be neglected because, as a problem, it may be difficult to recognize. A deficient scope statement creates surprises in cost and schedule performance and may be manifested as other problems, such as disputes over project changes. A *deficient statement* can be defined as one in which there is a lack of appreciation for the technical issues, complexities, and other implications. The potential for cost and schedule overruns can be attributed to inadequate project definition.

Finally, scope management has been neglected because project managers tend to regard decisions about the features and components of the product as "technical" issues. Hence, it becomes a problem of specialists such as engineers, architects, systems analysts, and programmers, to name a few. These are the creative members of the project team who provide innovative ideas about the technical, physical, and aesthetic characteristics of the outputs. Their ideas, however, are subject to review and acceptance by project management. It is the project manager's duty to ensure that the work of the creative professional is examined for reliability to the client's requirements and for compliance with the agreed standards of quality.

An indication of the degree to which scope management has been misclassified as a technical issue is the fact that configuration management and its associated methods, one of the most powerful tools available for scope management, is virtually ignored generally. Configuration management, along with quality assurance, is a supporting or service discipline that is often essential for project management success.

THE WBS - WORK BREAKDOWN STRUCTURE

The work breakdown structure (WBS) is well recognized as a tool for integrating information on project time and cost performance. Its more fundamental role as a framework for configuration control and scope management has not received the same attention. The logical basis, on which the elements of the hierarchical tree structure are subdivided, in fact, reflects a subdivision of scope. The feature that makes every work package or WBS element unique is its distinct deliverable or output. Once a framework is created through partitioning the scope, the structure is used to identify and classify the work effort through which the deliverables will be obtained. The hierarchical structure also serves as the information framework that guides the detailing of the components and features of the end product. As additional detail is conceived, the WBS is correspondingly expanded to lower structural levels.

The WBS is a work or scope breakdown[9] structure. Work packages are planned as means to achieve the outputs reflected in the WBS. A WBS displays the product(s) to be developed or produced and relates the elements of work to be accomplished to each other and to the end product. WBS should be an end item-oriented structure that links objectives and that transcribes the objectives in terms of successively smaller subdivisions of the deliverable end result. The caution should be taken against patterning the structure along functional organizational lines, since this leads to a loss of control. The primary focus is on outputs, and the designation of responsibility for the end items follows. To generate a WBS, one subdivides scope and deliverables in successively more detail until one arrives at elements that can be produced as manageable units of work.

The method of subdividing the required results or end conditions into progressively smaller elements of scope has proven to be an indispensable device for coordinating and communicating the objectives of complex projects. This principle of subdivision has been carried out with good results, down to the very lowest levels of the structure. Each critical path network activity, task, work package, or work item is defined in relation to a unique, specific deliverable. The rule, simply put, is that each element must have a scope.

In "Project X-1", we had to develop a software application, which was a workflow management system for retail pharmacies. In this example, I have explained how we used WBS in order to divide the project functionalities into smaller WBS components, which helped us in providing accurate effort estimates, assignment of the task to the team members, configuration management, and tracking the progress of the tasks. The workflow management system had major modules or components such as Patient information, Prescription information, Adjudication, Imaging, Dispensing, Checking, Inventory, Dashboard, and POS (Point of Sale). All these components were broken down into smaller components. Consider the Dispensing module or component for instance. This was further divided into smaller components, and each of these components resulted in tasks and deliverables for the team members. The subcomponents of Dispensing were Dispense by drug number, Dispense by stock bottle, Manual dispensing, Verify stock bottle, Resend dispense, Reject dispense, Dispense from device-1, Dispense from device-2, Dispense from shelf, Stop dispense, Handle device exception, and so on.

Some of the project outputs may not be for delivery to the client, but are needed within the project team to support the decision-making process or the performance of the work on real deliverables. Such internal deliverables are tangible outputs nonetheless and do provide the specification of scope about which the work content of WBS elements is planned.

Application and Use of the WBS

The use of the WBS for scope management goes well beyond its use as a framework through which the required work effort may be assigned to deliverable items. It serves also to portray and trace the family relationships among functional components of the configuration. The hierarchical breakdown reflects the progressing design of the end product.

So that it may serve as the information framework for configuration management purposes, it is required that certain elements in the WBS be designated as configuration items, meaning components that are to be developed through the project to satisfy specified end use functions. A configuration item is the object of design activity during the project. In response to a specified operational need, first a set of performance parameters is determined for an item, and then a hardware and software configuration is conceived. As the design work progresses, the WBS is successively extended to lower levels, reflecting the designer's choices of the subcomponents and sub-subcomponents within an item.

The designation of certain WBS elements as configuration items does not restrict the use of other elements for management purposes. Integration of components, testing, project administration, and training, for example, are all accommodated in the WBS. For these kinds of elements, the degree of breakdown may be less than for configuration items. The overriding requirement remains, however, that for each element, there must be certifiable outputs or deliverables, be they documents, services, or physical items.

The act of subdivision should never change the scope of an element or configuration item. It merely expands the detail through elaboration. The WBS traces out an audit trail and a set of baseline standards whereby it can be verified that the authorized project scope was neither increased nor diminished in the course of designing and producing the end item.

CONTROLLING SCOPE OF A PROJECT

This section outlines a framework of principles and procedures for controlling the scope of a project. The control process is described in the context of a generalized model of the life cycle stages of a project. The stages are marked by the issuance of a series of logically related activities. Each stage is a further step in the evolution of the configuration of the deliverable end result. The progression is from a set of user or client requirements to a functioning product, system, or facility. The stages trace the evolution of the project scope. The process for controlling the evolution of scope centers on two sets of mechanisms:

- The first set ensures that the configuration of the end product, at each stage of its evolution, does not deviate from the client's requirements. An agreed upon requirements statement and a series of design reviews and freezes are the key tools in this case.

- The second set of mechanisms provides for amending the configuration in a disciplined fashion. Inevitably, changes arise, either because the requirements change or because the design does not work. Procedures are described for reviewing and approving changes and for incorporating them in the baselines.

The Life Cycle Model

A generalized life cycle model consisting of five major stages can be seen in the following picture. It indicates how a project should be managed. At the conclusion of each stage is a planned review and approval checkpoint. Only when the results of the work performed in one stage are formally accepted is authority granted for the project team to proceed with the next stage. The client or project sponsor, and typically, representatives of the users or beneficiaries of the project, are participants in the planned reviews.

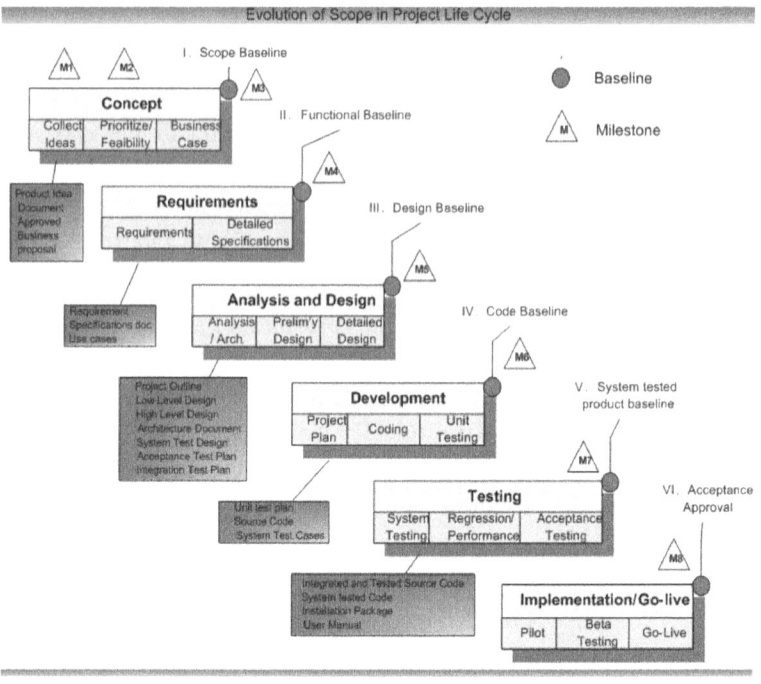

The life cycle model is based on V Model, generally followed for a typical software development project. The picture portrays the kinds of intermediate deliverables that should be issued at each of the milestone review points. The items shown are documents that trace the evolution of the end product configuration and are the basis upon which the project team's management of the project scope may be evaluated. Not shown on the diagram are other deliverable documents that describe the project team's strategy for managing the work effort in the subsequent stages of the project. Items such as cost estimates, working schedules, and staffing plans should be part of the same review process. These other intermediate deliverables are themselves components of the project scope. For simplicity, the illustration deals only with those items that describe the end product configuration.

Evolution of Scope

The division of the life of a project into a series of distinct stages provides the project manager and the sponsor with a mechanism for guiding and controlling the evolution of the project scope. *Evolution* here means elaboration or progressive expansion of detail. The project objectives do not change at each successive stage, but the definition becomes more exact. The elaboration of scope is a process of creation and innovation. The design process can be characterized as a series of choices from among creatively conceived alternatives. The top down or hierarchic approach to design development casts the design choices into the question: What is the best way to subdivide a component or system into subcomponents or subsystems, each with a distinct function to perform? The expansion of the WBS to a lower level reflects the decision taken in response to this question. As illustrated in picture, the detailing and expansion of the WBS follows the elaboration of configuration detail through design choices.

Baselines and Freezes at Milestones Three and Four

The standard against which design choices are evaluated and controlled is the approved set of requirements: the scope baseline shown at milestone three on the life cycle diagram. At this point in the life of the project, a feasibility study has been conducted. A concept or a system has been chosen from among the alternatives that could satisfy the need for change, originally expressed as a problem or an opportunity. The requirements statement should make specific reference to a chosen concept.

Once the requirements statement has been approved by the client or sponsor, the project team develops a more elaborate conceptual design. The deliverable at milestone four in the illustration assigns the agreed requirements to major functional components or subsystems of the end product. The deliverable, once reviewed and approved, constitutes the "functional baseline." At milestone four, the project outline or functional baseline, if it is compliant with the statement of requirements, is formally "frozen." That is to say, the design decisions taken to date must be respected in all subsequent design work. The functional baseline is the fixed framework within which future design choices must be made. Each of the chosen subsystems or components in the design is represented by a corresponding WBS element.

Baselines and Freezes: Milestones Five through Eight

During the preliminary engineering stage, subsystems are optimized and performance requirements are translated into technical specifications for sub-subsystems or subcomponents. As shown in the illustration, the WBS is expanded at milestone five to reflect these preliminary and detailed design decisions. In many organizations, the cost estimate prepared from the preliminary design is the basis for the major funding authorization for a capital project. Once the preliminary design has been reviewed and found compliant with both the statement of requirements and the functional baseline, it is "frozen" as the basis for the detailed design.

In the detailed design stage, detailed specifications are prepared as a basis for the construction of the product. The design provides detailed instructions to the programmer: flow charts of processing logic for each module, naming conventions, programming language, and required documentation. The detailed design is reviewed against the requirements and the previous design baselines. If compliant, the detailed design is "frozen" as the "product baseline." The deliverables issued at this point, milestone five, would include system test designs, high level and low-level system design, and acceptance test plan. The WBS, as suggested in the picture, will typically be expanded to lower levels again during the course of final design.

During the implementation stage (coding and system testing), hardware and software items are inspected for compliance with the product baseline. This scope management activity is often called "quality control." At milestone six (completion of code construction) and seven (system testing), the completed deliverable is certified as compliant with the detailed design and the requirements.

Milestone eight marks the conclusion of the project. The acceptance test cases are taken as the basis to mark the acceptance of the project results. Both the beneficiaries and the sponsor agree that the project scope objectives have been fulfilled, if the acceptance criteria defined for the project is met. The acceptance checklist should be drawn from the statement of requirements. The final approval should make direct reference to the documented scope baseline. In the startup stage, the users—those who will inherit the results of the project—rehearse regular operation and maintenance with guidance and support from the project team. The users satisfy themselves that they have been adequately trained and that they have the necessary manuals and documents.

The project manager, as the single point of responsibility for project team performance, should lead the review process at all the key milestones. The sponsor and users must give formal consent on the produced artifacts at the end of each milestone.

Managing Changes

Changes are inevitable. A set of procedures for the tracking and control of changes is the final essential mechanism for the management of project scope. As a matter of principle, changes should be kept to a minimum on a project. This is a debatable principle, since the incorporation of changes may be crucial to project success and may be the correct decision in the client's business interest. The operative management policy, perhaps, should be to minimize the disruptive impact of changes through early identification and thorough evaluation before implementation.

The first commandment of baseline management is that change does not just happen; it happens by permission. Thus, project management has a duty to be in control of changes.

A change means any amendment to a baseline that has previously been authorized or frozen. A clear distinction must be made between scope changes and design changes. Scope changes are amendments to the requirements statement and represent a change in project objectives. A change in scope is grounds for an accompanying change in deadlines and budgets. A design change, on the other hand, is a modification to the planned configuration of the end product needed to produce a workable result. For a design change called an "internal scope change" in some organizations, the client should not be expected to provide additional funding or an extension of time.

The authority to accept or approve a change must be the same authority that established the baseline in the first place. Thus, scope changes require the approval of the sponsor. The request for a scope change, typically initiated by a user, should be stated in writing, and that no action should be taken to implement the change without written approval from the client. The client's approval, in turn, should be granted only with knowledge of the cost and schedule impacts. The rule that consistency among the cost, schedule, and scope baselines must always be maintained should be followed. Thus, the authorization for a scope change must be accompanied by the approval of commensurate budget and target date changes. Design/code changes are typically proposed by members of the project team, either to overcome a problem or to respond to new knowledge about the project environment. Conditions that give rise to design changes include errors, omissions, incorrect assumptions in the design, or new technology. The project manager and the panel of team members that authorized the design baselines affected by a change are the authority for acceptance. Again, the impacts of a potential change, both on configuration and on cost and schedule, should be analyzed prior to the decision to accept or reject.

The information system and administrative procedures required to support change control on a project should provide for the following, in addition to the review and approval mechanisms described above:

- The early detection and communication of potential changes so that all team members are alerted to them and so that responsibility may be assigned for analyzing and implementing the changes.

- The incorporation of the changes in all affected baselines in a timely fashion so that all team members work to a uniform set of requirements and specifications.

SUMMARY OF PROJECT SCOPE MANAGEMENT PRINCIPLES

This is a summary of the essential principles of effective scope management on a project.

- Identify the scope objective as one of achieving the agreed results or outputs of the project. Scope is separable from cost and schedule as a measure of project performance; it can be independently monitored and audited.

- Document a scope baseline early in the life of the project. Prepare a comprehensive statement of client requirements, both for the final product and for the intermediate output. Adopt a structured, "top-down" approach to designing the configuration of the final product. Organize the life of the project into distinct, sequential stages corresponding to steps in the evolution of the configuration: concept, functional design, detailed specification, and physical product.

- Design the project WBS to reflect the progressive subdivision of the configuration of the end product. WBS elements should correspond to configuration items. WBS levels should correspond to the stages of design development for configuration items.

- To assure compliance with the scope baseline and to monitor progress in accomplishing the scope objective, conduct a planned review at the conclusion of each stage of product development. Freeze the configuration as a baseline following each successful review.

- Inspect the physical, deliverable items for compliance with the detailed requirement specifications.

- Be in control of changes. At each stage of the life cycle, maintain procedures, information systems, and administrative mechanisms for the timely identification, screening, evaluation, approval, and incorporation of changes to the required or planned project outputs.

- Maintain change processing mechanisms that separate scope changes from design /code changes; only scope changes may amend the agreed baselines for the scope, cost, and schedule objectives. Promptly revise all requirement and design baselines affected by an authorized change, and promptly communicate approved changes throughout the project organization, so that team members always work to a consistent and valid set of baseline standards.

CHAPTER 2
ASSUMPTIONS AND CONSTRAINTS

Definition

Few projects begin with absolute certainty. If we had to wait for absolute certainty, most projects would never get off the ground. As projects are planned and executed; some facts and issues are known, others must be estimated. Estimation is an art, with many fine points to refinement between certainty and wishful thinking. The project manager has to manage and mitigate, using informed assumptions and constraints.

Assumptions and constraints form the basis for project planning, filling in the gaps between known proven facts and total guesswork. Each assumption is an educated guess about a likely condition, circumstance or event, presumed known and true in the absence of absolute certainty. Each constraint is a limiting condition, circumstance, or event that sets boundaries for the project process and expected results. Once identified, these assumptions and constraints shape a project in specific, but diverging ways—assumptions bring possibilities and constraints bring limits. Consider this example: A defined budget is a fact; let's say $100,000 has been allocated to complete a given project. The belief that the budget is sufficient to complete the project on time and as required is an assumption. This assumption should not be a guess; it should be the result of a planned, verified budget estimate. The need to modify deliverables and adapt the schedule to suit the budget is a constraint.

In summary, it can be said that assumptions are circumstances and events that need to occur for the project to be successful but are outside the total control of the project team. Assumptions are accepted as true and are often without proof or demonstration. Constraints are things that might restrict, limit, or regulate the project. The characteristics of assumptions and constraints are similar and can be represented by conditions, circumstances, or events. The impact of assumption is that it allows the project to proceed, whereas constraint restricts and limits project execution. From a process perspective, an assumption must be analyzed and monitored to ensure validity and relevancy as the project proceeds, whereas a constraint must be identified and incorporated into the project plan to ensure that the plan is realistic.

Referring to the "Project-X1" as an example, one of the constraints that project faced was with respect to development and testing of the software. The product development and testing was being done at offshore and the product involved interaction with lot of hardware devices such as dispensing machines, label printers, Point of Sale machines, etc. The product development and testing could not proceed until these devices were shipped to offshore to set up a pharmacy lab. Similarly, some of the assumptions in this project were that "the non-functional requirements will be provided by the customer at the beginning of the development activities. The vendor will perform the feasibility analysis on these requirements and respond to the customer on what can be achieved", "Customer would carry out acceptance testing at onsite at the end of each iteration. Vendor would provide two weeks of acceptance test support to the customer." and so on.

From initiation to closure of a project, assumptions and constraints set the stage for project planning and execution. As the project is planned, assumptions and constraints will be used to define and shape tasks, schedules, resource assignments, and budget allocations. As such, each is used to manage an otherwise uncertain future, laying out a roadmap for how the project will proceed. At a minimum, as the project begins, assumptions and constraints must be defined for one or more of the following elements:

- Effort: The estimated tasks and activities required to manage the project and produce deliverables.

- Schedule: The estimated tasks and events needed to complete the project, organized into a structured sequence to meet a specified project end date.

- Resources: The estimated staff resources needed to complete the project, according to number, type, work hours, and skills.

- Budget: The estimated cost of the project, allocated to tasks, resources and phases as needed to complete the project.

- Vendors and procurement: The anticipated performance of contractors, vendors, and suppliers to deliver goods and services according to contracts and project requirements.

- Management process: Management standards can serve as a constraint on project performance, adding quality control overhead.

The following could be considered a checklist while analyzing the assumptions and constraints for a project. Have known assumptions about the following categories of factors been considered and documented: scope, schedule, financing, resources, expectations, customers, technologies, vendors, partners and business relationships, sponsorship, and other assumptions? Have constraints in the following categories been considered and documented: timeframes and deadlines, funding, resources, skill levels, dependencies, legal, policy, technology, environment, and other constraints?

WHY IS THIS IMPORTANT?

Assumptions that prove to be incorrect can have a significant impact on a project. It is important that project participants, stakeholders, and executives understand and agree with the assumptions before the project begins. This way, it is more likely that an incorrect assumption will be detected before it can impact the project.

All projects have constraints, and these need to be defined from the outset. If the project manager understands the limitations under which a project must be conducted, including the project environment or parameters (timeframes and deadlines, funding, skill levels, resource availability, etc.), they will do a better job of developing the project plan. Early project risk analysis often uses the assumptions and constraints as a starting point. This provides a foundation for building mitigation strategies for the most significant assumptions that, if proven incorrect, could seriously impact the project. Likewise, it provides for the evaluation of constraints and the opportunity to manage them to positively impact the project or prevent a negative impact.

Instruction—Briefly and clearly describe any project assumptions related to business, technology, resources, scope, expectations, or schedules. List the project assumptions based on the current knowledge today. Describe the principal constraints and limitations impacting the project. Very often, these include timelines, resource availability or competence, funding, and other important environmental issues within the organization. It is important to include any major dependencies the project relies on either as assumptions or constraints. If assumptions and constraints are invalidated or change at a later date, adjust the activities and estimates in the project plan accordingly.

How to scale—List only major assumptions, or consider listing everything in detail. Assumptions and constraints tend to exist around resource availability issues. Give extra consideration to cost, timing, and people issues surrounding the project. Often during the project initiation phase, many aspects of a project may still be undetermined or unknown. Identifying the unknowns in a project and making assumptions about them is one of the first steps in developing clarity.

Checklists—A checklist can be used as a tool to make sure that all the aspects have been considered while documenting the assumptions and constraints for a project.

MANAGING ASSUMPTIONS AND CONSTRAINTS

Identify and Challenge—The first step in the "assumptions and constraints" management process is identification. As assumptions are identified, each must be viewed with an appropriate degree of skepticism. Assumptions cannot be mere guesswork or wishful thinking. For example, one can't just hope that the budget will be sufficient. It has to be examined and verified by the means of budget estimates to get as close to certainty as possible. In turn, constraints must also be viewed skeptically, with an eye toward possible elimination. Constraints pose restrictions, and any relief from these restrictive elements would be welcome. But, if constraints cannot be eliminated, then appropriate workarounds must be developed.

Assess—Assumptions should be evaluated from a long-term perspective, according to confidence level, and followed by a related "if-then" risk counterpart analysis. During the course of this analysis, the "impact of the incorrect assumption" must be determined. Impact can be weighed at various levels, from serious, such as threatening successful or timely project delivery, to moderate, such as absorbable impact on deliverables, schedules, or costs, to minor, such as insignificant impact on deliverables, schedules, or costs. Depending upon the assessed confidence level and related impact, a full risk assessment may be required. Lower confidence and higher impact would probably require further analysis and the related risk assessment. In contrast, constraints must be evaluated from a short-term perspective, according to immediate impact— i.e., how does a given constraint limit or refine the project in one or more respects? For example, product availability constraints can impact multiple elements of a single project. Product delays can elongate the project schedule, add to costs, and negatively impact resource availability. As constraints are assessed; all points of impact must be determined.

Incorporate—Once assumptions and constraints are identified and assessed, they must be incorporated into the relevant portion of the project plan. Assumptions, combined with known facts, will drive the formation of the project plan, providing the actionable basis for planned tasks, schedules, budgets, and resource assignments. Constraints must be factored into the project plan from the start in the form of stated workarounds. These workarounds will mitigate constraint impact by providing the means for the project to move ahead, despite the existence of constraining factors. Unidentified constraints will not just disappear, they will likely pop up at some later point as full-fledged project problems.

Control—Initial assumptions and constraints are rarely static. As the project evolves, assumptions will be proven true or untrue. Changing circumstances may eliminate or modify previously identified constraints. In either case, you must be prepared to react, with contingencies, workarounds, and modifications to plans and deliverables. To ensure a constant state of readiness, identified assumptions and constraints must be tracked and monitored throughout the project process. In addition, assumptions can be factored into the plan via checkpoints. These checkpoints can then be monitored to ensure that working assumptions are valid, and if not, to take corrective action.

Review—Once a project is complete, assumptions and constraints should be reviewed as part of an overall post-project review process, to evaluate all steps taken for identification, assessment, incorporation, and control. This review should consider quality, accuracy, effectiveness, and omissions—missed assumptions and/or constraints that should have been discovered as the project began.

CONCLUSIONS

Projects are filled with varying degrees of certainty and uncertainty. As projects begin, known facts must be supported by informed assumption and managed according to identified constraints. As the project proceeds, changes will occur, as reflected in an ongoing series of revised "assumptions and constraints." Using a structured process for identification, assessment, validation, and control will lead to certain success.

CHAPTER 3
RISK MANAGEMENT

A risk is something that may happen and, if it does, will have an adverse impact on the project. The phrase "that may happen" implies a probability of less then 100 percent. If it has a probability of 100 percent, in other words, it will happen; it is an issue. An issue is managed differently to a risk. A risk must also have a probability something above 0 percent. It must be a chance to happen, or it is not a risk. The second thing to consider from the definition is "it will have an adverse impact." If it will not have an adverse impact, it is not a risk. Suppose we said a risk was that we would find the project less complicated than we thought and could finish early. Unless finishing early has an adverse effect on the project, it is not a risk.

RISK MANAGEMENT PLAN

There are four stages to risk management, which are risk identification, risks quantification, risk response, and risk monitoring and control.

Risk Identification

In this stage, the risks are identified and named. The best approach is a workshop with business and IT people to carry out the identification. Use a combination of brainstorming and reviewing of standard risk lists. There are different types of risks[10], and it has to be decided on a project-by-project basis what to do about each type. Business risks are ongoing risks that are best handled by the business. An example of this is that if the project cannot meet the end of financial year deadline, the business area may need to retain their existing accounting system for another year. The response is likely to be a contingency plan developed by the business to use the existing system for another year. Generic risks are risks to all projects, for example, the risk that business analyst might not be available and requirements may be incomplete. Each organization will develop standard responses to generic risks. Risks should be defined in two parts. The first is the cause of the situation (vendor not meeting deadline, business analyst not available, etc.). The second part is the impact (budget will be exceeded, milestones not achieved, etc.). Hence, a *risk* might be defined as "The vendor not meeting deadline will mean that budget will be exceeded." If this format is used, it is easy to remove duplicates and understand the risk.

Risk Quantification

Risk needs to be quantified in two dimensions. The impact of the risk needs to be assessed, and the probability of the risk occurring needs to be assessed. For simplicity, each of the risk items can be rated on a one to ten scale. The larger the number assigned to a risk, the larger the impact or probability. If probability is high and impact is low, it is a medium risk. On the other hand, if impact is high and probability low, it is high priority. Failure Modes and Effects Analysis (FMEA) is a recommended methodology to analyze and manage risks in a project, which is discussed later in this chapter.

Risk Response or Risk Strategy

Once a risk has been identified and quantified, it can be responded to in four different ways.

- Avoid the risk—Do something to remove it. Use another supplier for example.

- Transfer the risk—Make someone else responsible. Perhaps a vendor can be made responsible for a particularly risky part of the project.

- Mitigate the risk—Take actions to lessen the impact or chance of the risk occurring. For example, if the risk relates to availability of resources, draw up an agreement and get sign-off for the resource to be available.

- Accept the risk—Analyze the risk, and find a mitigation strategy to handle the risk.

A risk response plan, or action plan, should include the strategy and action items to address the strategy. The actions should include what needs to be done, who is doing it, and when it should be completed.

Risk Control

The final step is to continually monitor risks to identify any change in the status or if they turn into an issue. It is best to hold regular risk reviews to identify actions outstanding, risk probability and impact, remove risks that have passed, and identify new risks.

FAILURE MODES AND EFFECTS ANALYSIS (FMEA)

Customers are placing increased demands on companies for high quality and reliable products. The increasing capabilities and functionality of many products are making it more difficult for developers to maintain quality and reliability. Traditionally, reliability has been achieved through extensive testing and use of techniques such as probabilistic reliability modeling. These are techniques used in the late stages of development. The challenge is to design in quality and reliability early in the development cycle.

Failure Modes and Effects Analysis (FMEA) is methodology for analyzing potential reliability problems early in the development cycle, where it is easier to take actions to overcome these issues, thereby enhancing reliability through design. FMEA is used to identify potential failure modes, determine their effect on the development and operation of the product, and identify actions to mitigate the failures. A crucial step is anticipating what might go wrong with a product. While anticipating every failure mode is not possible, the development team should formulate as extensive a list of potential failure modes as possible. The early and consistent use of FMEA in the development process allows the team to design out failures and produce reliable, safe, and customer pleasing products. FMEA also capture historical information for use in future product improvement.

Types of FMEA

There are several types of FMEA; some are used much more often than others. FMEA should always be done whenever failures would mean potential harm to the project or product being developed. The types of FMEA are:

- System—focuses on global system functions
- Design—focuses on components and subsystems
- Process—focuses on development and integration processes
- Service—focuses on service functions
- Software—focuses on software functions

Historically, project managers have done a good job of evaluating the functions and the form of products and processes in the design phase. They have not always done so well at designing in reliability and quality.

FMEA provides the project manager with a tool that can assist in providing reliable, safe, and customer pleasing products and processes. Since FMEA helps the project manager identify potential product or process failures, he/she can use it to:

- Develop product or process requirements that minimize the likelihood of those failures.

- Evaluate the requirements obtained from the customer or other participants in the design/development process to ensure that those requirements do not introduce potential failures.

- Identify design characteristics that contribute to failures and design them out of the system or at least minimize the resulting effects.

- Define methods and procedures to develop and test the product/process to ensure that the failures have been successfully eliminated.

- Track and manage potential risks in the project, tracking the risks contributes to the development of corporate memory and the success of future products as well.

- Ensure that any failures that could occur will not seriously impact the development or implementation of product/process.

Benefits of FMEA

FMEA is designed to assist the project team to improve the quality and reliability of product being developed. Proper use of the FMEA provides the project teams several benefits. Among others, these benefits include:

- Improve product/process reliability and quality
- Increase customer satisfaction

- Early identification and elimination of potential product/process failure modes
- Prioritize product/process deficiencies
- Capture engineering/organization knowledge
- Emphasize problem prevention
- Document risk and actions taken to reduce risk
- Provide focus for improved testing and development
- Minimize late changes and associated cost
- Catalyst for teamwork and idea exchange between functions

The FMEA is a living document. Throughout the product development cycle, changes and updates are made to the product and process. These changes can and often do introduce new failure modes. It is therefore important to review and update the FMEA when:

- A new product or process is being initiated (at the beginning of the cycle).
- Changes are made to the requirements of the product or process being developed.
- A change is made to either the product or process design. The product and process are interrelated. When the product design is changed the process is impacted and vice versa.
- New regulations are instituted.
- Customer feedback indicates problems in the product or process.

USING FMEA FOR SOFTWARE PROJECTS

Following are the sequential steps that should be considered while analyzing the risks using FMEA for software projects. The steps can be grouped in three categories, namely risk diagram, evaluation matrix, and action list.

Risk Diagram
- Identify project's main objectives.
- Recognize the risk groups and their corresponding effects.
- List the underlying risks of each group.

Evaluation Matrix
- Assign values for severity to each group or type of risks (evaluation matrix).
- Assign value for the probability of occurrence of each risk.
- Assign values for the ability of detection for each risk.
- Calculate the risk factor.

Action List
- List the risks in descending order according to the risk factor (action list).
- Define a common strategy for each group or each risk.
- Take possible actions for the selected risk based on the adopted strategy.

Risk Diagram

To come up with the risk diagram[11], several meetings of the risk management team members and other stakeholders in the project are needed. Following is an example of the approach that can be taken up to come up with a risk diagram. The diagram can be created and represented as the manager wishes to. In general, it is shown as a layered diagram with three levels—Objective, Failure Effect, and Failure Causes. Under objectives, all the project objectives are listed. The second layer, Failure Effect, has the list of the effect if the objective is not met. This is done for all the project objectives identified. The third and final layer, Failure Causes, has the reasons for possible failure of the objectives identified. Following is the layout of the risk diagram, shown by taking example of a software development project for a retail pharmacy.

Level 1—Objective
- Development of a complex module "X" in Retail Pharmacy Software

Level 2—Failure Effect
- Delay in time to market and loss of market share
- Budget overrun

Level 3—Failure Causes
- Lack of skills (technology, domain)
- Lack of subject matter expert
- Attrition

Evaluation Matrix

With the list of risks drawn up as described in previous heading "Risk Diagram," the FMEA criteria, severity, occurrence, and detection can be addressed. The table below shows the details of the risks associated with a given objective. The project objective is expressed in the failure mode column. The failure effect column reflects one of the possible consequences of the failure mode. The column with heading "S" is related to the value of severity. This is measured on a scale of one to ten, with one being the small impact and ten reflecting a great impact. The risk group column has the group of possible risks that can impact the objective of the project. The failure causes column has the risks that belong to a risk group. The column with heading "O" registers the value of the probability of occurrence, with one representing very low probability of occurrence and ten representing an event of extremely high probability. The control column is a means of identifying a risk that has occurred or is about to occur. The column headed "D" refers to detection value with one for risk easily monitored for listed controls and ten for risk monitored with difficulty for the listed controls. RPN column is the calculation of the risk index (or Risk Priority Number), calculated from the product of criteria severity, occurrence, and detection.

Failure Mode	Failure Effect	S	Risk group	Failure Causes	O	Control	D	RPN
Development of complex module "X" in Retail Pharmacy Software	Delay in time to market and loss of market share	9	Skill problems	Lack of skilled resources (Technology, Domain)	8	Team evaluation	1	72
	Budget overrun	9		Lack of subject matter expert	7	Team evaluation	2	126
		9		Attrition	6	Incentives	4	212

Action List

After calculating the RPN values as in the previous section, the risk strategies and action list can be identified. The action list can be presented in a tabular form, with Failure Cause as the first column of the table. In this column, the risks are listed in descending order, according to the RPN values. The second column RPN shows the RPN values for each of the failure cause or risk. The third column is Risk Strategy. This column mentions which of the four strategies are recommended (to prevent, to transfer, to mitigate, and to accept) to guide the action to be taken to deal with the risks. For example, for the Failure Cause column value attrition, the RPN value is 212, the Risk Strategy value is to mitigate, and the corresponding actions could be giving incentives to team members, creating a knowledge base, hiring new resources on contract basis. "Actions" is the last column in the table.

Once the action list is complete, the project manager has to work on these action items and assess the status of the risk from time to time. A risk can become an issue for a project if the risk has already occurred. Working on the action item well within time can avoid a risk becoming an issue. An issue could have serious impact on a project and generally needs immediate attention.

SECTION 3
APPROACH TO PROJECT
EXECUTION METHODOLOGY

CHAPTER 1
PROJECT MANAGEMENT PROCESS

Projects are the way that most new work gets delivered. All projects have certain characteristics in common:

- They all have a beginning and an end.

- All projects are unique. They may be similar to prior projects, but they are unique in terms of timeframes, resources, business environment, etc.

- Projects result in the creation of one or more deliverables.

- Projects have assigned resources—either fulltime, part-time or both.

All organizations have projects. Projects can be managed using a common set of project management[12] processes. In fact, a similar set of project management processes can be utilized, regardless of the type of project. For instance, all projects should be defined and planned, and all projects should have processes to manage scope, risk, quality, status, etc.

Some people are confused on the difference between project management and the project life cycle. It takes both types of work to complete a project successfully. The general difference is that project management is used to define, plan, control, monitor, and close the project. The work associated with actually building the project deliverables is accomplished through work that is referred to as the "life cycle." Project management is used to build the schedule, but the vast majority of the work in the schedule is the life cycle work associated with building the project deliverables.

Even though all projects are unique, there are still common life cycle models that can be used to build deliverables in similar ways. An example of a life cycle models is the generic waterfall model. In a waterfall model, a project goes through different phases in a sequential manner, starting with understanding the requirement of the solution, designing a solution, building and testing a solution, and then implementing the solution. Each of these major areas of focus is called a phase (analysis phase, design phase, construct phase, etc.).

There are other life cycle models other than classic waterfall. Although the waterfall model can be applied to all projects, other life cycle models might be more efficient and effective, based on the characteristics of the project. For instance, if a software package is being installed, a specific life cycle model for package implementation can be utilized that is light on the design and construct phases. Likewise, if a research and development (R and D) project is being conducted, a specific R and D life cycle model can be used that takes into account the fact that the work might be thrown away when it is done. Other important life cycle models can be used to accelerate projects with certain characteristics. Certain software development projects, for instance, may be able to utilize iterative development and agile techniques. The important point is that a common, scalable project management process can be used effectively on all your projects. The specific, detailed work to build project deliverables is referred to as the *life cycle*.

LIFE CYCLE MODEL PROCESS FRAMEWORK

Any development life cycle would follow a basic process framework as depicted in the following diagram. There are entry criteria to start any task, the task itself, and the exit criteria, indicating the conditions to be met for the task to be completed. The process framework is defined through a life cycle model describing the phases in which the project will be executed. Each phase represents a state of evolution of software and has associated project deliverables. Each phase is controlled using an ETVX (Entry criteria, Task, Validation, Exit criteria) model as shown below. Associated with each phase is

- Entry criteria—Conditions that must be satisfied before beginning of phase

- Tasks—A set of tasks to be carried out in the phase

- Verification—A set of verification tasks to verify the quality of deliverables

- Exit criteria—A set of conditions that must be satisfied before the phase is concluded

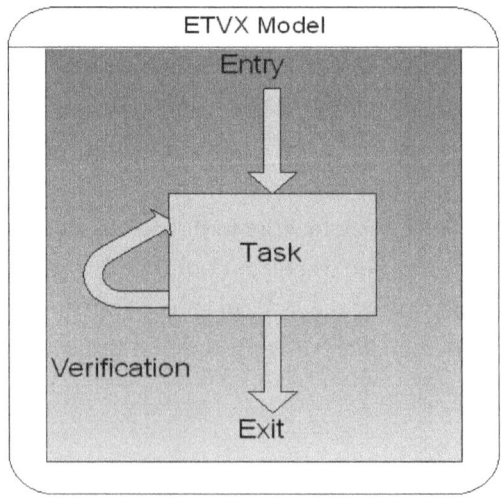

During the course of executing a phase, the tasks and verification produce outputs as work items. The task produces "product" work items and verification produces "process" work items/quality records. Typical examples of product work items are functional specifications, source code, test plans, and so on. Typical examples of process work items include development strategy, test strategy, configuration management process, quality control process, communication process and so on.

DEVELOPMENT LIFE CYCLE MODELS

A system development methodology refers to the framework that is used to structure, plan, and control the process of developing an information system. A wide variety of such frameworks have evolved over the years, each with its own recognized strengths and weaknesses. One system development methodology is not necessarily suitable for use by all projects. Each of the available methodologies is best suited to specific kinds of projects, based on various technical, organizational, project, and team considerations. Following are some of the different project types and project development life cycle models.

V Process Model

Just like the waterfall model, the V shaped life cycle is a sequential path of execution of processes. Each phase must be completed before the next phase begins. Testing is emphasized in this model more so than the waterfall model, though. The testing procedures are developed early in the life cycle before any coding is done, during each of the phases preceding implementation. Requirements begin the life cycle model, just like the waterfall model. Before development is started, a system test plan is created. The test plan focuses on meeting the functionality specified in the requirements gathered. The high-level design phase focuses on system architecture and design. An integration test plan is created in this phase as well in order to test the pieces of the software systems ability to work together. The low-level design phase is where the actual software components are designed, and unit tests are created in this phase as well. The implementation phase is where all coding takes place. Once coding is complete, the path of execution continues up the right side of the V, where the test plans developed earlier are now put to use.

Iterative Life cycle Model

This model has the following phases—Project Definition Phase, Analysis Phase, Design Phase, Code and Unit Test Phase, Integration and System Test Phase, and Acceptance Test Phase. This life cycle model can be defined as intuitive approach to the waterfall model/V process model, a.k.a. incremental or progressive life cycle model, examples include Rapid Application Development (RAD) and Rational Unified Process (RUP). As part of this model multiple development cycles take place, making the model a "multi-waterfall" life cycle; RAD includes business and data process modeling. Cycles are divided up into smaller, more easily managed iterations. Each iteration passes through each of the phases (requirements through testing). Working software is produced in the first iteration, and built upon during each iteration thereafter. The iterative life cycle model works best when requirements cannot be well defined up front. At first glance, this may appear to be a fast method of delivery to business partner, but it can become time consuming if the iterations are allowed to extend beyond the scope or duration set for each individual one. Each iteration is executed using the tailored V process model or waterfall model. Some of the advantages are: It generates working software quickly and early during the life cycle, more flexibility—less costly to change the scope or requirements, easier to test and debug during a smaller iteration, easier to manage risk, risks are identified and resolved during the iteration, and each iteration is an easily managed milestone. Some of the disadvantages are that each phase of iteration is rigid with no overlaps, and costly system architecture or design issues may arise because not all requirements are gathered up front for the entire life cycle.

Rational Unified Process

This is another form of iterative model but more controlled and organized. The process has two dimensions. The horizontal dimension represents time and shows the life cycle aspects of the process as it unfolds and is expressed in terms of cycles, phases, iterations, and milestones. The vertical dimension represents core disciplines, which group activities logically by nature and are described in terms of activities, artifacts, workers, and discipline. The dynamic organization of the process is along the time, wherein the software life ~~le is broken into cycles, each working on a new generation of

development cycle in four con-
phase, construction
1ases are concluded
ne at which certain
key goals must have
1er broken down into
nt loop resulting in a
1e final product under
iteration to iteration
process disciplines in
/ork and activities into
des business modeling,
1entation, test, deploy-
1nfiguration and change
ironment discipline.

Application Management Model

This defines the processes for engagements providing maintenance and support services. The Application Management Model is divided into four stages, with each stage having multiple phases.

- Stage 1: Post Proposal—Due diligence is performed, and initial planning for the project is carried out at this stage. Due diligence and project definition are the two phases in this stage.

- Stage 2: Transition In—The engagement is defined, and responsibility for maintaining the applications is transitioned from the client during this stage. The phases in this stage are Knowledge Acquisition and Pre-Steady State Phase and Process Alignment Phase.

- Stage 3: Service Delivery—This is the core phase of application management engagement, where application management services are provided. Depending on the engagement, the service provided during this stage could vary. The key phases in this stage are related to maintenance and enhancement services. The key phases are Impact Analysis Phase, Code and Unit Testing Phase, and Regression Test Phase.

- Stage 4: Transition Out—This is the final stage of application management engagement, where the responsibility for application maintenance is transitioned back to the client or to a third party. The two phases in this stage are Knowledge Transfer Phase and Project Closure Phase.

Migration/Porting Life Cycle Model

This generally has seven phases, as mentioned below: Project Definition Phase, Baseline Phase, Migration Design Phase, Impact Analysis Phase, Migrate and Unit Test Phase, System Test Phase, and Acceptance Test Phase.

Testing Process Model

There are many projects that concentrate only on the testing services. The testing services could be of various types, such as normal product testing, performance testing, automation testing, etc. All these services follow the same process model with some minor changes. The phases are Project Definition Phase, Knowledge Acquisition Phase, Test Design Phase, Test Development Phase, Test Execution Phase, and Acceptance Test Phase.

Business Intelligence (BI) Projects

Typically, the BI development projects are technology specific and follow the modified V process life cycle, involving the following phases: Pre-Sale Phase, Project Definition Phase, Analysis Phase, Architecture and Design Phase, Code and Unit Test Phase, Integration Test Phase, System Test Phase, and Acceptance Test Phase.

Oracle / SAP Application Data Migration Life cycle Model

These are again technology specific project models. The project phases here are typically derived from V process and/ or waterfall process model with some modifications. The phases included are Project Plan and Initiation, Requirement Analysis, System and Solution Design, Code and Unit test, System and Integration Test, User Acceptance Test, Go-Live, Post Production Support.

HOW TO CHOOSE THE LIFE CYCLE MODEL?

The following list suggests how a life cycle model should be chosen. As it can be seen, depending on the project type, a suitable life cycle needs to be selected. At times, it is possible that none of the following life cycle models are suitable for a given project. In such a case, one of the following life cycle processes could be selected and tweaked as per the need. The details could be mentioned in the Software Project Plan.

- Development projects, Re-engineering projects, Major enhancements projects—V Process, Iterative, Rational Unified process

- Oracle / SAP projects—Oracle / SAP application data migration

- BI development projects—BI Process

- Maintenance projects involving bug fixing and minor enhancements—Application Management, V process, iterative process

- Migration project/Porting projects—Migration/Porting

- Pure testing projects—Testing process model

For example, the "Phase–I" of "Project X-1" followed V process model. Most of the "Phase-II" was also based on V process model. Only the code development and testing activates were done using the iterative process model. The overall model was a combination of V process and iterative process model. The main reason for "Phase-I" to follow V process model was the interdependency of tasks on each other. For example, precise estimates were not possible until the scope definition and requirement detailing was complete. For "Phase-II", there were tasks which could be done in parallel. For example, the set of requirements those were independent of the other requirements could be coded and tested in a separate iterations. Hence, part of the project was done in iterative mode.

CHAPTER 2
DETAILS OF PROJECT EXECUTION

This chapter discusses the execution model and suitable processes pertaining to the project execution. The V process model has been used to describe this concept. As it is described in the previous chapter, most of the development life cycle models have the basic ingredients that are taken from the V process model or basic waterfall model. The development projects can be executed as per the V process model as shown below.

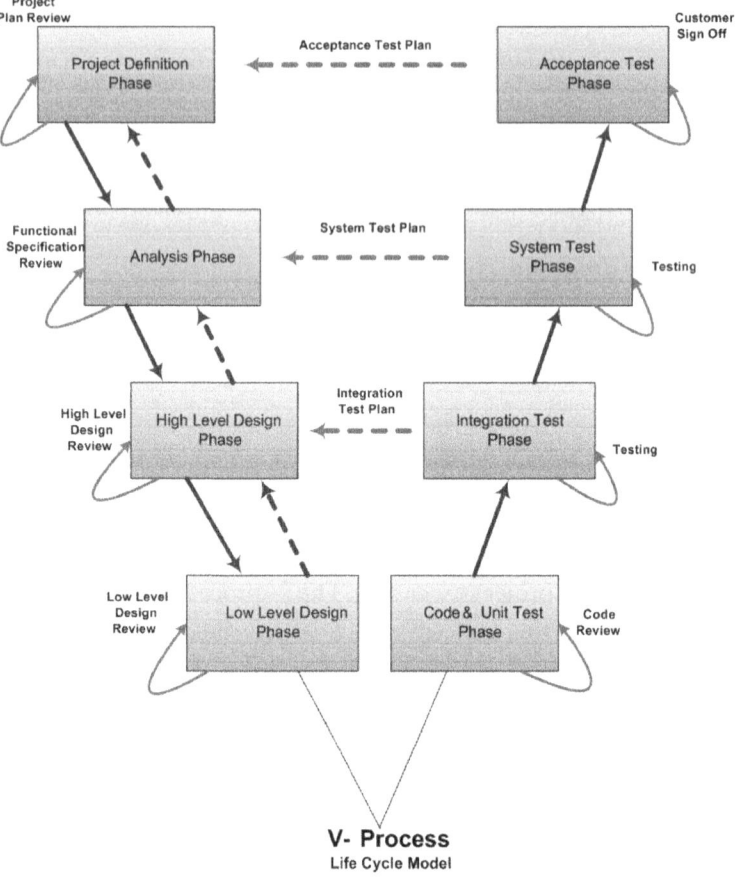

V- Process
Life Cycle Model

The phases in this model are as below:

- Project definition phase
- Analysis phase
- High-level design phase
- Low-level design phase
- Code and unit test phase
- Integration test phase
- System test phase
- Acceptance test phase

The V process model is ideal for projects in which the requirements can be identified completely at the beginning of the project and are not expected to change radically throughout the life of the project. It performs well for projects with clearly understood requirements or when working with well understood technical tools, architectures, and infrastructures.

PROJECT DEFINITION PHASE

The objectives of this phase are to identify the project's scope and understand the customer requirements, request infrastructure and human resources for the project, and define the Software Project Plan (SPP).

Entry criteria
Approved Statement of Work (contract with the customer), Requirement Specification, and the Ballpark Estimates

Tasks
Project Initiation (resource management team / project manager) - The resource management team is responsible for identification of the project manager. Once the project manager is identified, he takes care of project id allocation, understands project requirements, and prepares the project kickoff request and submits it for approval.

Requirement Specification (project manager)—This task involves preparation of the requirement specification (if not available from the customer), reviewing of requirements, obtaining clarification required from the customer, and signing off the requirements.

Develop Business Requirements (business analyst / project manager)—Includes identification and eliciting requirements, identifying business requirements, stakeholders, and their goals; eliciting customer needs and proactively identifying additional requirements not explicitly provided by the customer; identifying and documenting project constraints and assumptions; using clarification log to document clarifications if any; documenting the business requirement; and reviewing the requirements with the stakeholders.

Develop System Requirements (business analyst / project manager)—involves identifying functional requirements, identifying all stakeholders and eliciting inputs from all stakeholders, identifying system behavioral requirements, data requirements, user interface requirements, non-functional system requirements, system architectural requirements, system usability requirements, performance requirements, operational requirements, security requirements, legal requirements if any, globalization requirements if any, packaging requirements, identifying use cases, identifying prototype as needed, and documenting the identified system requirements.

Analyze the Requirements (business analyst / project manager)—Involves identifying stakeholder needs and expectations, constraints, external interfaces, objectivity, feasibility, completeness, availability, and testability.

Prioritize Requirements (business analyst / project manager)—Incorporates identifying key requirements that have strong influence on cost, schedule, functionality, risk, and performance; reviewing these requirements with all stakeholders; and achieving agreement among the stakeholders.

Verify and Validate Software Requirement Specifications (business analyst / project manager)—Involves verifying the Software Requirement Specifications (SRS) with the stakeholders through review, validating the SRS with the stakeholders through either of the validation methods comprising simulations, prototype, demonstrations and walkthroughs, and getting approval on the SRS from the stakeholders.

Establish Requirements Management environment (project manager / project lead, team lead)—The task involves creating requirements, Traceability Matrix, establishing traceability from business requirements to use cases to system requirements, baselining the requirements, requirements documents, and requirements traceability documents.

Software Project Planning (project manager, configuration management lead, quality team lead)—This task consists of following sub-tasks:

- List the assumptions made.

- Identify the deliverables for the project.

- Define the development process and specify deviations from the standard process, if any.

- Identify the project organization depending on the size of the project.

- Identify the risks and the risk management plan for the project.

- Review the estimated effort and schedule for the project provided in the estimation worksheet.

- Identify the project management process.

- Prepare the training plan for the project.

- Identify the hardware, software, and other project specific requirements for the project.

- List the invoicing schedule for the project.

- Identify the quality goals for the project.

- List the verification activities and mention deviation, if any.

- Identify the project metrics to be collected.

- Define the organization for configuration management activities.

- Identify the configurable items, libraries to store them, and version numbering scheme.

- Define configuration control mechanism.

- Define Configuration Status Accounting (CSA) mechanisms.

- Plan for configuration audits.
- Prepare a Software Project Plan (SPP) and submit for review.

Exit criteria

Completion of approved software project plan, and approved requirement specifications.

ANALYSIS PHASE

The objective of this phase is to obtain consensus on the system's requirements/functionality and scope, develop a functional specification for the system describing a logical model of what the system will do, develop a software architecture document, develop an architectural prototype, develop a user interface prototype of the system for user interface screens, develop Proof of Concept (PoC), help project team to understand functional requirements and help in designing the system, and prepare the acceptance test plan.

Entry criteria

Approved software project plan and approved requirement specifications.

Tasks

Prepare functional specification (project manager)—this involves review of the requirements specifications and any related project information, obtaining any clarifications required from the customer, defining the data and process models, and preparing the functional specification document for the project and getting it approved.

Preparing software architecture document (architects)—involves:

- Understand non-functional requirements (supplementary specifications) received from the customer
- Analyze functional requirements (use cases) to identify architecturally significant requirements (use cases)

- Identify technical risks and provide mitigation strategies, such as planning/implementing a proof of concept
- Plan and execute proof of concept to mitigate risk
- Realize the use case selected to define an architectural approach, and implement an architectural prototype
- Evaluate the architectural prototype against the nonfunctional requirement
- Compare alternate architectural approaches considered, if any, and provide recommendations
- Document the details in software architecture document, and get it approved

Prepare Architectural Prototype (architects)—Understand nonfunctional requirements, analyze functional requirements and identify architecturally significant use cases, realize the use cases selected to define an architectural approach and implement and architectural prototype, evaluate the architectural prototype against nonfunctional requirements, and submit the prototype for review and get approval.

Prepare Proof of Concept (architects / designers)—involves understanding the objective of Proof of Concept, planning and executing the PoC, analyzing the outcome of the PoC and making recommendations, documenting the analysis and results, and getting the approvals.

Acceptance test plan (project manager)—involves preparation of the acceptance test plan and getting it reviewed and approved by the customer.

Update traceability matrix (project manager)—includes updating the traceability matrix to trace from system requirements to functional components.

Exit criteria

Approved functional specifications, approved software architecture document, approved architectural prototype, approved PoC, and approved acceptance test plan.

Product work items
Functional specification—Solution architecture describing the hardware and software element, logical process mode including process hierarchy, data flow diagrams, process descriptions, the logical data model describing data entity relationship diagrams, entities and attributes, user interface specifications describing screen and report layouts, interfaces to external systems, security specifications, and audit trail requirements.

Acceptance Test Plan—Plan to test system based on the customer's acceptance criteria.

Software Architecture Document (SAD)—Contains various architectural elements of the system.

Architectural prototype—Realize the use case selected to define an architectural approach and implement an architectural prototype.

Proof of Concept (PoC)—obtain the feasibility of meeting performance requirements or usability requirements or validating the interface points or finding the suitability of a product to meet specific functional/non-functional requirements.

HIGH-LEVEL DESIGN PHASE
The objectives of this phase are to design the system architecture and identify interface between individual system components and develop a system test plan to test the system based on functional specification.

Entry criteria
Approved functional specifications, approved acceptance test plan, approved software architecture document, approved architectural prototype, and approved proof of concepts.

Tasks

Design system architecture and prepare high-level design specifications (project manager)—this task has following subtasks: Understand the functional specification and prototype (if any), obtain any clarifications required from the customer, define the high-level design specification, identify reusable components, and submit the high level design document for review and get approval.

Prepare System Test Plan (quality team lead)—The task involves preparation of the system test plan based on the functional specifications, review, and approval process.

Set up development environment (project manager)—This task involves setting up the development environment, setting up development database and test data, and acquiring development and testing tools required.

Update Traceability Matrix (project manager)—Update traceability matrix to trace from system functionalities/use cases to design components such as packages, subsystems, interface, etc.

Design Baseline (project manager)—Baseline-approved high-level design, system test plan, and traceability matrix.

Exit criteria

Approved high level design specifications, and approved system test plan.

Product work items

High Level Design Specifications—system architecture, component description and their interfaces, database design, and GUI design.

System Test Plan—Contains test conditions for functionality, security, navigation, database updates, multi-user testing, and performance.

LOW-LEVEL DESIGN PHASE

The objectives of this phase are to design individual functional components/programs, develop unit test plans to test individual functional components/programs, and develop integration test plans to test internal/external interfaces of the system.

Entry criteria
Approved high level design specification and approved system test plan.

Tasks
Prepare Low-Level Design (team members / project manager)—The task consists of understanding the functional specifications and prototypes, the high level design specifications, developing the low level design specifications, and getting it reviewed and approved.

Prepare Low-Level Design (team members / project manager)—Develop the approach to testing of programs and define the scope of unit testing, develop unit test plan for the component/program describing how the program will be coded and unit tested, and get it reviewed and approved.

Prepare Integration Test Plan (project manager)—This includes developing the approach for testing of programs and define the scope of testing, identifying the test environment and test tools, preparing unit test plan document, and getting it reviewed and approved.

Update Traceability matrix (project manager)—This involves updating the traceability matrix to trace from system functionalities/use cases to design components such as packages, subsystems, interfaces, etc

Design baseline (project manager)—Baseline-approved low-level design, unit test plan, integration test plan, and Traceability Matrix.

Exit criteria
Approved low-level design specification, approved unit test plan, and approved integration test plan.

Product work items
Low-Level Design Specifications—Initialization, process, and termination logic for the program, specific algorithm used, program interfaces, messages and file formats, control statements, boundary values, and error handling mechanisms and error messages.

Unit Test Plan—Test cases to validate the program logic, test cases for positive and error cases, and test cases for boundary values.

Integration Test Plan—Test environment requirements, types of tests to be performed, features and functions to be tested, test cases to validate the component against the high-level design specifications, and test cases and expected results.

CODE AND UNIT TEST PHASE

The objectives of this phase are to be code based on the low level design specification and coding standards, test the code based on the unit test plan, and review the code against coding standard.

Entry criteria
Availability of approved low level design specification, approved unit test plan, and approved integration test plan.

Tasks
Coding (team members)—Code the components based on the low-level design specifications, follow coding standards identified for the project.

Perform unit test (team members)—Create test data to test the components/program, execute test cases as per the unit test plan, document test results on defect tracking tool.

Perform code review (quality team lead)—Review code for conformance against coding standards and any other project specific standards, verify the component/program logic and algorithms and low-level design specifications.

Update traceability matrix (project manager)—Update traceability matrix to trace from system functionalities/use cases to design components such as packages, subsystems, interfaces, etc.

Perform Code baseline (team member).

Exit criteria
Completion of unit tested code.

Product work items
Unit tested source code, and unit test results—Test conditions marked "Pass" or "Fail."

INTEGRATION TEST PHASE

The objective of this phase is to integrate individual components and validate the integrated system against the high-level design by executing test cases defined in the integration test plan.

Entry criteria
Unit tested code and approved integrated test plan.

Task
Integrate (team member)—Integrate the individual system components.

Perform integration test (team member)—Execute test cases as per the integration test plan, record defects, fix defects, submit the code for review.

Exit criteria
Approved integrated test results.

Product work items

Integrated and Tested Source Code—Source code and any associated scripts and files.

Integration Test Results—Defects logged in the defect tracking tool, and test results—test conditions marked in "pass" or "fail."

SYSTEM TEST PHASE

The objective of this phase is to validate the system against the functional specifications by executing test cases specified in the system test plan.

Entry criteria

Integrated and tested source code, approved integration test results, and approved system test plan.

Tasks

Perform system test as per the plan (quality team lead / team member)—Install the package, execute all test cases as per system test plan, record defects in the defect tracking tool, fix defects, and document system test results for the first cycle of testing.

Perform performance test execution as per plan (quality team lead / team member)—conduct sanity checks before executing the actual test, ensure the performance test script, scenario, and the test environment are correct; design the performance test scenario in the tool; the identified performance test scenarios need to be implemented using the tool—for example, setting up scripts for different transactions to run at the same time, conducting dry runs for the performance test scripts as it is necessary to confirm the script credibility, refreshing data in performance test scripts' credibility, refreshing data in performance test scripts as this is required because there could be redundant or invalid or unique data in the script, doing the fine tuning to the code if needed to match the performance benchmark.

Package and delivery (project manager)—Create installation package for the system and prepare release notes.

User manual (team member)—Prepare the user manual, and submit it for review.

Note: The number of system test cycles and performance test cycles can be decided by the project manager based on the time available, need, and criticality of the project.

Exit criteria
Completion of approved system test results, approved performance test results, approved installation package, and approved user manual.

Product work items
System tested code—System tested source code and associated scripts and files.

System test results—Defects reported in the defect tracking tool and test conditions marked "pass" or "fail."

Installation package containing program executables, install scripts, and database creation and initialization scripts.

Release notes—Hardware/software environment, prerequisite for installation, installation instructions, and known bugs/limitations.

Delivery note—Checklist for delivery is available.

User manual—General guidelines and main menu item with description.

ACCEPTANCE TEST PHASE

The objectives of this phase are to verify the system based on the acceptance test plan and obtain the signoff from the customer.

Entry criteria

System tested code, approved installation package, approved system test results, and approved user manual.

Tasks

Perform acceptance test (customer team)—Set up the environment at customer location, install and set up the system for acceptance testing, Execute test cases as per the acceptance test plan, report defects through the defect tracking tool/change requests to the development team and get them resolved, and document the acceptance test result.

System acceptance test (project manager / team member)—Provide any support/bug fixes required to the acceptance test team, and package and deliver.

System acceptance (customer)—Submit the system to customer for signoff.

Archive/backup the delivered system (quality team lead / team member)—Copy the delivered system from the controlled library to backup media, label the backup media properly, and submit the backup media to in-charge—for Archival.

Collect project metrics (project manager)—Collect the project metrics identified in the software project plan, project closure report, submit the project closure report for review, and identify points for corrective/preventive actions.

CHAPTER 3
PROJECT CLOSURE

PROJECT CLOSURE PHASE

It is the last phase of the project life cycle. The commencement of the project closure phase is determined by the completion of all project objectives and acceptance of the end product by the customer. Project closure includes the following tasks:

- Release of the resources, both staff and non-staff, and their redistribution and reallocation to other projects, if needed.

- Closure of any financial issues like labor, contract, etc.

- Collection and completion of all project records.

- Archiving of all project records.

- Documenting the issues faced in the project and their resolution. This helps other projects to plan for such type of issues in the project initiation phase itself.

- Recording lessons learned and conducting a session with the project team on the same. This helps improve the productivity of the team and helps identify the dos and don'ts of the project.

- Celebrate the project completion.

The basic process of the project closure phase involves:

- Administrative closure is the process of preparation of closure documents and process deliverables. This includes the release and redistribution of the project resources.

- Development of project post implementation evaluation report, which includes project signoff, staffing and skills, project organizational structure, schedule management, cost management, quality management, configuration management, customer expectations management, and lessons learned.

Importance of Project Closure

By definition, a project has a beginning and an end. But without a formal closure process, project teams can fail to recognize the end, and then the project can drag on, sometimes at great expense. Project closure ensures that:

- Outcomes match the stated goals of the project.

- Customers and stakeholders are happy with the results.

- Critical knowledge is captured.

- The team feels a sense of completion.

- Project resources are released for new projects.

Which Projects Need Closure?

Every project requires closure. For large or complex projects, it's a good idea to close out each major project phase (for example, design, code and test, or training) individually. The closure process can also help by identifying lessons learned on projects that are canceled or deferred before completion. The outputs from project closure phase provides as a stepping stone to execute the next projects with much more efficiency and control.

Learn Lessons from Past Projects

Lessons learned form an integral part of the project closure phase. It helps answer the following typical question during project closure.

- Did the delivered product/solution meet the project requirements and objectives?

- Was the customer satisfied?

- Was project schedule met?

- Was the project completed within budgeted cost?

- Were the risks identified and mitigated?

- What could be done to improve the process?

Learning lessons from past failures is an important source of progress. Project managers should plan a formal session to discuss lessons learned during the closing phase. These should be documented and fed appropriately to the knowledge management system of the organization. It is important to make a note of the mistakes made during the course of the project so that these are not repeated again. Project managers are vulnerable to an unending repetition of errors. What makes it acutely painful is the loss that the project, its members, and the organization suffers. From time lost to unnecessary duplication of effort to financial losses from wasting time and resources, everyone loses. By something as simple as maintaining a managers' log that documents all errors, such losses can be avoided. If this log is updated and shared between all project managers at all times, they have a unique opportunity to learn from mistakes of others and their own. However, the process usually stops here, with mistakes documented for sake of formality and filed away, only to never be seen again.

What's needed is an incentive for project managers to act upon the lessons learnt. By instituting management level policies that reward efficiency and better results, organizations can cut down on process mishandling, time mismanagement, and resource wastage. Project management methodologies should be expanded to include not only complete sharing of information as mentioned above, but an emphasis on identifying, processing, and rectifying mistakes in project phases even before they can affect output. However, before any of this can happen, someone has to write them down.

Ending Projects Properly

Projects usually have a clearly defined end—a bridge opens for public use, a product launches, or new software rolls out to everyone in the organization. As a project manager, as the go-live stage is approached, and before the new challenges are taken up, it's important that the final step of project closure is not ignored. This means capturing the lessons learned during the project, so that the project team or other departments within the organization can benefit from them next time. And it also means taking stock of what has been achieved and celebrating the successes. The formalized project's acceptance is generally called the project closure process. This process verifies that the project has delivered the required outcomes and that stakeholder expectations have been met. It also makes sure that everyone involved in the project knows how to move forward. Without formal closure, there's a risk that issues may arise and no one will be assigned to resolve them.

Project closure has many different elements, and the best way to carry out a closure is to plan for it from the start. This provides the opportunity to decide which criteria will be used to show that the project is actually completed and budget the time and resources for the closing activities. As with all goals, it's important to know what has to be done to cross the project finish line. It should be noted that sometimes a project is cancelled before it's finished. When this happens, some parts of project closure become irrelevant. However, other elements may still need to be completed.

The following section describes the steps for closing a project properly. The following guidelines should be added for project closure to the overall project plan. These are based on the project closure outputs defined by the Project Management Body of Knowledge (PMBOK) Guide, and endorsed by the Project Management Institute (PMI).

PROJECT CLOSURE PROCESS

Finalize the Project's Documents

Project closure begins with wrapping up administrative documentation and providing a support plan for product maintenance. Much of a project's documentation is created over the life of the project. Document collection and update procedures are probably already well established. Even so, the following has to be done:

- Collect final time sheets, expense reports, and team status reports.

- Close or complete remaining tasks in the project schedule.

- Collect final cost and schedule metrics.

- Make final payments to vendors and contractors, and close out contracts.

- Review and update the issues log, highlight remaining issues, and decide how these issues are to be addressed.

- Prepare a plan for handling ongoing product support.

- Prepare a final project status report.

Capture the Knowledge

The project has likely produced documents that will be helpful during future projects, in troubleshooting the product, or in a future audit. Documenting of this valuable information is often deferred or overlooked because team members become busy with new projects, but the longer the wait, the less likely it is to capture all of the important data.

Prepare Final Project Report

As the project manager, most organizations will expect some sort of final project report. This document should be delivered to the project sponsor. The document should be a recap of the project. Begin with information from the project plan document, like the executive summary, project purpose, project objectives, project organization, and a project schedule (Usually include a comparison table of major milestone dates from the initial schedule baseline, as compared to the dates of the final working schedule at the end of the project).

Some detail should be provided on the effect of changes to the project, and those changes not covered by the project should be described. Recommendation should be made to address these as soon as possible. In addition to the above topics, final reconciliation of the project budget should also be included, along with a recap of the performance metrics taken during the project. Some organizations and some project sponsors will request a written report; others will request a presentation. Project sponsor should be asked for her/his preferred format of the final project report.

Once the Final Project Report is delivered and accepted by the project sponsor, the release/reassignment of all project team members is ensured, and all contracts are closed. The final chore as project manager is to make sure all project documentation is archived and accessible.

Set Up a Library

All key documents are stored in a project library that is accessible to future project teams. Possible document categories include: Project planning documents, status reports, design documents, test cases and test results, issues and resolutions, risk documentation, change requests, presentations, important communications (both those sent and those received), time and expense reports, contracts and invoices.

Ideally, the project library is set up at the beginning of the project, and team members add documents as they produce them. It's a good idea to maintain the library in an electronic format that is backed up at regular intervals—something as simple as a set of folders on the LAN or as robust as a knowledge management system. At the project's closure, the contents of the project library are reviewed and updated where necessary. Any relevant paper documents are collected and stored in an organized set of files or binders.

Document the Learning

Some of the most valuable knowledge that can be captured is in the form of lessons learned. This information can be gathered from several sources:

- Team members' survey about what worked and what didn't
- A meeting with your sponsor and executive stakeholders to capture their thoughts
- Objective feedback from consultants and vendors, both about your organization and about the project's execution

A formal lesson learned meeting can be conducted before reassignment of the project team members. Prior to the meeting, a brief "lessons learned questionnaire" can be distributed to all project stakeholders. Ideally, the questionnaire should solicit uniform, objective responses. Questions can be in the following broad categories:

- Management sponsorship
- Project objectives
- Project plan and schedule
- Project team

- Client/End User involvement
- Use of technology
- Client acceptance
- Project monitoring
- Project communications

Spaces for comments should be allowed under each topic/question. In addition, a simple answer scale, such as: 0 to signify "don't know or not applicable"and a scale of 1–5 to signify "strongly disagree to strongly agree."

As a project manager, if either time or assistance does not warrant the effort, simply ask for their perceived top three lessons learned from this project. Also, ask for their top three issues and how they would recommend planning for and eliminating those issues on a subsequent project. Use the information from these questionnaires to facilitate discussions and development of the lessons learned for your project. All meeting participants should be in agreement on these lessons learned and they should become a document in the project files. The top three to five lessons learned should also be mentioned in the final project report, to be delivered to the project sponsor. Provide a summary of the results to team members, either as a presentation at a meeting or as a formal document.

Receive Knowledge Transfer

Ensure that the consultants on the project don't walk away with most valuable asset—critical knowledge that your organization can use. The consultants should be released form the project only once they have transferred all of their important product maintenance knowledge to the team. The transfer might take the form of documents created by the consultants or training sessions that the consultants conduct.

Get Final Signoff

Schedule a meeting with the project's sponsor and key stakeholders to get their final signoff on the project. A formal signoff documents that the sponsor is satisfied, objectives have been met, and the project is truly complete. Of course, keeping the primary focus of the meeting on signoff is important. If time allows, however, the project manager might also want to briefly: Review final metrics, spotlight project highs and lows, acknowledge the contributions of team members, share the key lessons learned, and discuss related projects for the future (such as software upgrades, new features, and other opportunities for ongoing improvement).

Contract Closure

These activities formalize the acceptance of the project outcome and deliverables. There may be an actual contract document when dealing with external customers. If the project is for an internal department, an acceptance email may be sufficient. Either way, planning for contract closure is important. Here are some things to consider:

- Determine how acceptance criteria will be defined.

- Define exactly what the acceptance criteria are (again, this is usually defined in a Software Project Plan, as modified by the scope control process).

- Identify who is authorized to approve project completion, and determine that criteria have been met.

- Determine how inevitable changes to the contract will be controlled and managed.

- Decide what terms are needed if the project is not completed.

During the project closure phase, the project team is responsible for meeting predefined criteria. It's also important to make sure that the client or end user is fully satisfied with the results. If any changes have been made to the contract before project completion, the contract document may need to be updated appropriately. The business requirements analysis is a key input to the project closure process. With the use of these upfront planning tools, it will be easier to bring the project to a close.

Shut Down the Project Office and Archive

If the project team used a project management office or a dedicated work area, arrangements have to me made for returning that space to general use. For example, it could be: return rented furniture or computers, reassign temporary staff, close down LAN and e-mail accounts, and shut down utilities. When the shutdown process for the project office is organized, it can be helpful to review the original setup procedures.

Archive the project information so that it's an accessible resource for future project teams. This function is easy to overlook, especially as team members separate and move on to other work. As with the other project closure activities, the more proactive the planning is, the better the results are. If archive expectations are established at the start of the project, it is more likely that the information required will be collected and stored. The archive system should include these types of items:

- Project files—planning documents, risk documents, status reports, presentations, financial reports, contracts, and significant communications.

- Formal acceptance documents—statements issued by end users, approved change requests, and documented issues and solutions.

- Project closure documents—contracts, invoices, schedule of training provided, and an "open issues" file.

- Historical information—lessons learned, and a knowledge database.

These unique organizational assets should be gathered and stored electronically as well as physically. Computer files should be backed up regularly. With physical files, the information should be well organized and stored so that people can access it easily.

Recognize, Reward and Evaluate

As a project gets completed successfully, the team deserves some real recognition. As a project manager, you have the best understanding of who pulled the project out of each tight spot, which members have transformed themselves with new skills, and who might be ready for a new level of responsibility. Being in this position, the team's superiors should be reminded of what each team member has brought to the project.

Provide each team member with a performance evaluation: highlight contributions the member made, identify skills the member updated, and recommend new roles the member might be ready for. Provide a copy of this document to the member's supervisor. Make sure that the evaluation also reaches all department leads, as well as the human resources office, where this feedback can influence annual evaluations and salary discussions and aid in team members' transitions to new projects and new responsibilities.

Celebrate!

After putting in all those long hours, the team needs and deserves a celebration. A team dinner, a team outing, gift certificates, or other rewards are minor costs that generate a large return in terms of morale and job satisfaction. In addition to group acknowledgments, be sure to take each team member aside and thank him or her individually. Make a point of reminding the sponsor and other executive stakeholders of individual members' contributions and of letting them know how much a personal thank you would mean to your team.

An announcement to the organization is a good way to highlight the success of the project and its benefits to the company. For example, a senior company executive can send out an e-mail message recognizing the team's efforts, or an article can be published in the company newsletter touting the project's success.

CONCLUSION

Formal project closure ensures that project team has met its objectives, satisfied the customer, captured important knowledge, and been rewarded for their efforts. Once this is done, the next project can be moved on to with confidence. The end of a project is a significant event. Therefore, it needs its own set of processes and activities for formal closure. This shows that the project goal has been met, and it provides a sense of accomplishment for the project team. Closure also ensures that lessons learned are gathered and stored, and that end users' needs and expectations have been met. With an official close, it is understood that the stakeholders are satisfied. This enables reassigning the project team and reallocating resources to other projects—and starting the cycle all over again.

SECTION 4
ESTIMATION PROCESS

CHAPTER 1
ESTIMATION PROCESS OVERVIEW

This chapter is focused on describing the steps and procedures used in developing a software estimate. The software estimation process described here is intended to be a generic concept that can be applied to almost any project, anytime during its life cycle. It encompasses all of the necessary activities required to produce a software estimate for a software project throughout its life cycle and pertains only to the estimation of the costs associated with the software portion of a project (for example: requirements analysis, system design, coding, testing, configuration management, software quality assurance, etc.). There are many other costs associated with a project, such as hardware costs, overall project management costs, and travel costs that must also be considered when developing an overall project cost estimate.

PROCESS OVERVIEW

The software estimation process begins with the definition of the project's functional requirements. Without defining the requirements, it is impossible to determine the size, effort and cost estimate for the project. Once the functional requirements are known, the process of project estimation can begin. Two or more people should be involved in developing the estimation as two heads are always better than one. Never rely on any one person or method to develop software estimates. The organization's software process database should also be used to help calculate and validate software estimates.

Based on the available requirements, the first step is to develop the size estimates. Determining the size of the project is the process of quantifying the volume of work that has to be completed for the project. Traditionally, the size of the project is measured in Source Lines of Code (SLOC). Function or feature points could also be used to calculate the size of the work involved in a project. It is advisable to use more than one method to calculate size so that results can be compared. Once the size has been determined, the next step is to calculate the effort and cost estimates. Effort is usually calculated in person months (number of months required by a person to complete the project), which then can be translated into cost by using the applicable labor rates. These estimates can be used to arrive at the schedule estimates for the project. Estimates of critical computer resources should also be made. Items such as memory usage, processor usage, and timing requirements should be calculated and tracked. It is important to leave some reserve capacity in critical computer resources for future software upgrades.

Next step is to identify the risk associated with the project as these are likely to cause the estimates to change. Identified risks should be documented, tracked, and updated over the life of the project. The estimates should be updated based on the risk identified in the project. These updated estimates should then be validated. The purpose of the validation is to ensure that assumptions made for the estimates are accurate, that the estimate itself is reasonable and accurate, the methods used to develop the estimate are appropriate, all risks have been identified, and to confirm and record the official estimates for the project.

Software estimates should be continually tracked and updated throughout the life cycle of a project. Each time an estimate is updated, the assumptions and inputs should also be updated to reflect the most current information. A Software Estimation File (SEF) should be maintained that contains information such as estimation methods used, date of estimate, size estimate, effort estimate, cost estimate, project schedule, critical computer resources, and project risks. Software estimates should be submitted for use in the organization's software process database. Finally, data should be collected and analyzed from each of the above steps and should be used to improve the estimation process.

PROCESS PHASES AND DESCRIPTIONS

Projects should produce and document project plans, which include estimates of product size, project effort, cost, resources, staffing levels, schedules, and key milestones. Historically, the costs and schedules for most software projects have been greatly underestimated. There are many reasons for this including those listed below:

- Costs and schedules are often predetermined by an outside source.

- An in-depth analysis of the software development process is not undertaken or, in many cases, is not fully understood

- There is a general lack of acceptance that developing software is an expensive endeavor.

The software estimation process discussed in the following sections describes the steps required for establishing initial software Life Cycle Cost (LCC) estimates and then tracking and refining those estimates throughout the life of the project. Establishment of this process early in the project life cycle will result in greater accuracy and credibility of estimates and a clearer understanding of the factors that influence software development costs. This process also provides methods for project manager to identify and monitor the estimates, project schedule and project risk factors.

Process for Software Estimation Activities

Software estimation is a continual process that should be used throughout the life cycle of a project. The software estimation process consists of the following procedures:

- Estimate size.
- Estimate cost and effort.
- Estimate schedule.
- Estimate critical computer resources.
- Assess project risks.
- Inspect and approve.
- Track and report estimates.
- Measure and improve the process.

The process activities for developing the size, effort, and cost are shown before the schedule estimate in the following figure because this is the sequence often used by the cost models. However, a development schedule is often mandated during the scope definition activity of the project. The early establishment of a work breakdown structure (WBS) helps to divide the effort into distinct work segments that can be scheduled and prioritized. Detailed explanations of estimation requirements for each phase of a project are in subsequent sections.

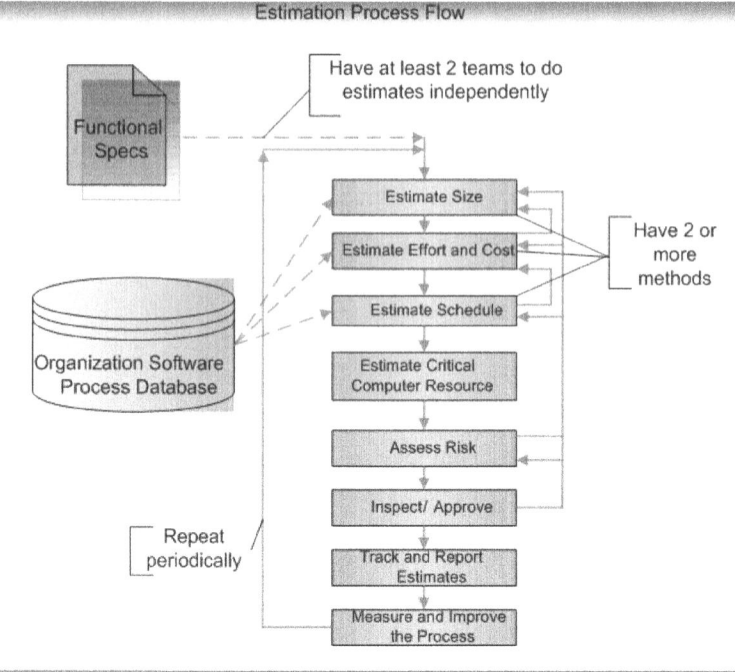

Estimation Process Flow

Have at least 2 teams to do estimates independently

Functional Specs

Estimate Size

Estimate Effort and Cost

Estimate Schedule

Have 2 or more methods

Organization Software Process Database

Estimate Critical Computer Resource

Assess Risk

Inspect/ Approve

Repeat periodically

Track and Report Estimates

Measure and Improve the Process

Estimate Size

Purpose

The purpose of developing the size estimate is to determine the magnitude of the effort. Size is a major input that cost models use to calculate the effort, cost, and schedule of a software project.

Responsible Personnel

Project manager, software engineers, and business analysts are responsible for determining the size of the software project.

Entry Criteria

Software functional requirements must be defined before size estimation can occur. Defining requirements early on in a project can be a very difficult task. However, without knowing what the requirements are, it is impossible to accurately estimate a project's size and cost. If all of the requirements are not known, then estimate based on the requirements that are known and make sure everyone knows that the estimate is based on only those known requirements. If an incremental or iterative development strategy is used, then base the estimate on the requirements that have been defined for that increment.

Input
Software Requirements Specification (SRS) and historical size data are the inputs needed to begin the size estimation.

Activities
Software product size is generally measured in Source Lines of Code (SLOC). The software should be developed using all new code or from combining new code with existing code. The estimate for the adaptation of existing code is as important as the estimate for new code. Adaptation of existing code often requires as much effort as if the code had been developed new. Size can also be measured by function points. Function point estimating is based on the functionality of a system and is most often applied during the Requirements Phase. Whichever method is used, care must be taken to consistently use standard definitions of size.

Estimates of software product size should be based primarily on organization's historical data and past experience. In addition, two or more software engineers with experience similar to the application under development should develop a top-down or bottom-up size estimate as described below:

- Develop a high-order architecture (top-down) diagram of the system, based on the requirements that define each Computer Software Configuration Item (CSCI) to be developed.

- Develop a functional WBS based on the CSCIs and the major functions within each CSCI.

- Develop a manual estimate of SLOC or function points to the lowest level of detail possible (bottom-up) for each major function within each CSCI based on experience with a similar application and historical data. A size-estimating tool may be used as a second input.

- Develop a nominal or expected size estimate plus a standard deviation, i.e., the lowest possible size and a highest possible size to reflect the uncertainty of the nominal estimate. The spread between the lowest and highest estimates may be as much as 30–50 percent in the early phases of a project, e.g., the Inception Phase. The range may be even wider if experience is scarce or there is high technical risk.

- Project managers and software engineers with similar project experience should review and refine the estimate until a consensus is reached. The lowest possible size estimates should be given special scrutiny as experience has demonstrated that size estimates are almost always low.

Some standard methods and tools for estimating size are the Wideband Delphi Technique, Pert Sizing Technique, Function Point Method, Sizing by Analogy, and automated size estimation tools. It is advisable to use at least two methods to develop the size estimate. Do not rely on any one method. Instead of calculating a single size count, use a range of values (maximum, minimum, and most likely). As the project progresses, size can be more accurately determined. Once coding has been completed on a project, automated SLOC counters can be used to calculate the size of the program.

Output
The outputs of this step will be the size of project in either SLOC or Function Points and a functional WBS.

Exit Criteria
The functional WBS has been documented in the Software Project Plan (SPP) and the size estimate has been recorded in the SEF.

Metrics
Metrics for this step includes a count of the SLOC or Function Points and the time and effort spent on calculating the size estimate.

Estimate Effort and Cost

Purpose
The purpose of this step is to determine the effort and cost required to complete the software portion of the project.

Responsible Personnel
The project manager, software engineers, and two or more software estimators are responsible for determining the cost and effort of the software project.

Entry Criteria
The size estimate and functional WBS must be completed before effort and cost estimation can occur.

Input
The size estimate, functional WBS, and historical cost data are the inputs needed for this step.

Activities
Choose an estimation method. If a parametric cost model is being used, then the environmental parameters for the project must be determined and entered into the model. Examples of parameters are program complexity, programming language, requirements volatility, analyst capability, and execution time constraint. The estimate should include all labor activities charged directly to the task. These activities normally include the following items:

- Engineering labor charges for software requirements analysis, design, code, test, and integration
- Documentation effort
- Configuration management

- Software quality assurance
- Management effort charged directly to the task

Run estimation calculations using two or more estimation methods. Some of the standard and acceptable methods for estimating cost and effort are shown below:

- Algorithmic Models—Consists of one or more algorithms that produce an effort estimate as a function of a number of variables or cost drivers. This is the most prevalent method utilized by software estimation models.

- Expert Judgment—Relies on one or more people who are considered experts in some endeavor related to the problem at hand, e.g., the software application or effort estimation. This is the most widely used method of manual estimation.

- Analogy—Comparison of the proposed project to completed projects of a similar nature whose costs are known. This method emphasizes the need for software costs historical databases. The more data that is available, the more accurate the estimates will be. The organization's software process database is a source for this historical cost data.

- Top-Down—An overall cost estimate for the project is derived from global properties of the software product. This estimate will usually be based on previous projects and will include the costs of all functions in a project, e.g., integration, documentation, software quality assurance, and configuration management.

- Bottom-Up—Each component of the software product is separately estimated and the results aggregated to produce an estimate for the overall job. These estimates often overlook many of the system-level costs such as integration, software quality assurance, and configuration management.

- Automated Estimation Models—A number of computerized models are available that estimate cost and schedule from user inputs of size and environmental cost factors.

Most of these are algorithmic models that use lines of code as the measure of size.

A high level estimate of cost should be generated early in a project's life cycle, as soon as the general software requirements are defined. Early on in the project, a manual estimate can be done. It will give the estimators an understanding of the process and parameters that the automated tools utilize. After a manual estimate is completed, a second estimate should be developed using an automated tool. The results of the two estimates should be compared, and reasons for any large variances should be resolved. How large a variance is acceptable depends upon where a project is in the life cycle. Early in the project, estimates within 20 percent are reasonable. As a project matures, the estimates should converge. When using an automated estimation tool, results improve when the model is calibrated to better reflect historical cost data from the project domain, if available.

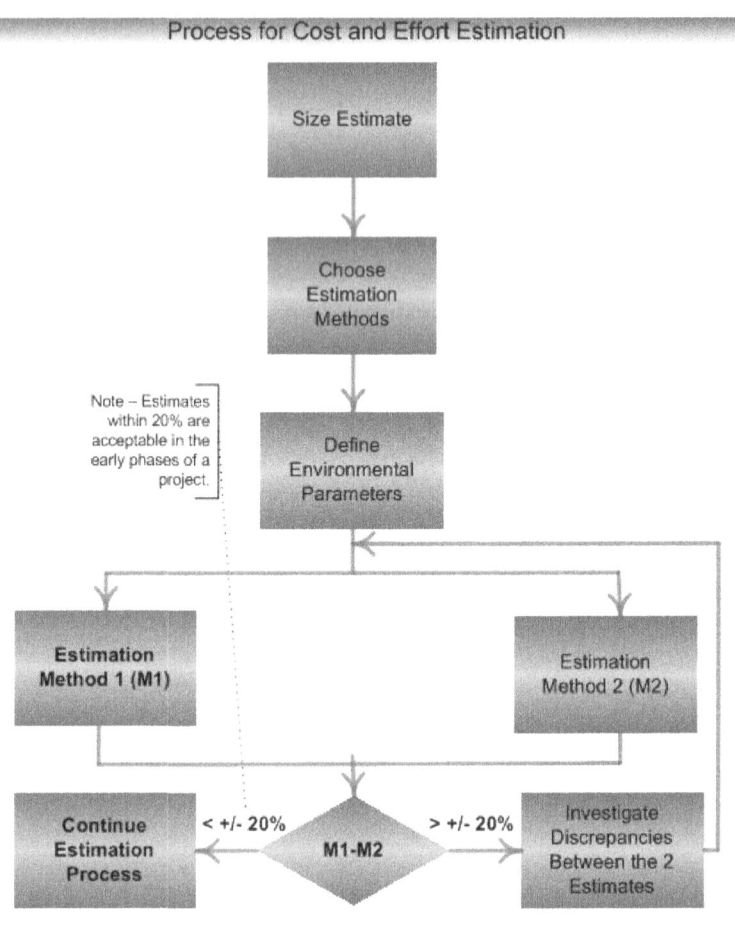

Process for Cost and Effort Estimation

Output

Effort and cost estimates for the software project are the output of this step.

Exit Criteria

Effort and cost have been determined and documented in the SEF and the SPP. If more than one method was used, then any discrepancies between the estimates have been resolved.

Metrics
Metrics for this step include the cost and effort estimations, and the time and resources expended developing estimate.

Estimate Schedule

Purpose
The purpose of this step is to determine the length of time needed to complete the project and when major milestones and reviews will occur.

Responsible Personnel
The project manager, software engineers, and software estimators are responsible for determining the schedule of the software project.

Entry Criteria
The functional WBS, size, cost and effort estimates must be completed before the schedule estimation can occur.

Input
The size, cost and effort estimates, functional WBS, and historical schedule data are the inputs needed for this step.

Activities
Schedule estimates can be derived by using either manual or automated estimation models. A combination of both manual and automated methods is recommended. Manual methods should be based primarily on past experience or historical data from the organization's software process database. One or more software engineers with experience, with the specific application under development, should use the size estimate and experience, with similar projects to develop a schedule estimate as follows:
- The WBS should be expanded to delineate the order in which functional elements will be developed. The order of

development will define which functions can be developed in parallel as well as dependencies that drive the schedule.

- A development schedule should be derived for each set of functions that can be developed independently, i.e., a schedule for each build of an incremental development.

- The schedule for each set of independent functions should be derived as the aggregate of the estimated time required for each major phase of the development, including analysis, design, code and unit test, integration, and test.

- The total project schedule should reflect the aggregate of the product development, including documentation and formal review requirements.

The steps outlined above are typical of manual estimates. Automated tools provide a schedule estimate, along with the cost and effort estimate. Automated tools allow the user to tailor the schedule to observe the impact on cost. However, most automated tools allow only a small amount of flexibility in shortening schedules.

Output
Schedule estimates for the software project, including major milestones and reviews, are the output of this step.

Exit Criteria
The schedule has been determined and entered into the SEF and the SPP. If more than one method was used, then any discrepancies between the estimates have been resolved.

Metrics
The project schedule estimate, and the time and resources spent developing schedule estimate are the metrics collected from this step.

Estimate Critical Computer Resources

Purpose
The purpose of this step is to determine the critical computer resources needed to complete the project and compare that estimate to the actual critical resources available.

Responsible Personnel
The project manager and software engineers are responsible for this estimate.

Entry Criteria
The functional WBS must be completed; requirements defined and critical computer resources limits known before the critical computer resources estimation can occur.

Input
The critical computer resource limits and software requirements are the inputs needed for this step.

Activities
There are several methods for calculating critical computer resources. Some of the methods are historical experience, simulations, prototyping, and analysis. The method used for the calculation of critical computer resources is project-specific. Critical computer resources include items such as memory usage, throughput capacity, timing, and hard drive usage. Different projects have different critical computer resources, so projects may estimate and track different critical computer resource items. It is important to plan for the availability of excess critical computer resources in anticipation of future program updates.

Output
The estimate of the critical computer resources for the software project is the output of this step.

Exit Criteria
The critical computer resources have been estimated and have been compared against critical computer resource limits.

Metrics
Metrics for this step include the project critical computer resource estimates and the time and resources spent developing critical computer resource estimates.

Assess Risks

Purpose
The purpose of this step is to determine what the project risks are and what their effect is on the software size, effort, cost, schedule, and critical computer resource estimates.

Responsible Personnel
The project manager and software estimators are responsible for assessing the risks on the project.

Entry Criteria
The software estimates and functional WBS must be completed before the risk assessment can occur.

Input
The size, effort, cost, schedule, critical computer resource estimates, and WBS are the inputs needed for this step.

Activities
Determine project risk factors and update estimates based on the known risks. For example, if requirements volatility is a risk, then provide one estimate assuming low requirements volatility and one assuming high requirements volatility. In this way, the sponsor will know the project risks and the effects of those risks on the cost and schedule of the project. Estimates for the amount of code that can

be reused are a source of error and risk in estimating software cost. Estimators tend to be overly optimistic about the effort that will be necessary to adapt the existing code. Other risks that commonly impact the size, cost, and schedule estimates are optimistic assessments of the software development environment and staff and misunderstood or constantly changing requirements.

Project risk assessment and its impact on the estimates is a continuous process. The risk assessment update should not concentrate only on the risk areas identified originally. For instance, an off-the-shelf-software package may not be performing as originally assumed. If such an occurrence may cause a problem, such as a slip in schedule, it should be noted. Each time an estimate is done, the assumptions and inputs should be updated to reflect the most current information. Once the potential risks are identified, metrics should be defined and tracked to identify when and how the project may be overrunning size, cost, or schedule. Risk factors should be recorded and tracked in the SEF as well as in the SPP.

Output
The project risks and revised software estimates are the outputs of this step.

Exit Criteria
Project risks have been documented in the SEF and the SPP. Software estimates have been revised to reflect the impact of project risk factors and have been documented in the SEF and SPP.

Metrics
For this step, include the number and classification of risks and the time and effort expended on risk analysis and in developing alternative size, cost, and schedule estimates.

Inspect and Approve

Purpose

The purpose of this step is to detect any defects in the estimates and to get upper management commitment. The objectives of the inspection and approval of the estimate are listed below:

- Confirm the software architecture and functional WBS.

- Verify the methods used for deriving the size, cost, and schedule estimates.

- Ensure that the assumptions and input data used to develop the estimates are correct.

- Ensure that the estimate is reasonable and accurate given the input data.

- Formally confirm and record the official estimates for the project.

Responsible Personnel

The project manager, software engineers, software estimators, quality assurance personnel, and senior management are responsible for inspecting and approving the estimates.

Entry Criteria

The software estimate must be completed before the inspection and approval can occur.

Input

The software estimates, including input parameters, project risks, project constraints, and any assumptions associated with the estimate, are the inputs needed for this step.

Activities

Inspection and approval should be accomplished by a peer review. The peer review should be attended by the personnel that developed the estimate, at least one other software engineer from the same project, a software engineer with experience on a similar project, and a management representative, division level or higher, or a person from an independent SQA organization.

Software estimators, the project manager, quality assurance personnel and senior management representative will sign the estimate after the inspection is complete and all defects have been resolved.

Inspection and approval activities can be formal or informal. What is important is that the estimates are reviewed independently. Most project managers do not inspect and approve their estimates. This invariably leads to poor and inaccurate estimates. Also, senior management is oftentimes unaware of the estimates that project managers are submitting. Estimates can be improved simply by having the appropriate personnel participate in the validation process.

Output
The signatures of the software estimators, project manager, senior management, and SQA on the software estimate are the outputs of this step.

Exit Criteria
Software estimates have been reviewed and approved by the software estimators, project manager, quality assurance personnel, and senior management representative.

Metrics
Metrics for this step include the number of defects found in estimate and the effort and resources expended in inspecting and approving the estimates.

Track and Report Estimates

Purpose
The purpose of this step is to check the accuracy of the estimate over time and develop a historical file of the estimates.

Responsible Personnel

The project manager, software engineers, and software estimators are responsible for tracking and reporting the estimates.

Entry Criteria

The software estimate must be completed and approved before tracking and reporting can begin.

Input

The approved software estimates, SEF, SPP, and WBS, are the inputs needed for this step.

Activities

Compare current estimate to previous estimates. Resolve any discrepancies with previous estimates and document tracking data in the SEF and the SPP.

Estimates should be tracked over time. Comparing planned versus actual estimates over time allows the estimators to see how well they are estimating and also to see how their project is changing over time. The development of the SEF allows the estimator to develop a historical database of estimates. This historical database can be used by the estimator to either calibrate cost models or for purposes of comparison when performing estimates for future projects.

Estimation data, both planned and actual, should be provided to the organization's Software Process Database for the benefit of other projects in the organization. The SEF should contain summaries of all estimates, tracking summaries, copies of memos, etc. that relate to the estimation process, and copies of detailed estimate data, i.e., assumptions, inputs and results. Specifically, the SEF should contain the following items:

- Method of estimation

- Dates of estimates

- Proposed dates for major reviews

- Number of computer software configuration items
- Number of software units or components
- Number of objects (if Object Oriented Analysis/Design methods used)
- Estimated size for new and reused code
- Estimated schedule for each major phase
- Estimated cost
- Project risks
- Estimates of critical computer resources

Estimation information does not have to be put in a stand-alone SEF. It can be included in the SPP as well.

Output
Updated tracking data documented in the SEF or SPP and an evaluation of comparisons between current and past estimates documented in the SEF or SPP are the outputs of this step.

Exit Criteria
Estimates have been tracked, and any discrepancies between present and past estimates have been resolved.

Metrics
Metrics for this step include the variation of estimates over time and the effort and resources expended in tracking and reporting the estimates.

Measure and Improve Process

Purpose
The purpose of this step is to use the metrics collected during each step of the software estimation process to improve the process.

Responsible Personnel

The project manager, software engineers, and software estimators are responsible for measuring and improving the software estimation process.

Entry Criteria

Estimations have been completed and approved, and metrics have been collected during each step of the estimation process.

Process Input

Metrics from each of the steps of the software estimation process and previous estimates are the inputs needed for this step.

Process Activities

Two forms of measurement will be accomplished. The first, called process effectiveness metrics is used to track the effects of the process on the project. The second set of metrics, called process cost metrics, is used to provide management with insight into the cost of implementing and performing this process. The long-term benefit of collecting these metrics is to determine a correlation between the overall accuracy of the estimates and the cost of developing the estimates. This information is another input to the resource requirements of a project and should be identified as such.

The collection of metrics will begin as soon as the process is implemented and will continue throughout the development cycle. Collection of the metrics will continue through the final phases of development, even though estimation activity declines in those phases. The two types of metrics are described below:

Process Effectiveness Metrics—The purpose of the Process Effectiveness Metrics is to identify the elements of the estimation process that enhance the estimation process and those elements that are of little or no value to the planning and tracking processes of a project. Process elements or activities that enhance the process are those that provide the greatest accuracy regarding the actual cost and schedule, as well as cost and schedule to completion of a project. Conversely, those elements or activities that do not enhance the accuracy of the estimates need to be isolated and eliminated. The Process Effectiveness Metrics consist of the variances between most recent estimates and the baseline estimates.

Process Cost Metrics—The purpose of the Process Cost Metrics is to quantify the cost of the process and identify ways to increase the cost-effectiveness of the process. Elements or activities that cost-effectively enhance the process will remain intact, while those that are of little or no value to project will be eliminated. Process elements or activities that are cost-effective are those that provide meaningful input to the process with a minimum amount of work effort. Conversely, those elements or activities that require effort but do not return meaningful data need to be isolated and eliminated.

The elements and definitions of the Process Cost Metrics are divided into two categories: effort to perform the estimates and the cost of tools. The effort metrics include the person hours for the following items: size estimate and cost/schedule estimate. The cost of the tools is a summation of the following items: purchase price, training cost, license renewal, special hardware, and consulting fees. These metrics should be collected for each estimate developed. Collecting and analyzing metrics are important to process improvement efforts. Use metrics to evaluate every step of the process. Change process steps as needed, and don't be afraid to delete steps if they are found to have no added value.

Output
Process improvement activities that have been planned and documented are the outputs of this step.

Exit Criteria
Metrics have been analyzed, and process improvement activities have been planned.

Measure and Improve Process Metrics—Metrics for this step include the effort expended analyzing metrics and planning and implementing process improvement activities.

An example of software estimation

I have considered "Project X-1" to demonstrate the estimation process that was followed for the project. During the "Phase-I" of the project, requirements were detailed out and documented. Based on the detailed requirements, a navigable user interface prototype was developed to get a feel of the screens and application flow. Signed-off requirement documents and prototype were taken as the input for estimation for "Phase-II" of the project. "Phase-II" involved design, coding, testing, and deployment of the application.

For the workflow management system that was developed, let me consider the "Checking" module for explaining the estimation process that was adopted for this project. The purpose of "Checking" module or component was to verify the correctness of medicines and quantity against the prescription. The prescription image was available to the technician from the "Imaging" module where the prescription was scanned. The vial containing the medicine was made available in the packing box (A device to store vials) form the "Dispensing" module. Using these inputs, the technician could verify if the medicine dispensed for the given prescription was correct or not.

Project size: The size was measured using WBS units, which is based on the functional point estimation process. As per this process, the functional requirement is divided into smaller units or components and each of these components is identified as simple, average, and complex based on the complexity level involved. The type of component is also identified. It could be a transactional component, or query component, or report component, or process component. A numeric value called "WBS unit" is assigned to each component based on the complexity level (simple, average, complex) and the type (transaction, query, report, process). For instance, a simple component of type transaction is given a value of 6, an average component of type transaction is given a value of 12, and a complex component of type transaction is given a value of 22. These values are derived from our organization database and are based on the project experiences that we had in the past.

As per the above process, the "Checking" module was divided into smaller components such as "View prescription queue", "View packing box", "Integration with packing box", "Status of prescription in packing box", "Select prescription to verify", "Display incomplete order screen", "View partials", "Audit log", and so on. Each of these components were assigned a complexity level and identified for the type. Accordingly, each component had a WBS unit assigned. The sum of all these "WBS units" resulted in the total size of the "Checking" module or component.

Effort estimate: Once the size of the component was available, the effort required to design, develop, test, and deploy the component could be derived using a formula. This formula considers the following factors.

Effort (In person days) = [(Size of the component in WBS units) / (Productivity)] + COCOMO drivers

The productivity factor is a percentage number between 1 percent and 100 percent. It denotes the productivity level of the team working on the project. For example, a working day consists of 8 hours of work. The team may not be spending all the 8 hours on the work. The effective working hours could be only 6. In that case, the productivity of the team is 75 percent.

Similarly, the COCOMO drivers are the factors which decide the additional effort required for developing the component or product. Some of these factors are, "Similar project done in past", "Stakeholder relationship", "Skill levels of team members",

"Organization maturity in processes", " Annual personnel turn-over rate" and so on. Each of these drivers is given a numeric value between "very low" to "extra high" for a given project. Based on the value assigned, the effort value is considered in the total effort required to develop the component or project. The effort estimate can be used to calculate the cost required for the development work. The cost depends on the service rate that is charged to the customer.

CHAPTER 2
SOFTWARE ESTIMATION PROCESS
IN SOFTWARE LIFE CYCLE

The estimation process is described in this section for each phase up to the Software Unit (SU) or system integration and test phase of a typical software development project. As the project progresses through the phases, the estimation process graduates from a process of project planning to a process of project management and tracking. Software estimation inputs and outputs are included for each of the major phases and address the general needs for a standard full-scale development project.

The entry criteria required for estimates consists primarily of a set of minimum input data necessary to satisfy the data requirements of a size, cost, and schedule estimate for that phase. The exit criteria are generally a set of products that must be complete before the estimation activity is considered complete for that phase. The software estimation process is summarized in following picture and table. This exhibit highlights the steps necessary to establish a formal project estimate and for revising and tracking the estimate throughout the life of the project.

ESTIMATION PROCESS ACTIVITIES BY PROJECT LIFE CYCLE PHASE

The explanations of the estimation activities corresponding to the phases of the software development life cycle are described below. Entry and exit criteria are also included for each of the major phases. The picture below provides the summary of the process.

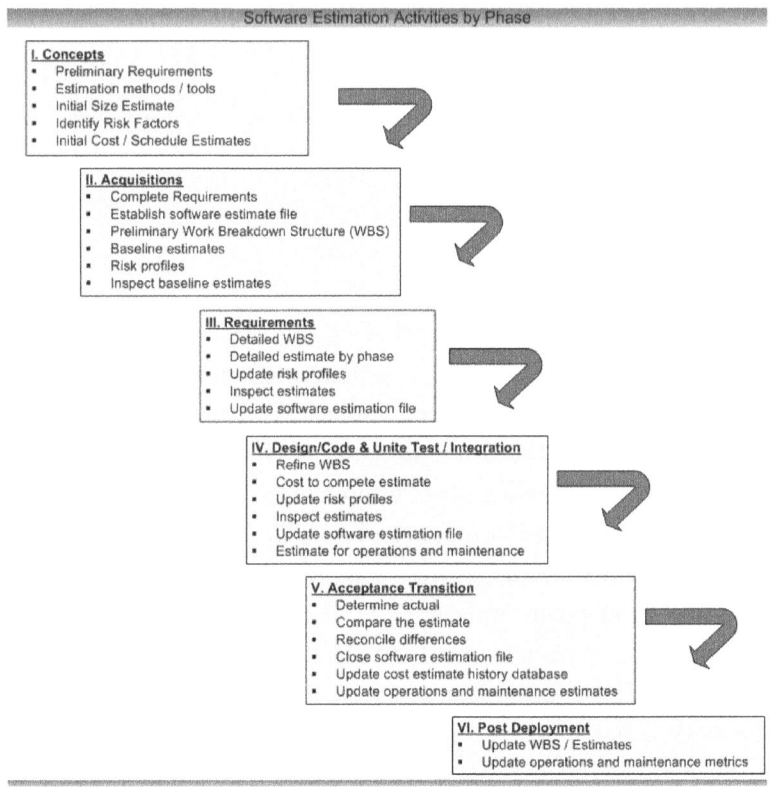

Concept Phase

It is during this phase that the functional description of the system is loosely defined. There is often a great degree of uncertainty about the probable requirements of the project and thus, much uncertainty of the final product's size. Usually during this period, several options are analyzed and then evaluated for technical and cost advantages and disadvantages.

Entry Criteria

The entry criteria for this early phase are that the preliminary functional requirements be available. A preliminary, top-level estimate can be derived without a detailed understanding of the final product. The estimate cannot be expected to be extremely accurate but can provide a range of costs suitable for long-term budget and cost estimating.

Tasks

Define preliminary system requirements; an initial set of requirements should be documented. These preliminary requirements are usually ambitious and should be treated as a wish list of functionality. The requirements should be prioritized in separate categories that denote those functions that are absolutely necessary from those that are nice-to-have. The functions should be defined in such a manner as to reflect similar existing functions as much as possible.

Establish method of estimation. Early in the life of the project, methods of developing software estimates should be explored and experimented with, using representative data. Once a method is adopted, it should be used in a consistent manner until estimates are replaced by actual data or until the method is found to be deficient or can be improved.

Identify similar functions. Software systems that perform functions similar to the desired functions should be identified. Functions that do not resemble some existing function should be broken down to as low a level as possible to separate out all of the new functionality. Reducing the number of unknowns in a new system will decrease the uncertainty of the estimated cost of the project.

Develop size estimates from historical data. A most likely size estimate should be developed for each major CSCI. An upper and lower size estimate should also be defined that reflects the degree of confidence in the most likely estimate. Software size estimates can be derived manually or with the help of software sizing tools. Historical data should be used as much as possible. Size information that can be gleaned from existing systems will be the most accurate.

Develop size estimates for new functions. For functions that do not have a similar existing function, size estimating by analogy can be utilized, i.e., identify functions that have some similarity. Functions that have the greatest range of uncertainty in size should be decomposed into smaller units that reflect an increased confidence in the size estimate. An additional reference point can be derived with a software size estimation tool.

Develop preliminary estimates. Size, cost, and schedule estimates should be developed for the total proposed functionality. Estimates should be developed manually from the estimates of product size and complexity derived in earlier steps. The total estimate should be developed in a bottom-up approach, i.e., cost and schedule estimates should be developed for each of the major functions, as defined earlier. Once a manually derived estimate is complete, a second estimate should be developed with an automated estimation model. This second estimate will serve as a sanity check of the manual estimate. Commercially available models offer the benefit of varying input parameters to quickly observe the effect on a project's cost and schedule.

Define areas of risk. Risks can be separated into several categories. Three categories most often addressed are technical, personnel, and requirements. All three of these categories will impact the cost and schedule of a project. Defining and addressing specific potential impacts to cost and schedule early will highlight issues that need to be addressed and tracked throughout the project. When an overall baseline estimate is complete, the impacts on the estimate as a result of the risk areas identified should be applied. A best-case scenario will demonstrate the lowest cost and shortest schedule, if all elements of the project proceed without perturbation. A worst-case scenario will demonstrate the potentially high cost and long schedule that will result if numerous problems occur and risks are not abated.

Review and refine estimate. The development of the requirements and the cost estimate to complete the project is an iterative process. The implementation of the requirements is dependent upon many factors, including cost and schedule. Thus, the impact on cost and schedule should be closely tracked as alternative requirement sets are considered. Each set of requirements should result in a revised project cost and schedule estimate.

Exit Criteria

The software estimation activity for this phase is complete when a top-level size, cost, and schedule estimate for the total software project has been completed. The exit criteria also includes a prioritized list of the potential software functions, definition and analysis of potential high-risk cost and schedule factors, and a plan for developing all future estimates for the project. The plan will describe estimation methods and tools to be utilized by the project, as well as the method of tracking to be used. This information should be included in the SEF and the SPP. The estimate should be approved and signed off by the software estimators, project manager, senior management, and quality assurance representative.

Acquisition Phase

It is during this phase that the system specification or requirements specification of the system is defined. The requirements specifications are in considerable detail, still there is often a great degree of uncertainty about the probable size of the final product. Usually during this period, several options are defined and then evaluated for technical and cost advantages and disadvantages.

Entry Criteria

Preliminary estimates based on the preliminary requirements from the preceding phase should be available. The preliminary estimates should address the total size, cost, and schedule of the software product. The functional description and requirements should now be complete and concise enough to refine the previous estimates to a range of +/-20 percent of the expected values.

Tasks

Define the Software Requirements. This is not necessarily a formal step in developing an estimate; rather, it is something that must be generated for any project. The requirements must be clearly understood before even the most cursory estimate can be accomplished.

Establish software estimation file. Project estimates and all supporting data should be formally documented and maintained. These initial estimates can be informally documented at this time, i.e., the format can be refined at the beginning of the Requirements Phase. The information can be provided in the SEF and the SPP. The documentation should include a description of all input data, clear and concise definitions of data items, acronyms relative to the project, assumptions and constraints, the estimation method used, and tool outputs if an automated estimation tool was used.

Develop preliminary WBS. A Work Breakdown Structure (WBS) should be developed that shows the activities related to the development of each major software function. At this early stage in the project, it is sufficient to show the major activities and products identified in the software development process. The WBS, along with the method used to track the cost and schedule status of each WBS line item, should also be documented in the SEF and the SPP. If a project management tool is used, hard copies of the baseline plan and each major revision should also be retained in the SEF.

Develop baseline software estimates. Estimates should be developed and documented that reflect the baseline project software requirements. The methods used during the Concept Phase should be reviewed to determine their adequacy. The methods that are going to be utilized throughout the remainder of the project should be agreed to at this time. Copies of all estimates, manual or otherwise, should be retained in the SEF.

Develop risk profile. A risk assessment profile shall also be developed that shows a range of cost and schedule estimates to assess the impact on the project for variations of unknowns in the project. Typical variables that should be considered in developing a risk profile include code size growth, complexity, requirements volatility, data security requirements, and number of organizations or vendors involved.

Conduct formal review. A formal review, such as the peer review process, can be followed to review the estimation methods. The estimates will be reviewed for reasonableness of assumptions and input data. Risk profiles and assessments will also be reviewed.

Refine and record estimates. Estimates should be refined and recorded as often as any changes in requirements occur or whenever any change in direction or scope of the project occurs. All estimates and revised schedule milestone dates should be recorded.

Exit Criteria
The software estimation activity for this phase is considered complete when size, cost, and schedule estimates have been completed and a top-level WBS has been defined. These estimates and the WBS can be included in the SPP. A separate SEF can also be established and should contain the estimates and all information and assumptions used to develop the estimates. If a separate SEF is not established, then all of the estimation information should be recorded in the SPP. The exit criteria also include a prioritized list of the potential software functions and a risk analysis of cost and

schedule risks. The estimate should be approved and signed off by the software estimators, project manager, senior management, and quality assurance representative.

Requirements Phase

During this phase, detailed software requirements activity begins. It is important to ensure that all functional software requirements are traceable to the next higher-level specification. It is during this phase that a good functional breakdown of the software product is developed. Functions should be prioritized to develop a thorough and realistic cost estimate for the project. A concise and clear set of prioritized requirements will also enhance the completeness of a risk assessment. A complete estimate of size, cost, and schedule should be developed for all development and acquisition options. Such estimates should be developed immediately prior to any formal requirements reviews.

Entry Criteria

The SPP should be available and include an estimate for the total software product, a WBS, and a preliminary cost and schedule risk analysis. The functional description for the product should be clear enough to develop preliminary estimates for the size, cost, and schedule of the CSCIs.

Task

Develop WBS. Early in the Requirements Phase, a WBS should be generated that reflects adequate detail to generate an estimate down to at least the CSCI level. The initial WBS should address the cost and schedule associated with each major software function or CSCI.

Develop and record baseline requirements phase estimate. New estimates should be generated and recorded. Each new estimate should be compared with the last estimate and with the baseline estimate from the previous phase. New estimates should be based on the revised WBS and requirements.

Update and revise risk assessment. The cost estimate should be reviewed as often as the risk assessments are refined. The high-risk variables that should be constantly reviewed; include code size, complexity, requirements volatility, data security requirements, state-of-the-art, and number of organizations or agencies involved.

Conduct formal review. A formal review, such as the peer review process can be followed to review the estimation methods. The estimates will be reviewed for reasonableness of assumptions and input data. Risk profiles and assessments will also be reviewed.

Refine and record estimates. Estimates should be refined and recorded as often as any changes in requirements occur or whenever any change in direction or scope of the project occurs. All estimates and revised schedule milestone dates should be recorded in the SEF and the SPP.

Exit Criteria

The software estimation activity for this phase is considered complete when a detailed size, cost, and schedule have been completed for each CSCI. The CSCI estimates should be calculated for each phase of the project. The CSCI estimates should be rolled up into an estimate for the total software product. The previously developed prioritized list of the potential software functions and analysis of cost and schedule risks shall also have been updated to reflect the most recent information. The WBS should be refined to include detailed planning information, down to the CSCI level. The SPP and SEF shall be updated. The estimate should be approved and signed off by the software estimators, project manager, senior management, and quality assurance representative.

Design Phase

The Design Phase begins after the software requirements have been defined, reviewed, and documented in the software requirements specification document. A formal approval on the requirements document is necessary. There are two major activities that occur during the Design Phase, the High Level Design (HLD) and the Low Level Design (LLD). During these two major activities, medium to large projects require periodic technical progress reviews. These reviews often result in refined requirements, better understanding of the original requirements, or sometimes a redirection. Size, cost, and schedule estimates should be revised based on the LLD, HLD, and other technical reviews.

Entry Criteria

The minimum entry criteria for this phase are the SPP and the approved software requirement specifications document available from the completion of the Requirements Phase. Detailed size, cost, and schedule estimates by phase to the CSCI level and the WBS to the CSCI level should also be available from the previous phase.

Tasks

Develop detailed WBS. Early in the Design Phase, the top-level WBS should be expanded to reflect the software design down to the SU level. The WBS should contain adequate detail to generate an estimate down to at least the SU level. The detailed WBS should address the cost and schedule associated with each major function, CSCI (or module), and SU (or components). The format of the WBS should be such that the aggregate costs of SUs can be rolled up to produce the total cost of each CSCI.

Develop and record baseline design phase estimate. New estimates should be generated and recorded. This will often be a revision of the last estimate from the Requirements Phase. The revised estimate should be compared with the baseline estimate from the previous phase. Any new estimates should be based on the revised WBS and a better understanding of the requirements.

Update and revise risk assessment. The risk assessment profile should be reviewed as often as the software estimates are refined. The high-risk variables that should be constantly reviewed include code size, complexity, requirements volatility, data security requirements, state-of-the-art, and number of organizations or agencies involved.

Conduct formal review. A formal review, such as the peer review process can be followed to review the estimation methods. The estimates will be reviewed for reasonableness of assumptions and input data. Risk profiles and assessments will also be reviewed.

Refine and record estimates—Estimates should be refined and recorded as often as any changes in requirements occur or whenever any change in direction or scope of the project occurs. All estimates and revised schedule milestone dates should be recorded in the SEF and the SPP.

Exit Criteria

The software estimation activity for this phase is considered complete when a detailed size, cost-to-complete cost, and schedule estimate has been completed for each CSCI. The cost-to-complete estimates should be calculated for the remaining phases of the project. The CSCI cost-to-complete estimates shall be rolled up into an estimate for the total software product. The estimates and WBS should include information to the SU level of detail. The previously developed prioritized list of the potential software functions and analysis of cost and schedule risks should also have been updated to reflect the most recent information. The SEF and SPP should be updated as appropriate. The estimate should be approved and signed off by the software estimators, project manager, senior management, and quality assurance representative.

Code and Unit Test Phase/Integration Phase/ Acceptance and Transition to Operation Phase

The processes for these subsequent phases are accomplished in the same manner as described for the design phase. By the time the project reaches these phases, estimates should be giving way to actual effort, and the processes should be instantiated to the degree that minimal effort is involved in updating the cost-to-complete estimates.

Post Deployment Phase

There are various methods for estimating the cost of software maintenance. The most often used method is to calculate maintenance cost as a percentage of the software development cost. This can be accomplished by estimating the Annual Change Traffic (ACT), i.e., an estimate of the amount of code that will be changed each year. This method is acceptable during the early phases of the project's life cycle. As the project's development nears completion, however, more precise methods should be employed.

Maintenance costs may be broken down into three categories: corrective, perfective, and adaptive. Corrective maintenance involves fixing errors. In adaptive maintenance, changes are made to accommodate different data or processing environments. Perfective maintenance includes changes that improve the program. The total cost of software maintenance is the sum of these costs. As in software development estimates, the maintenance cost estimates should be derived based on past experience. The cost of corrective maintenance will depend on the quality of the software. Software that is fielded with a great number of defects will result in a great number of software trouble reports that, in turn, could potentially result in high maintenance costs. However, maintenance activities typically do not get funded adequately to eliminate all errors as they are reported. The highest priority defects are fixed first, followed by the lower priority defects.

ADDITIONAL MODES OF SOFTWARE DEVELOPMENT

The process described above is tailored to the standard waterfall, full-scale development method that is most commonly used when discussing project planning and management concepts. However, other types of development that are common include prototyping, evolutionary acquisition, technology insertion, incremental development, and Research and Development (R and D) or agile. Some general considerations that should be made for the estimation process under each of these modes are discussed in the sections that follow.

Prototyping

Prototyping, as a method to evaluate the feasibility of technical ideas and theories, has become increasingly popular and is a widely used development mode. Developing a prototype is usually a distinct portion of the life cycle and thus, sound software engineering practices should be followed, including the development of a well thought out estimate. Just as the prototype will provide insight into the design and implementation issues, the estimate and cost of producing the prototype will provide insight into the cost of the overall project.

Developing a cost estimate for a prototyping project should be accomplished in the same manner as for a full-scale development project. The primary cost savings resulting from prototyping is the lack of formal reviews and documentation required. Also, there is a minimum of systems engineering and formal testing involved.

Evolutionary Acquisition

Evolutionary Acquisition (EA) is becoming the rule more than the exception in large-scale development efforts. The thesis of "build a little, test a little" is seen as a way to develop systems that better satisfy user requirements and more easily take advantage of technical advances. The underlying factor in EA is to field a well-defined core capability quickly in response to a validated requirement, while using a phased upgrade program to eventually enhance the system to provide the overall system capability.

The process for estimating an EA project can be accomplished in the same manner as for a standard waterfall project. An EA project requires the same formality as any other method of development. Estimates should be developed for each phase or development cycle of an EA project, just as they would be for a large full scale development project. During each phase of an EA project, two separate estimates shall be required, an estimate for the current phase and an estimate for the total project as it is understood and defined at that time.

Incremental Development

The incremental development approach is a top-down implementation of distinct functional elements of the product. The development of each increment is accomplished as a separate waterfall type of development. This strategy allows visibility into potential design, interface problems, etc., early in the development cycle. It also provides the opportunity to incorporate user experience into the final product. The incremental development methodology differs from the evolutionary approach in that under the incremental strategy, the end product is well defined.

Estimates should be developed for the total project, as well as for each of the increments. Each increment should be identified and sized. The estimates for each increment should be accomplished as for an individual waterfall development project. The estimate for the total project will have to show the overlapping of the increments. How the individual increments overlap may differ from project to project. The establishment of size, cost, and schedule estimates for each increment will provide an overall estimate of the total project. As the first increments are completed, then the assumptions and estimates for the subsequent increments, as well as for the total product, can be revised to reflect a more accurate assessment.

Technology Insertion

Technology Insertion is the enhancement of an existing system through the introduction of new technology. The new technology to software systems is often the result of improved hardware. The new hardware is usually characterized by higher throughput, increased memory size, and will often have an improved operating system. New hardware often provides the opportunity to also introduce a new version of the application software. The new version is usually characterized by improved functionality. The new software version is typically comprised of a significant amount of new code and modified existing code.

Technology Insertion projects are usually conducted the same as new development projects and thus will follow the generic estimation process contained herein. The primary difference, however, is the amount of existing software that is planned for reuse. The project managers are often optimistic regarding how much existing code can be used. The estimators should be conservative in their reused code estimates.

One of the most common reasons for this development of new code is to take advantage of operating system and hardware enhancements. Another reason is that new programmers in the project may recode in accordance with more modern software engineering practices.

The uncertainty in the amount of effort for the reused code should be reflected in the cost and schedule risk analysis. A range of estimates should be generated that reflects the optimistic viewpoint and the conservative viewpoint. A detailed analysis of the existing code should be performed as early in the project as possible to ascertain the degree of rework actually required. An accurate estimate of the reuse effort will not be possible until the existing code is actually inspected by the programmers and business analysts.

CONCLUSION

Software estimation activities follow the same basic process throughout the development, i.e., develop cost and schedule estimates based on estimates of product size. The differences lie in the level of certainty that can be expected during each of the phases. The estimates derived during concept phase are used to develop capability versus cost tradeoffs. These early estimates are based on gross assumptions of size that are usually based on similar systems that are operational or under development. The methods discussed herein for the full scale development mode also apply to the Research and Development mode. However, during the early phases of a Research and Development project, the emphasis is more on concept and technology tradeoffs versus estimating the cost of a specific design.

CHAPTER 3
STANDARD METHODS OF ESTIMATION

SIZE ESTIMATION

Wideband Delphi Technique

There are various forms of Delphi technique but in general it is a consensus-based technique for estimating effort and cost. In this technique the participants are encouraged to discuss the problem with each other. This technique, summarized below, requires participation from a group of participants with a diversity of software related experience.

- Coordinator presents each expert with the project's specification and an estimation form.

- Coordinator calls a group meeting, in which the experts discuss product issues related to size.

- Each expert fills out the form anonymously.

- The coordinator prepares a summary of the estimates on an Iteration Form and returns them to the experts.

- The coordinator calls a group meeting, primarily to discuss the most widely varied estimates.

- The experts review the summary and submit another anonymous estimate on the Iteration Form.

- Steps four through six are repeated until a consensus of the lowest and highest possible estimates are reached.

PERT (Program Evaluation and Review Technique) Sizing

This method involves deriving three estimates: an expected size of the product, a lowest possible estimate, and a highest possible estimate. These three estimates are used to arrive at a PERT[13] statistical estimate for the expected size of the product and a standard deviation. For example, for a new communications routine, if

a = the lowest possible size (10 KSLOC),

b = the expected size (12 KSLOC),

c = the highest possible size (15 KSLOC).

The Pert equations estimate the -

Expected Size (E) = $[(a+4b+c)/6] = [(10+4*12+15)/6]$ = 12.167 KSLOC and

Standard Deviation (SD) = $[(c-a)/6] = [(15-10)/6]$ = 0.833

This means that about 68 percent of the time, the size will fall between 11.334 KSLOC (12.167-.833) and 13 KSLOC (12.167 +.833). This approach assumes that the estimates are unbiased, while in fact, experience shows that estimates tend to cluster more toward the low limit than toward the upper limit.

Function Points

Function point [14]metrics is a method of estimating size during the requirements phase, based on the functionality to be built into the system. Initial application requirements statements are examined to determine the number and complexity of the various inputs, outputs, calculations, and databases required. Points based on established values are assigned to each of these counts and then added to arrive at an overall function point rating for the product. The general approach is shown below:

- Count the number of inputs, outputs, inquiries, master files, and interfaces required.

- Multiply these counts by the following factors: Inputs-4, Outputs-5, Inquiries-4, Master Files-10, and Interfaces-10.

- Adjust the total of these products +25 percent, 0, or -25 percent, depending on the estimator's judgment of the program's complexity.

Function points have been found to be helpful in estimating size very early in a software product's development. However, after more is known about the product, function points can be converted to SLOCs, which is the software size metric more widely used.

Sizing by Analogy

This approach involves relating the proposed project to previously completed projects of similar application, environment, and complexity. The organization's software process database can be used to compare size data from similar projects. The basic steps of sizing by analogy are shown below:

- Develop a list of functions and the number of lines of code to implement each function.

- Identify similarities and differences between previously developed database items and those database items to be developed.

- From the data developed in bullet points one and two, and select those items that are applicable to serve as a basis for the estimate.

- Generate a size estimate.

The accuracy of the derived estimate will, obviously, depend on the completeness and the accuracy of the data used from the previous projects.

Automated Size Estimation Tools

Computerized models are commercially available that help develop size estimates. Some of the basic methods that tools utilize are the Sizing by Analogy, Function Point Analysis, Linguistic Approach, Size-In-Size-Out, PERT, and Comparison of Project Attributes.

Reused Code

The only way to estimate the amount of code to be reused is for the programmers and business analysts to examine the existing code in detail. The examination should derive estimates for three factors to help estimate the effort. The three factors are the percentage of code that will be redesigned, percentage to be recoded or modified, and percentage to be retested. These estimated percentages are used by cost models to arrive at an equivalent line of code estimate.

The equivalent lines of code estimate represents the amount of new code that could be developed for the same effort it would take to modify the existing code. Some models allow the user to enter these three percentages, while other models assume a standard percentage of effort to develop equivalent lines of new code.

REVIC is one such model that provides a single "weighted average" distribution for effort and schedule along with the ability to let the user vary the percentages in the system engineering and development test and evaluation phases. The REVIC model has also been enhanced by using a Program Evaluation and Review Technique (PERT) statistical method for determining the lines of code to be developed. The main difference between REVIC and COCOMO is the coefficients used in the effort equations. The REVIC model allows the user to enter the three factors. When the three percentages are used, the equivalent new lines of code are calculated as follows:

([%Redesign + %Recode + %Retest]/3) * Existing Code = Equivalent LOCs.

For example, consider a product which had 10,000 LOCs and require 40% redesign, 50% recode, and 60% retest, then the equivalent new line of code would be calculated as:

([40% + 50% + 60%]/3) * 10,000 = 5,000 Equivalent LOCs.

EFFORT AND COST ESTIMATION

Manual Method

The manual estimate of software effort should be based on a combination of the Top-Down and Bottom-Up approach and should be based primarily on the size estimates and schedule requirements. Two or more software engineers with experience with the specific application under development should develop a top-down and bottom-up estimate, based on the size estimates and schedule requirements as follows:

Top-Down: A derivation of an estimate of the total effort based on the estimated size of each major function. This can be accomplished manually or with an automated estimation tool. As in estimating size, the effort estimate should also be based on experience with a similar application. Each estimate should consist of a nominal, or most probable, estimate plus lowest and highest possible estimates to reflect the uncertainty of the size estimates. The spread between the low and high estimates may be as much as 30 to 50 percent in the early phases of a project, e.g., the Concept Phase. Functions for which experience is scarce or for which there is high technical risk should be given an even wider range.

Bottom-Up: Derive an estimate for the project by summing up the effort associated with each low-level task. This is best accomplished by developing a Work Breakdown Structure (WBS), which includes not only the details of the software architecture hierarchy, but also details on the software development organization.

- The WBS should include activities such as integration, documentation, software quality assurance, and configuration management. While all of these costs may not be known early in the project, at least the identification of these activities will ensure that they are considered.

- Estimate the effort related to the amount of time to prepare for and attend formal project reviews. The cost of reviews is often significantly higher than anticipated.

- The estimates should be reviewed by software engineers who have worked on similar applications.

Software Estimation Tools

A number of automated software estimation tools are available that allow a user to quickly derive effort and schedule estimates, based on size estimates and cost driver attributes. There may be fifteen to fifty cost driver attributes that reflect the development environment, depending on the model used. Common cost driver attributes include programmer and analyst experience and capability, database size, use of modern programming methods, use of automated tools, memory, and timing constraints. Some tools have unique attributes, such as requirements volatility and the number of organizations involved.

Generally, a tool should be used after an estimate has been manually derived. Automated tools provide a good method to crosscheck manually derived estimates. Manual estimates are usually low because of several reasons. The most prevalent reason is optimism on the part of the project manager, who has forgotten all of the effort that went into design, test, documentation, configuration management, and quality assurance. Project managers do not remember all of the time spent debugging, preparing for project reviews, or how often the requirements were modified. Another common reason for underestimating is unclear or misunderstood requirements. The use of an automated tool requires the user to consider all of the above, plus project attributes such as personnel experience, security complications, requirements volatility, number of sites, hardware constraints, and schedule requirements. However, caution must be exercised when using tools. Because of their ease of use, these tools can give a wide range of estimates by varying just a few parameters.

SECTION 5
PROJECT MONITORING AND CONTROL

CHAPTER 1
PROJECT TIMETABLE

HOW-TO: WRITE A PROJECT PLAN

This chapter suggests possible ways to plan and schedule projects. Project planning can help make employees more efficient. Instead of each going off to do their own thing, a project schedule brings people together. It is a rallying point of focus. Project manager should make sure that the project plan serves his purposes, rather than the other way around. It is appropriate to use a project management tool to plan and manage the project tasks.

Project Team Consideration

When creating a new project plan, first consider which employees are involved. Assign active and available resources to the project. People only see the projects that are relevant to them. Later project tasks can be scheduled to the resources selected for the project.

Project Phases or Task Breakdowns

Generally, a project follows a life cycle depending on the nature of the project, and the life cycle consists of phases. This gives the opportunity to break a long project into more manageable pieces. During the planning phase, the task breakdown based on the project phases should be considered. These may be referred to as summary tasks or subsystems. They are really just headings for all the real project tasks and help in collecting work into manageable areas. The WBS created for the project can be a good input source of making project plan.

Once a few subsystems are created under the project, it may be found that even they can be broken down further. So, this might lead to creating subsystems under subsystems. This breaks down the subsystem further. In many cases, one level of project breakdown is enough. The project plan should be kept easy to navigate.

Task Definition and Estimate

After laying out major project breakdowns, the next step is to create the actual tasks team members will do. These tasks will be located under the project phases that were created earlier. Each phase may contain several tasks. Each task is unique and it requires a certain amount of effort to complete. The effort taken for completing all the tasks is measured in person hours or person months. This effort is distributed over a period of time to complete the project tasks and is called elapsed time. This is the duration of the project. In the beginning of the project, this is really just a forecast, providing an estimate of how much effort and time the tasks will take. Later, when the project schedule is shown in the timesheet, the time taken for actual work for each task is collected. So, a task has both forecasted work and actual work. This provides the percent complete for each task and ultimately for the entire project.

Task Assignment

After defining a series of tasks under each project phase, it's time to consider resource assignment, or resource scheduling. It's the act of assigning team members to tasks. Identify what each of the team member is capable of, and accordingly assign them to the project tasks. It is essential to ensure that none of the team member is overloaded with work and there is optimum distribution of work among the team members.

Resource scheduling has several benefits. It provides details on the tasks that a certain team member is working on. It helps in tracking progress of each task. It also provides information on how much work each team member is loaded with in the team.

Timesheet

Timesheet is a tool to capture the actual effort spent on a task. Each team members fills the time spent against the task allocated to him or her. The timesheets can be filled on a daily or weekly basis. It has to be a regular activity so that the data collected is accurate. The project manager should also let team members know about the importance of filling the timesheet and how it contributes in measuring the actual effort spent on the project. Generally, team members consider filling timesheet as additional burden and tend to ignore it. To help the team members, the project manager should limit the timesheets to the projects that team members are assigned to and the tasks that are relevant to them at this time. In other words, don't show them projects that they don't work on. It only clutters things. Also, they should not be shown tasks they are not assigned to or are not scheduled to work on. The timesheet should be kept as tight as possible. There are various tools that can be used to track the time.

WHAT IS A PROJECT PLAN?

The Project Plan is the central document by which the project is formally managed. A *Project Plan* is a document that lists the activities, tasks, and resources required to complete the project and realize the business benefits outlined in the project business case. A typical project plan includes:

- A description of the major phases undertaken to complete the project

- A schedule of the activities, tasks, durations, dependencies, resources, and timeframes

- A listing of the assumptions and constraints identified during the planning process

To create a project plan, the following steps are undertaken:
- Reiterate the project scope.

- Identify the project milestones, phases, activities, and tasks.

- Quantify the effort required for each task (This is obtained from the estimation process).

- Allocate project resource.

- Construct a project schedule.

- List any planning dependencies, assumptions, and constraints.

- Document the formal Project Plan for approval.

When to Use a Project Plan?

Although a summarized project plan is identified early in the project definition phase (within the business case), a detailed project plan is not usually created until the project scope has been formally defined and the project team appointed. The project plan is completed early in the project planning phase and is, typically, prior to a quality plan and the formalization of a supplier's contract. Unlike other documents in the project life cycle, the project plan is referenced constantly throughout the project. As the project is undertaken, the project manager tracks the percentage of task completion and the task completion date (actual versus planned) to assess overall project performance. These statistics are communicated to the project sponsor and senior management within a regular project status report.

Sample Project Plan

				Version 1						
%	Status	Flag	WBS	Tasks	Start	Finish	Duration	Owner	Priority	Milestone
			1	Initiation	1/1/08	3/8/08	49 days	Owner1,Owner2,Owner3		
100%	COMPLETED		1.1	Collect project ideas	1/1/08	2/1/08	24 days	Owner1,Owner2,Owner3		
100%	COMPLETED	⏴	1.2	Prioritize project ideas	1/2/08	2/4/08	24 days	Owner1,Owner2,Owner3		Yes
100%	COMPLETED		1.3	Gather customer requirements	1/3/08	2/5/08	24 days	Owner1,Owner2,Owner3		
100%	COMPLETED		1.4	Select and justify a project	1/4/08	2/6/08	38 days	Owner1,Owner2,Owner3		
100%	COMPLETED	⏴	1.5	Submit and approve the Request for Proposal	1/5/08	2/5/08	22 days	Owner1,Owner2,Owner3		
20%	BEHIND SCHEDULE		1.6	Identify the project sponsor and project manager	1/30/08	3/6/08	28 days	Owner1,Owner2,Owner3		
30%	ON SCHEDULE	⏴	1.7	Get the project team in place	1/7/08	2/7/08	24 days	Owner1,Owner2,Owner3	M	
60%	ON SCHEDULE		1.8	Prepare the Requirements Document	1/8/08	2/6/08	24 days	Owner1,Owner2,Owner3		
10%	DATE TBD		1.9	Conduct project kickoff meeting		2/6/08	0 days	Owner1,Owner2,Owner3		
50%	CANCELLED		1.10	Conduct project brainstorming meeting				Owner1,Owner2,Owner3		
90%	ON SCHEDULE		1.11	Develop Statement of Scope	1/11/08	2/11/08	22 days	Owner1,Owner2,Owner3	NONE	Yes
			1.12	WBS Development	1/13/08	2/15/08	25 days	Owner1,Owner2,Owner3		
80%	ON SCHEDULE		1.12.1	Conduct Work Breakdown Structure meeting	1/13/08	2/13/08	23 days	Owner1,Owner2,Owner3	?	
30%	ON SCHEDULE		1.12.2	Build Work Breakdown Structure (WBS)	1/14/08	2/14/08	24 days	Owner1,Owner2,Owner3		
10%	ON SCHEDULE		1.12.3	Update WBS in Microsoft Project	1/15/08	2/15/08	24 days	Owner1,Owner2,Owner3		
100%	COMPLETED		1.13	Outline project plan	1/16/08	2/16/08	23 days	Owner1,Owner2,Owner3		
100%	COMPLETED		1.14	Assign resources to project plan tasks	1/17/08	2/17/08	22 days	Owner1,Owner2,Owner3		
			2	Analysis	1/19/08	2/22/08	25 days	Owner1,Owner2,Owner3		
0%	FUTURE TASK		2.1	Create Entity Relationship Diagram	1/19/08	2/19/08	22 days	Owner1,Owner2,Owner3		
100%	COMPLETED		2.2	Create Data Flow Diagram	1/20/08	2/20/08	23 days	Owner1,Owner2,Owner3		
0%	FUTURE TASK		2.3	Define data dictionary	1/21/08	2/21/08	24 days	Owner1,Owner2,Owner3		
0%	FUTURE TASK		2.4	Perform object-oriented analysis	1/22/08	2/22/08	24 days	Owner1,Owner2,Owner3		
			3	Design	1/24/08	3/5/08	30 days	Owner1,Owner2,Owner3		
0%	FUTURE TASK		3.1	Design data model	1/24/08	2/24/08	22 days	Owner1,Owner2,Owner3		
0%	FUTURE TASK		3.2	Write functional specifications	1/25/08	2/25/08	22 days	Owner1,Owner2,Owner3		
0%	FUTURE TASK		3.3	Design storyboards and/or prototypes	1/26/08	2/26/08	24 days	Owner1,Owner2,Owner3		
0%	FUTURE TASK		3.4	Write detailed design specifications	1/27/08	2/27/08	23 days	Owner1,Owner2,Owner3		
0%	FUTURE TASK		3.5	Write documentation plan	1/28/08	2/28/08	24 days	Owner1,Owner2,Owner3		
100%	COMPLETED		3.6	Write beta test plan	1/29/08	2/29/08	24 days	Owner1,Owner2,Owner3		
0%	FUTURE TASK		3.7	Write SQA test plan	1/30/08	3/1/08	23 days	Owner1,Owner2,Owner3		

Ready

CHAPTER 2
RESOURCE REQUIREMENTS

DEFINITION

How many people does it take to design and construct code, test the product, write a user's manual, install a computer network, or analyze a customer's needs? These questions may not be pertinent to every project, but it's important to know what physical resources it will take to complete any activity related to a project.

Physical resources can include any or all of the resources listed below, depending on the nature of the project.

- People: This is the most important resource of all. It is also the most diverse resource the manager has to deal with. People come with a wide variety of skills. The manager's job is to match the possible skill sets with the project tasks.

- Facilities: These are where the project activities will be performed. The project manager has to take into account what kind and how many of these facilities are required. Availability of facilities can have a big impact on the project schedule and has to be taken into account.

- Equipment: Specialized equipment may be needed for some projects. This equipment may have to be bought, rented, borrowed, or built. The project manager has to make sure that the equipment will be available according to plan.

- Materials: If a project produces anything tangible, the raw materials to produce the product need to be managed. Materials have to be managed to ensure they are available when needed.

Project managers should develop a list of all the resources needed to complete a project. This list is known as resource requirements. Resource requirements are descriptions of the types of resources required and quantities needed for each element of the work breakdown structure and are important inputs to activity duration estimation.

Resource capabilities are another input that should be considered when estimating activity duration. Resource capabilities can have a direct effect on an activity's duration. For example, a person with more experience and skills will complete a job faster than someone who is unskilled. The capacity of the materials used for a project also will affect an activity's duration. For example, a machine that runs at only 50 percent capacity will take twice as long to complete the activity as a machine that runs at full capacity. Resource capabilities not only affect the duration of an activity, but they can also affect the resource requirements. For example, if team members are unskilled, more of them will be needed to complete a project on time. If team members have more experience, fewer people will be needed. A project manager should look at all the aspects of a project's resources when estimating activity duration. Remember, resource capabilities can have a far-reaching effect on the duration of a project activity.

FACTORS TO BE CONSIDERED

Generally, for a project, the available human resources (people) in the organization are assigned to work on it. In the ideal scenario, a project manager would like to identify the resource requirements and then look for people with the necessary skills to fill those roles. But, that is not the case in reality. Some fit the requirements, and some have huge gaps in their skills and experience. The following section describes how such situations can be handled.

Accepting the Inevitable

Resource management may entail saying no to the resources allocated, but in most cases, the direction will be to make the most of what is given. This requires a different approach to managing the project from what might be the textbook approach. The gaps and limitations need to be covered, and that will make the whole process more difficult.

Define the Resource Requirements

For a project manager, the first step is to define the resource requirements in isolation from the people involved. To do this, create a roles and responsibilities listing for the project. Do not be constrained by the people that are already allocated, but start with the ideal way in which the project should be organized. It is often useful to look at previous projects to see what roles and responsibilities existed. Once the roles and responsibilities are listed, look at the people who have been nominated to fill those roles, and see how they fit. In the end, the gap analysis of the resources involved will be available, which will indicate the skills they bring versus the resource requirements for the project.

Match Resource Skills

Also, a project manager should look at the resources available and the individual skills they possess. It may be possible to rearrange the responsibilities to suit the particular people. For example, it is possible that a junior resource has a reputation of being an excellent documenter. Some of the responsibilities could be changed around to put more of the documentation responsibility with that person. It will free up other resources to focus on developing requirements rather than developing final documents.

The Gaps in Resources

By now, there should be a clear picture of where the resource gaps are. The first port of call is to discuss the issue with the sponsor or project steering committee. It may be enough to convince them to change the allocation of project resources. If not, the manager will need to make plans to cover the gaps. Some strategies that could be looked at are:

Part-time resources—Look for people who have the required skills, and see if they can be allocated on a part-time basis.

External resources—Perhaps there are people from outside the company who could assist in particular areas. If project lacks anyone with risk management expertise, there are numerous people available in the market that could carry out a risk assessment.

Training resources—Another solution is to train some people to fill the gap. If project needs the resource to develop use cases for the requirements and they have no knowledge of use cases, a training program may be the answer.

Find another way—The answer may be to do things in a different way. For example, if a manager is looking to implement a software package but lacks development resources, perhaps the best solution is to outsource the management of the package. The manager should seek out an ASP (Application Service Provider) who will run the software and hardware for him.

Alternative funding—If the resource constraint is the result of a funding decision, perhaps there is another way to fund the resource. For example, if the project does not have the necessary testing skills, perhaps the services of a test specialist could be funded from a department's operational budget, or another project.

Constrain the activities—Perhaps there are a number of developers with experience in "X" programming language and there is a need for developers for providing a number of solutions involving both "X" and "Y" programming languages. One approach is to constrain the selection activity by not considering "Y" programming language solutions.

Identify the Impact

Most of the solutions outlined above will have an impact on the project. It might be cost or time or the scope of the proposed solution. Each of the impacts should be documented and formally agreed by the sponsor and steering committee. If the organization decides to limit the resources and the skills they provide, they should also be prepared to agree the limitations to the project that may result from their decision.

Evaluating Personalities

What we have discussed so far is related to the skills of resources. There is another aspect, which is how well the team will work together. People management is one of the important tasks that any project manager will have to do. It is possible that the project is assigned resources who have problems working together. To handle such situations, the manager may need to have enough rights to control the resources and direct them to work toward the common goal without bringing in the personal differences. There could be other scenarios, where the project manager, with enough empowerment, is equipped to handle the situation well. The project manager may have to discuss this scenario with the senior management and/or sponsors to get such privileges. The soft skills of the project manager also play an important role in managing such situations.

Summary

Project resource management is a complex task and usually not treated with the importance it deserves. It is often a case of being given some people and being told to get on with it. You still, however, need to identify the gaps in resource skills and take actions to plug them. Don't just focus on the resource skills required. Also, get some indication of personal issues, and try not to fly in the face of the obvious. If two people can't work together in a normal environment, they probably won't work together in a high-pressure project environment. Finally, don't just accept resources and ignore what the project needs in terms of roles and responsibilities. If a responsibility is not allocated, at some point, it will escalate into a problem. Addressing it early in the project life will avoid or lessen the impact.

CHAPTER 3
ROLES AND RESPONSIBILITY

Projects of different sizes have different ways and requirements on how the people are organized. In a small project, little organization structure is needed. There might be a primary sponsor, project manager, and a project team. However, for large projects, there are more and more people involved, and it is important that people understand what they are expected to do and what role they are expected to fill. This chapter identifies some of the common and not so common project roles that may need to be required for a project.

A vital aspect of ensuring that the project stays on track is clarifying project roles and responsibilities with all involved in the project. Many projects fall short of expectations because too many things fall through the cracks. And nobody catches the droppings because either they did not know they were meant to or because they thought that no one would notice. This trap can be avoided by clarifying who is responsible for what right at the outset of the project.

PROJECT ROLES

Project roles will vary, depending on the size and complexity of the project and the industry you are in. The project governance model your organization uses is especially important here. Who will be responsible for overseeing the project deliverables and performance and overcoming obstacles—the project sponsor or a complete steering committee? Which project team members will be working on the project full-time, and which will also share a reporting line with their line or practice manager? These are some of the questions to be asked. In a typical software project, following are the roles that are required to execute a project.

Analyst: The analyst is responsible for ensuring that the requirements of the business clients are captured and documented correctly before a solution is developed and implemented. In some companies, this person might be called a business analyst, business systems analyst, systems analyst, or a requirements analyst.

Change Control Board: The change control board is usually made up as a group of decision makers authorized to accept changes to the projects requirements, budget, and timelines. This organization would be helpful if the project directly impacted a number of functional areas and the sponsor wanted to share the scope change authority with this broader group. The details of the change control board and the processes they follow are defined in the software project plan.

Client: These are the people or groups that are the direct beneficiaries of a project or service. They are the people for whom the project is being undertaken. These might also be called customers.

Client project manager: If the project is large enough, the client may have a primary contact that is designated as a comparable project manager. As an example, if a software project is outsourced to a vendor, the project manager from the vendor side would have over-all responsibility for the software solution. However, there may also be a project manager on the client side who is needed to support this initiative. The vendor project manager and the client project manager would be peers who work together to build and implement the complete solution.

Designer: The designer is responsible for understanding the business requirements and designing a solution that will meet the business needs. There are many potential solutions that will meet the client's needs. The designer determines the best approach. A designer typically needs to understand how technology can be used to create this optimum solution for the client. The designer determines the overall model and framework for the solution, down to the level of designing screens, reports, programs, and other components. They also determine the data and system performance needs. The work of the designer is then handed off to the programmers and other people, who will construct the solution based on the design specifications.

Project Manager: This is the person with authority to manage a project. This includes leading the planning and the development of all project deliverables. The project manager is responsible for managing the budget and schedule and all project management procedures (scope management, issues management, risk management, etc.).

Project Team: The project team consists of the full-time and part-time resources assigned to work on the deliverables of the project. This includes the analysts, designers, programmers, etc. They are responsible for:
- Understanding the work to be completed.
- Planning out the assigned activities in more detail if needed.

- Completing assigned work within the budget, timeline, and quality expectations.

- Informing the project manager of issues, scope changes, risk, and quality concerns.

- Proactively communicating status and managing expectations.

The project team can consist of human resources within one functional organization, or it can consist of members from many different functional organizations. A cross-functional team has members from multiple organizations or different departments of an organization.

Sponsor *(Executive Sponsor and Project Sponsor)*: This is the person who has ultimate authority over the project. The executive sponsor provides project funding, resolves issues and scope changes, approves major deliverables, and provides high-level direction. They also champion the project within their organization. Depending on the project and the organizational level of the executive sponsor, they may delegate day-to-day tactical management to a project sponsor. If assigned, the project sponsor represents the executive sponsor on a day-to-day basis and makes most of the decisions requiring sponsor approval. If the decision is large enough, the project sponsor will take it to the executive sponsor for resolution.

Stakeholder: These are the specific people or groups who have a stake, or an interest, in the outcome of the project. Normally, stakeholders are from within the company and could include internal clients, management, employees, administrators, etc. A project may also have external stakeholders, including suppliers, investors, community groups, and government organization.

Steering Committee: A steering committee is a group of high-level stakeholders who are responsible for providing guidance on overall strategic direction. They do not take the place of a sponsor but help to spread the strategic input and buy-in to a larger portion of the organization. The steering committee is usually made up of organizational peers and is a combination of direct clients and indirect stakeholders. The members on the steering committee may also sit on the Change Control Board, although in many cases, the Change Board is made up of representatives of the steering committee.

Suppliers/Vendors: Although some companies may have internal suppliers, in the life cycle step process, these terms will always refer to third-party companies, or specific people that work for third parties. They may be subcontractors who are working under your direction, or they may be supplying material, equipment, hardware, software or supplies to your project. Depending on their role, they may need to be identified on your organization chart. For instance, if you are partnering with a supplier to develop your requirements, you probably want them on your organization chart. On the other hand, if they are a vendor supplying a common piece of hardware, you probably would not consider them a part of the team.

Users: These are the people who will actually use the deliverables of the project. These people are also involved heavily in the project in activities, such as defining business requirements. In other cases, they may not get involved until the testing process. Sometimes, you want to specifically identify the user organization or the specific users of the solution and assign a formal set of responsibilities to them, like developing use cases or user scenarios based on the needs of the business requirements.

RESPONSIBILITY MATRIX

In a large project, there may be many people who have some role in the creation and approval of project deliverables. Sometimes this is pretty straightforward, such as one person writing a document and one person approving it. In other cases, there may be many people who have a hand in the creation and others that need to have varying levels of approval. The Responsibility Matrix is a technique used to define the general responsibilities for each role on a project. The matrix can then be used to communicate the roles to the appropriate people associated with the team. This helps set expectations and ensures people know what is expected from them. On the matrix, the different people, or roles, appear as columns, with the specific deliverables in question listed as rows. Then, use the intersecting points to describe each person's responsibility for each deliverable.

CHAPTER 4
COMMUNICATION PLAN

A communication plan is a written document that describes:
- What are the communication objectives?

- Ways in which those objectives can be accomplished?

- Who are the audiences?

- What are the tools and timetable?

- How to measure or evaluate the effectiveness of the process?

Software project engagements carry with them the element of risk. Organizations typically engage a consultant because a project is beyond their capabilities due to technical issues, scarcity of bandwidth, or skill sets within the organization, or because of organizational or political risk factors that convince the organization to engage an outsider. All of these risk elements make formal communication more critical.

This chapter focuses on the impact of good communication on an engagement and the elements that make up a communications plan.

COMMUNICATION SKILLS

In one of the surveys, I researched what helps or harms productivity .The participants in this survey were asked to rank the attributes that contribute to an employee's productivity. Among the attributes included were traits like maturity, decision making, ambition, capacity for hard work, flexibility, and confidence. All of these characteristics were deemed important and remain so today. In the context of this topic, however, the important point is that the number one attribute was the ability to communicate.

The result of this study is appropriate for employees and consultants. In a new project, the project team generally consists of various individuals, some from within the organization, and some hired from outside. Employees who have worked together for years are like old friends, in the sense that they have developed shorthand of communications, so they often understand each other without a lot of formal communications. Consultants and new employees usually come into engagements without that depth of shared experience, so all communications must be explicit. With this scenario, it is imperative that there should be strong communication process laid out, which would help in the success of project.

Communication plans should be divided into two categories: project communications and ingredient communications. Project communications include the interaction that is required in order to deliver the engagement with quality. Included in this category is the project plan itself, the memos and status reports that the team distributes to one another, the team meetings, and the minutes that are issued from them. As far as ingredient communications are concerned, it includes the executive briefings, auditorium presentations, newsletters, lunch-and-learn sessions, posters, brochures, focus groups, and feedback mechanisms, like e-mail and voicemail suggestion boxes. The following explores all these elements in a bit more detail.

Project Communications

In terms of project communications, the project plan itself is probably the most meaningful communication item in the entire collection. By committing to paper the deliverables, the responsible parties, the scheduled delivery dates, and the dependencies, the overall engagement is planned. The entire project may be large and difficult to visualize, and hence break it down into its component parts, thus making it much easier to comprehend and discuss at the level of detail necessary.

To be a meaningful part of the communication program, the project plan must be revised, reviewed, and revisited throughout the project and used as the axis around which all subsequent communications revolve.

Memos and status reports are the next most important project communications channel, as they give team members the chance to raise issues, unexpected results, and impacts on the project that were not foreseeable before they occurred. The most important thing to keep in mind about internal memos and status reports is that they need to be true and tough. The inclination to sugarcoat or otherwise shirk the responsibility for facing the unpleasant truth is one of the key points of engagement failure. It is critical that these communications be focused on the facts and the problems, not the personalities or the team dynamics. That being said, however, the ability to take the emotion out of communication, while still imparting the unpleasant facts and their implications, is one of the central traits (soft skill) of a mature and effective consultant or team member.

Project meetings are also an important focus point for communications. Meetings that are well run, with agendas, time contracts, full team participation, and an opportunity for honest and open exchange, can impart the overall vision to the team, build commitment, and ensure success. It's very easy for team members to lose sight of the holistic goal, and team gatherings are a great opportunity to remember collectively what we are all working toward. Meeting leaders should use the agenda to facilitate the discussion, to encourage everyone to participate, to get status reports from all so that everyone builds an overall vision of the project, and to expose and resolve open issues. Formal meetings should be captured in minutes, especially action items and deliverables. The meeting is the cornerstone for project team building and for issue resolution as a team.

Ingredient Communications

Ingredient communications are specifically designed to inform the client and all the engagement stakeholders. Some of the elements that an ingredient communication program should contain are:

- Executive briefings. The executive sponsors of the project should be briefed periodically on the status of the project. This communication should be kept at a high level, typically in the form of a short presentation that focuses on the strategic, not the tactical, issues.

- Assembly presentations. Some projects, such as large relocation projects or company-wide information technology initiatives, should be presented to the rank-and-file employees, typically in the form of an auditorium presentation. This type of communication is typically focused on two aspects: features and benefits, and any disruption or dislocation that the project will cause.

- Newsletters. Newsletter formats allow for periodic, informal communications that can keep the organization in the loop on the status and schedule of the project. This is also a good forum for executives of the company to sell the project through things like open memos or "From the President's Desk" inserts.

- Lunch-and-learn sessions. In some organizations, like those that have their own cafeteria, it is useful to set up a mini trade show environment, where representatives from the project team can meet with the employees and answer questions, address concerns, and sell the project in an informal, unscripted environment.

- Focus groups. Like the executive presentation, it sometimes makes sense to deliver focused presentations to specific groups or teams within the organization to address their specific concerns and questions. For instance, the Infrastructure group might be interested in the impact a new system will have on their processes and activities, while the business analysis team might have their own concerns.

Other communication conduits include customer surveys, electronic suggestion boxes, and intranets. The key point about all this is that project execution and management, although obviously a technical discipline, is a communications discipline as well, and the projects and engagements that succeed are the ones that not only include sharing and collaborating technical expertise but also the ability to share knowledge, to converse, to create a shared vision, to build team spirit and consensus—in short, to communicate.

PROJECT COMMUNICATION PLAN

A well-planned project has a well-planned communication strategy. A project should have a master communication plan that lays out what communication streams are to be used, reporting standards, responsibilities, etc. The following communication information should be contained within the project communication plan:

- Project communication strategy
- The kickoff meeting
- Roles and responsibilities of the team
- Project status meetings and frequency
- Change control communications
- Project review meetings

- Transition from deployment to operations
- Closure meeting

The following are guidelines and options when creating a project communication plan.

What	Who/ Target	Purpose	When/ Frequency	Type/Method
Initiation Meeting	Stakeholders	Gather information for Initiation Plan	Before project start date	Meeting
Distribute Project Initiation Plan	Stakeholders	Distribute Plan to alert stakeholders of project scope and to gain buy in.	Before project kick-off meeting and before project start date	Document distributed via hardcopy or electronically.
Project Kick Off	Stakeholders	Communicate plans and stakeholder roles/responsibilities and encourage communication among stakeholders.	At or near Project Start Date	Meeting
Status Reports	Stakeholders and Project Office	Update stakeholders on progress of the project.	Regularly Scheduled. Monthly is recommended for large/midsize projects.	Distribute electronically
Team Meetings	Entire Project Team. Individual meetings for sub-teams, technical team, and Functional teams as appropriate.	To review detailed plans (tasks, assignments, and action items).	Regularly scheduled. Weekly is recommended for entire team. Weekly or bi-weekly for sub-teams as appropriate.	Meeting
Project Advisory Group Meetings	Project Advisory Group and Project Manager	Update Project Advisory Group on status and discuss critical issues. Work through issues and change requests here before escalating to the Sponsor(s).	Regularly Scheduled. Monthly is recommended.	Meeting
Sponsor Meetings	Sponsor(s) and Project Manager	Update Sponsor(s) on status and discuss critical issues. Seek approval for changes to Project Plan.	Regularly scheduled Recommended biweekly or monthly and also as needed when issues cannot be resolved or changes need to be made to Project Plan.	Meeting
Executive Sponsor Meetings	Executive Sponsor(s) and Project Manager	Update Sponsor(s) on status and discuss critical issues. Seek approval for changes to Project Plan.	Not regularly scheduled. As needed when issues cannot be resolved or changes need to be made to	Meeting

Communication is the most important component within any project. The success of most projects, whether handled by a dedicated project team or a cross-departmental team, depends upon a set of crucial communication skills and techniques. Interestingly, it has been observed that communication and human interaction make or break a project. Project communications refer to the specific behavior and techniques used to motivate, lead, delegate, and report back to all stakeholders working on the project.

There are three clear communication streams that managers need to establish once the project has started. Managing and improving these channels can dramatically increase the chances of success of a project.

Upward Stream
- Communicate to Senior executives
- Highlight issues, risks, and expectations
- Tools used – Exception reports, Weekly Status reports, Project charter, E-mail updates, Meetings, Communication plan
- Strengthens the buy-in from top

Communication Streams

Lateral Stream
- Communicate to clients, vendors, and functional managers
- Involves negotiation for resources, budgets, and time allocations
- Tools used – Communication plan, E-mail, Statement of Work, Contracts
- Requires diplomacy and tact

- Provide direction to project team
- Highlight tasks pending, scheduled tasks, dates, and general team meetings
- Tools used – Verbal exchange, Agendas, Minutes, E-mail, Project meetings, Project plan, Issue logs
- Requires delegation skills

Downward Stream

Communication affects performance. Therefore, there need to be effective communications ingrained to make sure that the team working on the project operates with high performance. Without well-established streams, it is likely that the project will fail. Successful project managers typically have good communications skills that include being able to effectively present the issues, listen and act on feedback, and foster harmony among team members.

REINFORCING PROJECT COMMUNICATIONS

Project communication isn't always as easy as it may seem, but it is a foundation that can be used to build the team, demonstrate leadership, and provide timely project direction. By means of effective communication plan, the project communication can be reinforced. An effective communications plan will:

- Facilitate team development: Proper communication actually provides the basis for the project team to work together and understand objectives and tasks to be completed. Better communication means better performance.

- Be used throughout the software development process: From defining the user requirements to implementing the product, a proper communication plan aids in informing all project stakeholders what communication streams will be used on the project, who will report to whom, and the frequency, type, and format of project meetings.

- Make it easier to update stakeholders: Frequent communications keep stakeholders in the loop.

- Save on creating additional project documentation: By taking effective communication steps from the day the project starts, a reduction may be seen in the project documentation.

Project Communication Tools

Below are some of the communication tools that project managers have available.

- E-mail—Allows project teams to communicate text, audio, and video files between the team members

- Interoffice memos—Provides a formal forum to communicate key dates, policies, and procedures

- Instant Messaging (IM)—Allows team members to communicate real-time

- Project status meetings—Provides regular status updates and reviews of the project

- Telephone/video conferences—Provides a medium to involve team members located in other geographic regions

- Intranet, Internet boards—Formally communicates status, progress, highlights, and objectives to all

- Project road show—Provides feedback to stakeholders or users

- Walkabout—Involves a hands-on, face-to-face approach with your team and clients

Effectively Improving the Communications

The project manager should determine which tools to use to remedy poor project communications. Communications are essentially closed when information comes in but doesn't go out. This occurs when some team members have access to accurate information and others don't. It's a key responsibility of project managers to provide regular and consistent feedback, such as status reports, issue logs, risk logs, meeting notes, or a project website, where project information can be published. A common repository for project information should be developed to avoid miscommunication and confusion on the team.

On the other hand, it should also be ensured that the correct and precise information is published across to the project stakeholders, without overloading them irrelevant and repetitive information. Skillful project managers know how to plan their communications, understand what type of information each team member needs, and utilize a wide range of communication methods.

Achieving Balance in the Communication Process

The key factor is that managers should facilitate project communications and encourage openness and allow the teams to be empowered with the right information to do their tasks. It is important to know if communications are being managed effectively. Here are some clues to look for that could signal impending project failure:

- Micromanaging everything on the project: Generally, managers create very detailed and complex project plans and start pushing themselves and the team to get every task done in the most incredible detail. This style of project manager actually stifles the entire communication process as a result of getting too involved with the details. The team soon realizes that a dictator has taken over the project, and they typically refrain from saying too much. This style of management leads to mistrust and eventual frustration. The project manager usually only releases information on an as-needed basis and, as a result, the team becomes less creative or unwilling to come up with great ideas. Remember that project managers need to foster more open and transparent communication.

- Allowing too much communication: Sending too much communication can actually hamper the amount of work that gets done. Sharing every piece of data and information with everyone is the norm for this type of manager. Team members are actively encouraged to speak their minds, share their pains, and, eventually, a regular-hour workweek is made even longer, all due to over communication. The downside here is that when breakdowns do occur because of technical challenges, the project manager will have a tough time trying to bring the project back on track, due to communication paralysis.

The correct balance is needed on a project team when it comes to communications. The important factors involve communicating how the project will be managed, including how information will flow into and out of the project. There should be a clear and concise communication plan to address project responsibilities and the types of communication that will take place.

CHAPTER 5

STATUS REPORTING AND PROJECT TRACKING

STATUS REPORTING

The purpose of status reporting is to manage the expectations of the sponsor and the stakeholders. In many cases where conflicts arise, it is not because of the actual problem but because the client or manager was surprised by it. Managing expectations through status reporting will keep such surprises from happening. Proper communication is a critical factor in any project. At a minimum, all projects should communicate accurate status on an ongoing basis throughout the life cycle of the project. The status reporting process should include team members sending status updates to the project manager and the project manager sending status updates to management stakeholders. On a small project, the status update might be informal, but as the project gets larger, it should become more formal, taking the form of a Status Report.

Status Report Structure

A project status report contains multiple sections as described below. Depending on the project and stakeholders' needs, a manager may chose to define the status report format, but in general, most of the reports will have following sections:

Opening project status information
This opening information helps managers to keep the right project in mind, assuming that they are managing multiple engagements. The information includes the name of the project, the project manager on the project, and a project description—a brief explanation of the project and reporting period.

Status summary
This section of the report provides summary information regarding the overall project. The summary is obtained from the team members by asking questions in such a way that the answers are either a yes or no. Examples of project summary questions include:
- Will the project be completed on time?
- Will the project be completed within budget?
- Are scope change requests being managed successfully?
- Are project issues being addressed successfully?
- Are project risks being managed successfully?
- Are all client concerns being addressed successfully?
- Provide more information on any questions above that were answered no.

Accomplishments
- List the major accomplishments from previous reporting period.
- List the major planned accomplishments for the current reporting period.
- Describe anything else that the reader should know that have not been reflected in the status report so far.

Risks/Issues

This section contains the major risks and issues that are being faced by the team. The severity of the risk and issues should also be mentioned so that they can be addressed accordingly.

Attachments

This section of the report includes other information of interest such as:

- Budget and effort hours summary
- Spending for the previous period and project to date
- Estimated total spending at project completion
- Earned value
- Issue log
- Scope change log
- Project work plan
- Project metrics/statistics

COMMUNICATION GUIDELINES

While status-reporting requirements may vary by project complexity, duration, and scope, regular reporting routines should always be established. These routines should be set as soon as the project starts, should always be enforced consistently, and should include the following:

Methods and Protocols—The specification of meeting methods and protocols, including the usage of group meetings, one-on-one meetings, phone conferences, email, memos, forms, or project management software.

Content Guidelines—The specification of the format and content of status reporting, including information to be included in reports and standardized agenda formats for meetings.

Scheduling Guidelines—Determination of the expected frequency, timing and duration for meetings, phone conferences, and the submission of status reports are necessary. While flexibility must be considered, these guidelines can help staff members better allocate their time and will help the project manager schedule sufficient time for status review, analysis, and feedback.

Feedback Guidelines—Status reporting should be a two-way street. Staff status reports should be acknowledged, and feedback should always be provided whenever appropriate. In addition, a regular routine for management reporting should be established to keep team members advised on the status of global project issues.

Consolidation Guidelines—Depending on the size and organization of the project team, status report consolidation may be necessary and appropriate. For example, individual status reports may have to be viewed as a whole if progress statistics are to have any real meaning.

Emergency Escalation Guidelines—If an important deadline is missed on Tuesday, the news should not be held for the Friday status report. Policies and guidelines should be established for emergency communication and problem escalation.

OTHER IMPORTANT ASPECTS OF STATUS REPORTING

No matter what format and process is chosen for status reporting, it will never be an exact science. Since projects are completed by people, behavioral factors must always be considered. Although well intentioned, team members may sometimes be reluctant to give totally accurate feedback. After all, no one likes to deliver bad news. Project members may honestly feel that problems can be solved or that individual delays can be overcome without management intervention. It may just seem easier that way. To combat this situation, a project manager needs to not only set the rules for status reporting, but also set the stage for honest and realistic reporting through the following three steps:

- Combine reporting methods for an effective blend of meetings and written status reports. Staff members may be even more reluctant to deliver bad news in a meeting, and a written report, even a brief one, can provide a much needed heads-up to a project manager.

- Remember that formal status reporting is not a replacement for personal communication. Informal discussions and spontaneous brainstorming should always be encouraged. Important information can sometimes be uncovered at the most unexpected times.

- Pave the way for open communication. Be sure to include standardized questions in your status report format, designed to get to the heart of the matter in status reporting.

This direct approach can facilitate the delivery of bad news in sufficient time for corrective action. And this, after all, is the ultimate goal of status reporting.

Status reports are not merely paperwork required by the project or organization. A proactive project manager embraces them, since they are one of key means for managing expectations. Project managers that carefully manage expectations will be much more successful than those that communicate poorly.

Project managers walk a fine line when it comes to requesting and actually getting status reports from staff members. On one hand, status-reporting procedures should not be too cumbersome or intrusive. Project staff may come to resent the attention and the perceived lack of trust and confidence. However, no project manager can afford to be caught unaware by performance or scheduling problems. They must rely on the team to provide timely, effective, and realistic feedback, and the quality and quantity of that feedback cannot be left to chance.

PROJECT TRACKING

Project tracking is essential to monitor project progress and identify any project slippage or time delay. Effective project tracking allows the project manager to see emerging problems and deal with them before they become big problems or impact the project schedule. Given the high project failure rate, it is important to ensure that a method exists to relate the project plan—schedule, tasks, and named resources—to time tracking of that project schedule and its tasks.

Effective Project Tracking

For project managers, the key elements of performing effective project tracking are:

- Clear project tasks with a named resource for ensuring its completion to schedule.

- Commitment of named resource to complete task according to schedule.

- Regular project team meetings to discuss and update on progress and identify any dependencies and potential risks.

- Regular verbal updates of progress with all named resources and identification of any dependencies and risks, especially competing project tasks or worse external factors, such as competing projects. These are additional to project team meetings and designed to ensure that the project manager is very closely in touch with project progress.

- Accurate and regular project reporting of progress and percentage completion of tasks based on team and individual updates.

Recording Time Tracking

Projects involving more than a few people quickly develop a long list of tasks and dependencies, and these must be held in some dedicated software tool as opposed to some manual, paper-based method or a spreadsheet. This is because it becomes very complex very quickly to keep a project plan up to date. Project time tracking is primarily about recording the time taken by individuals to complete their tasks. Ideally, timesheets for recording time are linked into the same software tool that records the project tasks, so that updating the timesheet automatically updates the percentage completion of the assigned tasks. If not, then the project manager must update the project plan with project progress.

Managing Time Delay

The real value to effective project tracking and especially time tracking, is to see any time delays really early. This gives the project manager more options for dealing with the time delay without impacting the project schedule. Every time delay matters, but not every time delay requires corrective action. A simple rule of thumb is:

- A one-time delay to an important task triggers an offer of help and if refused, the project manager maintains a watching brief and special attention on that task's completion.

- A second time delay to the same task triggers immediate project manager action help to solve the issue and to mitigate any further risk of a time delay that impacts the project schedule.

- A third time delay to an important task is significant enough to consider replanning, and the project manager should convene a project team meeting of the experts and key stakeholders to consider the options.

Project Monitoring

All of these project tracking and time tracking activities will ensure that the project manager is in touch with progress and able to react to deviations from the project plan very quickly. Reacting to a time delay is critical to a successful project, and effective project monitoring is an important part of project risk management. Effective project tracking allows the project manager to see emerging problems and deal with them before they become big problems or impact the project schedule.

CHAPTER 6
MEETING MANAGEMENT

Meeting management tends to be a set of skills often overlooked by managers. It should be kept in mind that meetings are very expensive activities when one considers the cost of labor for the meeting and how much can or cannot get done in them. So meeting management should be taken very seriously. The process used in a meeting depends on the kind of meeting that a manager plans to have, for example, a staff meeting, planning meeting, problem-solving meeting, etc. However, there are certain basics that are common to various types of meetings.

BASICS OF MEETINGS

The following section discusses the key points that constitute the basics of any meeting.

Selecting Participants

The decision about who is to attend depends on what has to be accomplished in the meeting. This may seem too obvious to state, but it's surprising how many meetings occur without the right people there. Project manager should not be depended on his own judgment about who should come. Several other team members should be asked for their opinion as well. If possible, each person should be called to tell them about the meeting, its overall purpose, and why their attendance is important. It should be followed up with a meeting notice, including the purpose of the meeting, where it will be held and when, the list of participants, and whom to contact if they have questions. A copy of the proposed agenda is also sent along with the meeting notice. Someone should be designated to record important actions, assignments, and due dates during the meeting. This person should ensure that this information is distributed to all participants shortly after the meeting.

Developing Agendas

The agenda is developed together with key participants in the meeting. The overall outcome from the meeting and what activities need to occur to reach that outcome should be thought of. The agenda should be organized so that these activities are conducted during the meeting. The agenda should be designed so that participants get involved early by having something for them to do right away and so they come on time. Next to each major topic, the type of action needed, the type of output expected, and time estimates for addressing each topic is included. Participants should be asked to commit to the agenda. Some of the key things to be considered are:

- Keep the agenda posted at all times.

- Don't overly design meetings.

- Be willing to adapt the meeting agenda if members are making progress in the planning process.

- Think about how the meeting is labeled, so that participants come in with that mindset.

- Have a short dialogue around the label to develop a common mindset among attendees, particularly if they include representatives from various cultures.

Opening Meetings

The meeting should always start on time. This respects those who showed up on time and reminds latecomers that the scheduling is serious. Once the forum is set, the agenda is reviewed at the beginning of each meeting, giving participants a chance to understand all proposed major topics, change them, and accept them. Note that a meeting recorder will take minutes and provide them back to each participant shortly after the meeting. The roles of the participants should be clarified in the meeting, if needed.

Establishing Ground Rules for Meetings

There need not be new ground rules each time a meeting is being arranged. However, it pays to have a few basic ground rules that can be used for most of the meetings. These ground rules cultivate the basic ingredients needed for a successful meeting. Four powerful ground rules are: participate, get focus, maintain momentum, and reach closure. List the primary ground rules on the agenda. Keep the ground rules posted at all times.

Time Management

One of the most difficult meeting tasks is time management. Time seems to run out before tasks are completed. Therefore, the biggest challenge is keeping momentum to keep the process moving. The attendees should be asked for their help to keep track of the time. If the planned time on the agenda is getting out of hand, the group should be made aware of it, and their input should be taken to get a resolution.

Evaluations of Meeting Process

It is amazing how often people will complain about a meeting being a complete waste of time, but they only say so after the meeting. Their feedback should be asked for during the meeting, so that the meeting process can be improved right away. When you evaluate a meeting only at the end of the meeting is usually too late to do anything about participants' feedback. A roundtable approach can be adopted to quickly have each participant indicate how they think the meeting is going.

Evaluating the Overall Meeting

Some time should be reserved toward the end of the meeting to evaluate the meeting. This is a very important part of the meeting, where the discussions are summarized and action items are listed out. The owner of each of the action item is decided. The participants should also be encouraged to rank the effectiveness of the meeting during this time.

Closing Meetings

It should be made sure that the meetings end on time on a positive note. At the end of a meeting, actions and assignments should be reviewed, and the time for the next meeting should be set aside, if required. Each participant should be asked if they can make it or not for the next meeting. It should be clarified that meeting minutes and/or actions will be reported back to members in at most a week.

MEETINGS—PREPARATION AND MANAGEMENT

In any organization, meetings are a vital part of the organization of work and the flow of information. They act as a mechanism for gathering together resources from many sources and pooling them toward a common objective. Meetings are generally disliked and mocked because they are usually futile, boring, and inconvenient. For a manager, the challenge is to break this mold and to make the meetings effective. As with every other managed activity, meetings should be planned beforehand, monitored during for effectiveness, and reviewed afterwards for improving their management.

A meeting is the ultimate form of managed conversation. A manager can organize the information and structure of the meeting to support the effective communication of the participants. Some of the ideas below may help in planning and organizing an effective meeting:

- Canceling a meeting—As with all conversations, it must be asked: is it worth spending the time? If the meeting involves the interchange of views and the communication of the current status of related projects, then it may be required to spend some quality time. Canceling a meeting should be considered if it has little tangible value.

- Participants—A meeting loses its effectiveness if too many people are involved. If someone has no useful function, they should not attend the meeting. Some may not like this, but most people are only too happy to be released from yet another meeting.

- Duration of meeting—It may seem difficult to predict the length of a discussion, but the manager should have an idea on how long the meeting will take. Discussions tend to fill the available time, which means that if the meeting is open ended, it will drift on forever. Manager should stipulate a time for the end of the meeting so that everyone knows, and everyone can plan the rest of their day with confidence. It is wise to make this expectation known to everyone involved well in advance and to remind them at the beginning of the meeting. If some unexpected point arises during the meeting and if the new discussion looks likely to be more than a few moments, stop it and deal with the agreed agenda. The new topic should then be dealt with at another planned meeting.

- Agenda—The purpose of an agenda is to inform participants of the subject of the meeting in advance and to structure the discussion at the meeting itself. To inform people beforehand, and to solicit ideas, the draft agenda should be circulated in advance. Still before the meeting, send the revised agenda after accounting for changes suggested by the participants with enough time for people to prepare their contributions. The agenda states the purpose of each section of the meeting. There will be an outcome from each section. The understanding of the meeting should be sufficiently precise that it can be summarized in short form. This form of display will emphasize to all that meetings are about achieving defined goals.

- Some other points to be considered are allowing enough lead time to plan the meeting, choosing an effective meeting format, choosing the right speakers and chairpersons, putting together a realistic agenda, keeping the audience fresh, and evaluating the meeting.

A manager must provide the necessary support to coordinate the contributions of the participants. If the structure is right at the beginning, a meeting can effectively run itself.

MAINTAINING COMMUNICATION

Communication is best achieved through simple planning and control. This section looks at approaches that might help a manager to do this and specifically at meetings, where conversations need particular care. Most of the conversations drift along in a meeting, without any result. In business, this is wasteful. To ensure an efficient and effective conversation, there are three considerations. The manager should:

- make his message understand to the participants

- receive and understand the intended message sent to him

- exert some control over the flow of the communication

The manager should develop the skill to listen as well as to speak. The following subsections describe how the three considerations could be practiced when conducting a meeting and handling the conversations in the meetings:

Most Important Tools

- Clarification—clarify the purpose of the meeting.

- Summary—at each stage of the proceedings, summarize the current position and progress.

- Focus on stated goals—at each divergence or pause, refocus the proceedings on the original goals.

- Code of conduct—to begin the proceedings by establishing a code of conduct, often by merely stating it and asking for any objections

- Matching method to purpose—depending on the purpose of a meeting, a certain method could be used to conduct the meeting. For instance, if the purpose is to convey information, the meeting might begin with a formal presentation, followed by questions. If the purpose is to seek information, the meeting would start with a short and clear statement of the topic or problem and then an open discussion supported by notes on a display, or a formal brainstorming session, and if the purpose is to make a decision, the meeting might review the background and options, establish the criteria to be applied, agree who should make the decision and how, and then do.

- Audiovisual support—Audiovisual devices could be used for a larger group. Consider using a wireless microphone, as it is essential for individuals addressing the group to move around easily. Set projectors and projection screens at different angles so that speakers can check their slides without turning their backs to the audience. Make sure a technician is assigned to the meeting, as technical difficulties can occur even if the equipment is checked in advance using the speakers' presentation materials. With larger groups, make sure there are one or more remote microphones available for audience questions.

Support

The success of a meeting will often depend upon the confidence with which the individuals will participate. Thus, all ideas should be welcome. No one should be laughed at or dismissed. This means that even bad ideas should be treated seriously and at least merit a specific reason for not being pursued further. Not only is this supportive to the speaker, it could also be that a good idea has been misunderstood and would be lost if merely rejected. But basically, people should be able to make naive contributions without being made to feel stupid. This is required to get good ideas from the team. Avoid direct criticism of any person. For instance, if someone has not come prepared, then that fault is obvious to all. Instead of criticizing, the manager should just try to understand why the preparation was not done. He could say: "We need to know this before we can proceed; could you circulate it to us by lunch tomorrow?" This will help the person to understand the importance of preparation for the meeting and at the same time, he will not feel humiliated.

Responding to Problems

A manager might deal with the various problems associated with the volatile world of meetings. One such problem is managing meetings in the given timeframe. Following are some examples that suggest how a meeting can be kept on track:

- If a participant strays from the agenda item, call him/her back, "We should deal with that separately, but what do you feel about _____?"

- If there is confusion, it could be asked, "Do I understand correctly that _____?"

- If the speaker begins to ramble, interrupt to say, "Yes, I understand that such and such, does any one disagree?"

- If a point is too vague, ask for greater clarity: "What exactly do you have in mind?"

- If someone interrupts, suggest, "We will hear your contribution after the current speaker has finished."

- If someone gestures disagreement with the speaker, then they should be brought into the discussion next by asking, "What do you think?"

- Ask question if the point is not understood: "I do not understand that, would you explain it a little more; or do you mean X or Y?"

- If there is an error, look for a good point first: "I see how that would work if X Y Z, but what would happen if A B C?"

- If there is a disagreement, be very specific: "I disagree because_____"

Ambiguity Avoidance

As a manager, your view of words should be pragmatic rather than philosophical. Thus, words mean not what the dictionary says they do but rather what the speaker intended. In everything a manager says or hears, he must look out for possible misunderstanding and clarify the ambiguity. The greatest source of difficulty is that words often have different meanings depending upon context and/or culture. If a potential misunderstanding is recognized, the conversation must be stopped, and a valid interpretation should be asked for.

A second problem is that some people simply make mistakes. A manager's job is not simply to spot ambiguities, but also to counter inconsistencies. The reason for mistakes could be many. For example, a speaker could intend one thing but say something else, the audience may not hear the speaker properly, the words used to describe an idea may not be appropriate in the give context, and so on. To make sure what speaker meant, some of these rules could be followed:

Rule 1: Play back for confirmation—simply ask for confirmation. It could be said, "Let me see if I have understood correctly, you are saying that…" and rephrase what the speaker said. If this playback version is acknowledged as being correct by the original speaker, then there is a greater degree of confidence in understanding what speaker said. For any viewpoint or message or decision, there should be a clear, concise, and verified statement of what was said.

Rule 2: Write back for confidence. It should be written down and sent to everyone involved as a double check. This has several advantages:

- Further clarification: is this what you thought we agreed?
- Consistency check: the act of writing may highlight defects/omissions.
- A formal stage: a statement of the accepted position provides a springboard from which to proceed.
- Evidence: people often fail to recall their previous errors. A message in written form acts as evidence of what was discussed.

Rule 3: Give background for context—providing a broader context in simple words helps in understanding the issue or suggestion. Thus, there is less scope for alternative interpretations.

Practical Points

For communication to be effective, the purpose of the conversation and plan for achieving it should be decided in advance. There is no alternative to this. Some people are proficient at "thinking on their feet"—but this is generally because they already have clear understanding of the context and their own goals. The following are a few techniques to help the conversation along:

Assertiveness—The definition of to assert is to declare or state clearly. This should be the aim. The following threefold plan of action that could be followed:

- Acknowledge what is being said by showing an understanding of the position, or by simply replaying it.

- The manager should state his own point of view clearly and concisely, with perhaps a little supporting evidence.

- The manager should state what he wants to happen next, that is, move it forward.

A manager will have to make many personal judgment calls when being assertive. There will certainly be times when a bit of quiet force from the manager will win the day, but there will be times when this will get nowhere, particularly with more senior management. In the latter case, the manager must agree to abide by the decision of the senior manager, but he should make his objection and reasons clearly known.

Confrontations—A manager may have a difficult encounter. In such a scenario, he should not lose his self-control, because it will not help. Even if a manager wants to be slightly volatile when the situation demands, it is fine, but he should be consistent and fair. He should be able to keep control on himself in such situations. A manager should avoid insulting, as it does not serve the purpose. In fact, it may complicate the situation. Hence, before a manager has to say anything, he should stop, establish what he wants as the outcome, plan how to achieve this, and then speak. Sometimes, the confrontations can happen between the participants, and managers have to carefully manage this situation. He should be aware of the viewpoints of both the parties involved and try to resolve the issue by providing appropriate suggestions.

Seeking information—There are two ways of phrasing any question: the closed question—which is likely to lead to a simple reply in form of yes, no, or maybe; the open question—which will hand over the speaking role to someone else and force them to say something a little more informative. A closed question may sound like: "Have you finished project X?" and the probable reply to this could be yes or no. These kinds of questions will not actually help in the flow of information. The same question in an open format would be, "What is left to do of project X?" Open questions are extremely easy to formulate. Establish the topic or aim of the question in the mind, and then start the sentence with the words: what, when, which, why, where, how.

Let others speak—Of course, there is more to a conversation than the flow of information. A manager may also have to win that information by winning the attention and confidence of the other person. There are many ways to handle this such as asking the right question: "What do you think about that idea?" "Have you ever met this problem before?" "How would you tackle this situation?" or by simply listening to the speaker with full attention.

To finish—At the end of a conversation, the manager has to give people a clear understanding of the outcome. For instance, if there has been a decision, it should be restated clearly in terms of what should happen and by when.

THE REASONS FOR INEFFECTIVE MEETINGS

Meetings are the most universal—and universally distasteful—part of business life. In a business world that is faster, tougher, leaner, and more downsized than ever, the sheer demands of competition can curb our appetite for meetings. In reality, the opposite may be true. As more work becomes teamwork, and fewer people remain to do the work that exists, the number of meetings is likely to increase rather than decrease. A variety of tools and techniques can make meetings less painful, more productive, and maybe even fun. Following are some of the reasons for a bad meeting[15] and how it can be handled:

Reason number one: People don't take meetings seriously. They arrive late, leave early, and spend most of their time scribbling.

Solution: Meetings are real work. There are as many techniques to improve the effectiveness of meetings, as there are items on the typical meeting agenda. Some companies punish latecomers with a penalty fee or reprimand them in the minutes of the meeting. But these techniques address symptoms, not the disease. Disciplined meetings are about mindset—a shared conviction among all the participants that meetings are real work.

Reason number two: Meetings are too long.

Solution: Track the cost of your meetings, and use a computer-supported environment to make them more productive. One reason meetings drag on is that people don't appreciate how expensive they are. As discussed earlier, a project manager should plan and organize meetings in such a way that they get over in time. He should control and provide direction to the meeting.

Reason number three: People wander off the topic.

Solution: It is the starting point for all advice on productive meetings—stick to the agenda. But it is hard to stick to an agenda that does not exist, and most meetings in most companies are decidedly agenda-free. The company can develop an agenda template that everyone in the company uses. The template could list the meeting's key topics, who will lead which parts of the discussion, how long each segment will take, what the expected outcomes are, and so on. Project manager has the challenge is to keep meetings focused without stifling creativity or insulting participants who stray.

Reason number four: Nothing happens once the meeting ends. People don't convert decisions into action.

Solution: Generally, people leave meetings with different views of what happened and what's supposed to happen next. Even with the tools of organization and sharing ideas—whiteboards, flip charts, Post-it notes—the capacity for misunderstanding is unlimited. The best way to avoid that misunderstanding is to convert from meeting to doing, where the doing focuses on the creation of shared documents that lead to action. Simple tools and techniques such as recording comments, outlining ideas, generating written proposals, projecting them for the entire group to see, and printing them so people leave with real-time minutes can be used to make meetings more effective.

Reason number five: People don't tell the truth. There's plenty of conversation, but not much openness.

Solution: Too often, people in meetings simply don't speak their minds. Sometimes, the problem is a leader who doesn't solicit participation. Sometimes, a dominant personality intimidates the rest of the group. But most of the time, the problem is a simple lack of trust. People don't feel secure enough to say what they really think. It is again a project manager who has to create an atmosphere of trust, where people can participate openly. The project manager can also make use of technology to promote openness. Many computer-based tools focus on anonymity, enabling people to express opinions and evaluate alternatives without having to divulge their identities.

Reason number six: Meetings are always missing important information, so they postpone critical decisions.

Solution: Most meeting rooms make it harder to have good meetings. Allow enough space in the meeting rooms for teams to store materials. Project teams generate lots more than minutes and memos. Meetings build models, fill up flip charts, and create artifacts of all sorts—information that's vital to future meetings.

Reason number seven: Meetings never get better. People make the same mistakes.

Solution: Monitor what works and what doesn't, and hold people accountable. In a meeting, someone can serve as an observer and create a list that would record what went right and what went wrong, and get included in the minutes. Over time, both for specific meeting groups and for the company as a whole, these lists can create an agenda for change. Good meetings are not just about work. They're about fun and keeping people charged up. It is about people freeing each other up to think more creatively.

CHAPTER 7
LEARNING ABOUT FACILITATION

Facilitation is helping a group to accomplish its goals. There are a wide range of perspectives about the ideal nature and values of facilitation, much as there are a wide range of perspectives about the ideal nature and values of leadership. The practice of facilitation usually is best carried out by someone who has strong knowledge and skills regarding group dynamics and processes. Effective facilitation might also involve strong knowledge and skills about the particular topic or content that the group is addressing in order to reach its goals. A project manager should have these skills to manage a project successfully.

INTRODUCTION TO FACILITATION

It is assumed that anyone can perform basic meeting, team, or group facilitation, given the right tools and opportunity. Facilitators can serve many different roles, including developmental intervention in meetings, running workshops, conducting experience-based training, and guiding team development. The focus of this chapter is on the role of the facilitator in relation to meetings. It is recognized that many meetings involve teams. However, there also exist many situations where meetings are held to share information and make decisions, in which the participants are not recognized as a team.

About the Facilitator

A facilitator is someone who uses knowledge of group processes to formulate and deliver the needed structure for meeting interactions to be effective. The facilitator focuses on effective processes, allowing the participants to focus on the content or the substance of their work together. Other roles exist for meeting participants besides facilitation. These include taking notes, recording, timekeeping, and leading discussions. The facilitator's role is unique, although no more or less important, since their primary focus is on the meeting processes. Facilitation can involve many different levels of knowledge and skill, can include work on all kinds of problems and challenges, can assist the group in fulfilling its desire, or can include pushing participants to new levels of understanding. Most importantly, however, facilitation includes both an ability to recognize when effective meeting processes are needed and an ability to provide those processes. These actions that define facilitators are based on an intuitive sense that something in the meeting is amiss. Though this intuition is fundamentally important to good facilitation, it must be emphasized that intuition alone does not replace an understanding of the skills and techniques that are the foundation for the role.

Need of a Facilitator for Meetings

People come together and meet for a variety of reasons. Sometimes, the participants are referred to as teams, groups, or committees. It is generally recognized that teams have a common bond, interdependency, and/or commitment to a goal. Groups, on the other hand, are usually not as cohesive, not accountable to each other, and may meet on a less regular basis. In either case, the techniques discussed here apply equally to teams or groups because both need to meet to be effective. The basic assumption underlying meetings is that two or more heads are better than one, and better decisions can be made if there is more input. However, to assure that better decisions are made, the meeting often needs to be facilitated. In fact, a well-facilitated team meeting generally is both more effective and more efficient. Meetings occur for a number of reasons where participants are called upon to:

- Make decisions.
- Share information.
- Plan work.
- Learn from one another.
- Create buy-in.
- Solve problems.

The results of these actions may be seen in the design of a new product, improvements to a system, development of a marketing plan, or suggestions for improving work conditions. No matter what the meeting's purpose, participants need to clearly understand the goal and how to work together. One misconception about meetings is that getting all the experts in the same room will automatically produce good results. In actuality, getting the experts together is just the beginning, the beginning of being able to work together effectively. The role of the facilitator is to help the participants learn how to work together by providing the structure and process, while they remain focused on the content. In any meeting, the facilitator must constantly balance process with content. Processes include the methods and tools used to help people interact productively with each other, including how decisions are made and making sure everyone has an equal voice. Content focuses on topics or subjects under discussion at any meeting. Determining the tools and methods to use that create this balance is an important task that the facilitator must perform. Time spent in thoughtful preparation goes far to assure a successful meeting.

FACILITATOR PREPARATION AND PLANNING

Preparation

Preparation involves deciding what methods and tools to use or provide. The following questions will aid in making this decision.

Why—Why is the meeting being held? What tasks are planned? What is the overall goal of the meeting? Is this meeting only a part of a larger goal? Has this been written down?

Who—Who is invited? If decisions need to be made, are the right people going to be present? Who is not going to be there? How does attendance affect successful completion of tasks? Who cannot come? Who is not invited? Why?

When—When is the meeting scheduled? How long should it be? Is there enough time? If it is close to lunch or dinner, should it be catered? Need to clearly understand the goal and how to work? How much time can be allotted for each agenda item?

Where—Where is the meeting to be held? Are there adequate resources (overheads, flip charts, white boards) available? How is the room arranged? Is the room appropriate for the task?

What—Consider possible group dynamics—Do the participants know each other? How well? What is the history of the participants? How long have they been meeting? Have they had specific problems working together in the past? What are potential problems with this meeting? Can they be mitigated or eliminated before the meeting begins?

PLANNING

Once information is gathered about the meeting, the facilitator can start planning. During the planning stage, the facilitator needs to decide which tool or technique to use where. There are a few tools that need to be reviewed and developed during planning. These include charters and meeting agendas.

Charters

For a team, the charter is the document that defines why the team exists and its overall goal. It defines the purpose of the meeting. It is used to ensure that the participants understand who is sponsoring the meeting, and that they clearly understand the focus of the time they will spend together. If a charter already exists, the facilitator needs to review it before the meeting. If a charter does not exist, the facilitator should discuss this item with the leader before the meeting and develop a purpose statement for the meeting. Typical items included in a charter or purpose statement include the participants, the sponsor, a description of the goal, and a due date.

Meeting Agendas

The meeting agenda is the document that defines what will be done at any particular meeting. It should include the date, time, and location of the meeting, the objective of the meeting, and the list of tasks to be addressed. In addition, it is a good practice to allot times for each task or agenda item to help assure that the meeting will end on time. The facilitator uses the agenda prior to the meeting to determine specific processes to be used and during the meeting to keep discussions on track. In addition, meeting agendas help participants know what to expect and how to prepare for the meeting.

MANAGING MEETINGS

Keeping the Meeting on Track

Keeping the team on track starts with good preparation and includes the use of appropriate process intervention. Process intervention is an interruption by the facilitator of the meeting process and conversation in order to refocus the participants and to rebalance group interactions. A facilitator's goal is to support the participants in achieving their desired outcomes by staying on track and balancing participation with results, so interventions must be supportive. Speak the intervention clearly, using assertive language, with supportive tone of voice and body language. Following are the five most common situations requiring intervention to keep the meeting on track:

- Side-bar conversations
- Staying on time
- Never-ending discussion
- Conflict
- Returning from breaks

Managing Data

One of the keys to meeting success is managing the information that the participants are dealing with and producing. It is up to the facilitator to make sure that everyone hears, sees, and understands what is presented, what is offered, what is going on, what is agreed to, and that work products and decisions are accurately captured.

One way to do this is to keep a running memory. The running memory is a consciousness thread used to keep individuals focused and working on one thing in a logical sequence. Running memory is the documentation that can be kept on flip charts, butcher paper covering the wall, chalk or white boards, electronic documents projected on a screen, or shared materials using web-based virtual meeting tools. It is where all comments, ideas, discussion, agreements, thoughts, votes, and decisions are kept.

Some facilitators use a recorder or scribe to keep running memory. This frees the facilitator to focus on group dynamics, traffic control, staying on topic, meeting process, honoring agreements about working together, and other aspects of facilitation. Recording the right things at the right level of detail, summarizing without changing essential words, and knowing when to check back with the speaker are all skills that require practice.

Meeting Review

Finally, it is important that a facilitator continue to learn and practice new techniques. Keep a generic meeting evaluation form, and have participants fill it out anonymously. Review the responses, and incorporate specific suggestions. Apart from using a written meeting evaluation, set aside a few minutes at the end of each meeting to ask the participants about what meeting processes worked and what did not. Ask for suggestions to improve the meeting process for the next time. Specific attributes of an effective facilitator include openness, honesty, fairness, consistency in actions, focus, active listening, accessibility, flexibility, assertiveness, and enthusiasm.

CHAPTER 8
CONFIGURATION MANAGEMENT

DEFINITION

Configuration Management (CM) provides a record of changes throughout the life of the product and shows any dependencies between products and their subsystems or components. It provides a mechanism for controlling the product's functional and physical characteristics throughout the project life cycle and enables an orderly transition from development to production and entry into service.

The standard definition for CM taken from IEEE standard[16] 729–1983 includes:

- Identification: an identification scheme is needed to reflect the structure of the product. This involves identifying the structure and kinds of components, making them unique and accessible in some form by giving each component a name, version identification, and configuration identification. For example, this addresses the question, "What version of the file is this?"

- Control: controlling the release of a product and changes to it throughout the life cycle by having controls in place that ensure consistent software via the creation of a baseline product. For example, this addresses the question, "How many changes went into the latest version of this product?"

- Status Accounting: recording and reporting the status of components and change requests, and gathering vital statistics about components in the product. For example, this addresses the question, "How many files were affected by fixing this one bug?"

- Audit and review: validating the completeness of a product and maintaining consistency among the components by ensuring that components are in an appropriate state throughout the entire project life cycle, and that the product is a well-defined collection of components. For example, this addresses the question, "Are all the correct versions of files used in this current release?"

Definition of CM From a User's Viewpoint

The definition includes terminology such as configuration item, baseline, release and version, and so on. At a high level, most designers of configuration management systems incorporate functionality of varying degrees to support these aspects. But at the implementation level, from the user's viewpoint, most configuration management systems have different functionality. Among the many reasons for these differences are disparate hardware platforms, operating system, and programming languages. But an interesting reason is due to the different kinds of users of a configuration management system. This stems from the role the user plays in the organization. In particular, a manager, a software engineer developing an application, an application customer, and an environment builder tend to see configuration management differently. As a result, they may want differing functionality from their configuration management system. For example, to a manager, the term *configuration management* conjures up the image of a Configuration Control Board. To a software engineer, the image of baselines arises. To a customer, versions of the application arise. And to the environment builder, mechanisms such as libraries and data compression arise. All these images obviously result in different requirements for a configuration management system and hence possibly different functionality.

It becomes clear that the definition of configuration management, as given by the IEEE standard, needs to be broadened to encompass the extra functionality found in configuration management systems. These concern:

- Construction: managing the construction and building of the product in an optimal manner. For example, this addresses the question, "What versions of files and tools were used to generate this latest release?"

- Process Management: ensuring the correct execution of the organization's procedures, policies, and life cycle model. For example, this addresses the question, "Were all the files tested and checked for quality before being released to the customer?"

- Teamwork: controlling the work and interactions between multiple developers on a product. For example, this addresses the question, "Were all the locally made changes of the programmers merged into the last release of the product?"

THE KEY PRINCIPLES OF CONFIGURATION MANAGEMENT

Configuration Management and Planning

In order to implement an effective configuration management process, it is necessary to first undertake a rigorous planning exercise, the aim being to plan and manage the configuration management process such that it delivers the outputs expected when required. The Configuration Management Plan (CMP) should be produced as part of the project initiation document or Software Project

Plan (SPP), for approval by the project owner at project initiation. Where appropriate, configuration management should continue throughout the life of the delivered end product, and therefore, the approach adopted should be transferable to the client organization at the end of the project. The application of effective procedures should ensure the accurate and up-to-date documentation and distribution of all relevant product components and project information. Configuration management should be applied to projects of any significant size and should be the day-to-day responsibility of a single individual, generally called as configuration management lead.

Configuration management is a method for administering an evolving, and often interrelated, set of products and project documentation. All of the products and documents that need administrative control are termed configuration items. Initially, the overall end product can theoretically be viewed as the only identifiable configuration item. However, an increasing number of configuration items that will usually be identified as the end product are subdivided into the manageable elements represented in the Work Breakdown Structure (WBS). A configuration item description record should be used to record the information needed to identify and track each configuration item through its development life cycle.

Configuration management provides a record of changes throughout the life of the product and shows any dependencies between products and their subsystems or components. The inputs and outputs generated by a typical configuration management system are shown in the following process diagram.

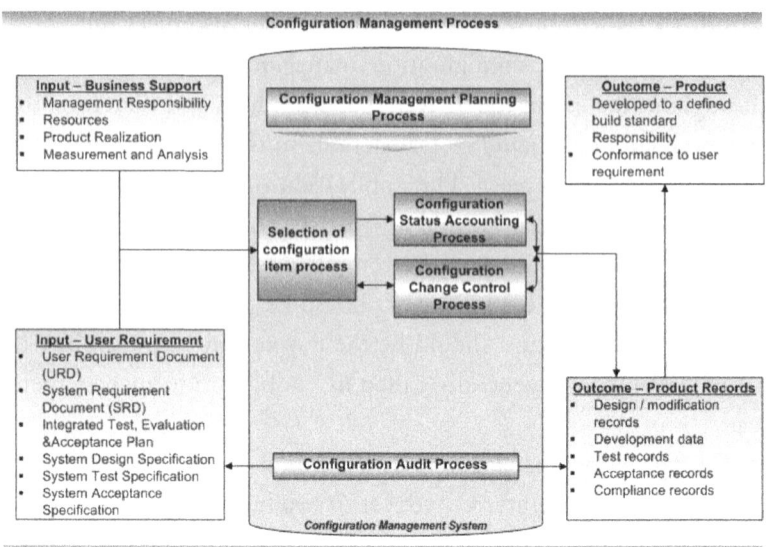

Input – Business Support
- Management Responsibility
- Resources
- Product Realization
- Measurement and Analysis

Configuration Management Planning Process

Outcome – Product
- Developed to a defined build standard Responsibility
- Conformance to user requirement

Selection of configuration item process

Configuration Status Accounting Process

Configuration Change Control Process

Input – User Requirement
- User Requirement Document (URD)
- System Requirement Document (SRD)
- Integrated Test, Evaluation &Acceptance Plan
- System Design Specification
- System Test Specification
- System Acceptance Specification

Configuration Audit Process

Outcome – Product Records
- Design / modification records
- Development data
- Test records
- Acceptance records
- Compliance records

Configuration Management System

Configuration Identification and Documentation

The application of configuration management controls at a system level rarely results in effective control. For this reason, it is normal to produce a WBS and then review it to identify those modules, sub-modules, and components for which the control of functional and physical characteristics are critical to product performance, safety, quality, and supportability. The output from the WBS review is a listing of components and subcomponents that will be subjected to configuration management practices throughout the project life cycle. These items are known as Configured Items (CI). The CI can pertain to computer software and hence referred to as Computer Software Configuration Item (CSCI). Similarly, a computer hardware configuration item is abbreviated as HWCI. Each CI should have a list of defined properties that together identifies its unique-ness. A change to any of these properties constitutes a change to the CI. For each CI, there should be associated configuration documentation defining the properties. Depending on the complexity, this may range from a full specification with detailed design drawings down to a brief descriptive brochure.

Configuration Control

Controlling the configuration management process is important to the success of a project. It refers to the procedures for the issue and submission of configuration items. These procedures should address both physical and electronically stored configuration items. In the first instance, a CI should be created and documented as the first version. The CI may then undergo a number of modifications as it is tested and errors corrected or as changes are requested. These subsequent submissions should be reflected by an increasing version number. The first baseline for a configuration item will be established when the specification of the item has been prepared, reviewed, and agreed upon. Subsequent baselines will normally be established at points at which the CI is ready to be used as a basis for further work, in which a major transformation of it will take place. A *Release* consists of a specified set of products from one or more base-lined configuration items, which are issued as a set for a specific purpose. Releases should be authorized by the project manager.

Issue and submission procedures are concerned with the submission of, and access to, the identified configuration items. These procedures will relate to administrative items, as well as those pertaining to the evolving products. Without careful control over the issue and submission of configuration items, the configuration management process can collapse. Only when the author of a new or revised product or document is satisfied that it is complete or ready for review, it should be resubmitted to the configuration lead. The submission procedure should not be used to introduce new configuration items. There are multiple tools available in the market to control the release or submission of the CI.

Configuration Change Management (CCM)

It is the process by which configurable items are managed throughout the product life cycle. The process shall:

- Identify the authority responsible for approving physical and functional changes throughout the product life cycle.

- Enable authoritative decisions to be taken on proposed changes to the product.

- Ensure that compatibility is maintained between the product configurable items themselves and those in any interfacing product or system.

- Establish CCM groups and/or committees as required.

- Determine the terms of reference for each group or committee and controls required to manage the CCM system efficiently and effectively.

When a document is the subject of an approved change request, the configuration lead should issue a copy to the appropriate person to carry out the work and notify all other copyholders of the impending change. On completion, it should be passed back to the configuration lead. Only after this step, the configuration lead should make it available for further changes. Ideally, when a new version of a configuration item is issued, earlier and now obsolete copies should be recalled and destroyed.

Configuration Status Accounting (CSA)

By this process, a product's build standard is formally documented and controlled. The process should be developed for all configurable items and be maintained for the life cycle of the product. CSA should record and make available the information necessary to manage the configuration effectively and maintain traceability of the configuration management documentation, the status of proposed changes to the configuration, and the implementation status of authorized changes. Configuration information should be presented in the formats specified in the configuration management plan. Procedures for CSA shall be detailed in the configuration management plan.

In relation to quality reviews, the configuration lead should be responsible for issuing a copy to each reviewer, in line with the issue procedures, and filing the original in the relevant development folder. The lead should never issue the master copies of baseline configuration items. It is important that current official copies are readily identifiable to avoid any obsolete documentation being used as the basis of future work. The configuration lead should maintain an issue log for each configuration item that records the identity and version of documents issued, the name of the recipient, the authority for and purpose of the issue, and the date of issue.

The configuration lead should be responsible for producing all scheduled and ad hoc reports on the status of the configuration items at any given point in time. Typical reports that may be required include numbers of change requests and project exception reports opened during a specific period, closed during a specific period, those currently open, and unresolved document update requests.

Configuration Audits (CA)

Configuration audits consist of cross checking the configuration item description records with the current version of the configuration item, as held in its development folder. These audits are normally carried out ahead of each project review, although they can be requested at any time by the project manager or the project owner. Configuration audits should establish that the current physical representation of each configuration item matches its current specification and that there is consistency in design between each configuration item and its parent, if there is a parent. Finally, it also establishes that the documentation is up to date and all relevant standards are being adhered to.

Configuration audits are the means by which a product's conformance to functional and physical parameters is confirmed. There are two types of CA:

- Functional Configuration Audit (FCA) is the examination of test data and quality records for a configured item to verify conformance with performance and functional characteristics.

- Physical Configuration Audit (PCA) is the examination of the "as built" configured item to verify conformance with build data. CA reports shall be formally presented to the appropriate authority for acceptance and evaluation of any need for corrective action.

ROLES AND RESPONSIBILITIES FOR CONFIGURATION MANAGEMENT

The project team shall ensure configuration management is controlled and managed and effectively applied by all stakeholders throughout all phases of the project cycle.

The Configuration Team Lead is ultimately responsible for the development and implementation of a CM strategy and for its implementation throughout the duration of the project life cycle. The Project Team Leader shall ensure that staffs have an appropriate level of CM competence and have, at their disposal, the necessary resources to carry out their tasks.

The project manager should support the configuration team lead in the configuration management process and its execution. The project manager's responsibilities include:

- Ensuring development, implementation, and operation of a documented strategy for managing the configuration of the project.

- Development of a project CMP, including the measurement of effectiveness to ensure the achievement of the stated aims and objectives.

- Ensuring that configuration management requirements are clearly defined, achievable, and translated into the appropriate project documentation, including measurable acceptance criteria.

- Keeping track of the project risks and ensuring potential configuration management risks are accounted for and managed appropriately.

The *customer* should fulfill the contractual configuration management requirements or dependencies in an economic and effective manner. It is the customer's responsibility to ensure that their configuration management controls continue to be effective and fully support the project configuration management strategy developed by the project manager.

The *end user* is responsible for the operation of the product, as well as for ensuring that delivered product is in full accordance with the required build standard. The end user is also responsible for the identification and proposal of product modifications that will improve operational performance.

As an example, in case of "Project X-1", an initial baseline version of the existing product was provided by the customer. This was used to start the development activity. At offshore and onsite locations, same directory structure was followed to store the source code files and other project documents. The files were checked-in and checked-out on a regular basis to avoid any configuration related issues. The offshore and onsite version control tools were synced to avoid any confusions and synchronization between the two environments used to happen on a weekly basis so that both the sites had latest version of the documents. A configuration team lead was assigned at both the ends to manage the configuration process.

CHAPTER 9
CHANGE MANAGEMENT

Developing and deploying large software applications, patches, and updates is a complex process that requires careful planning and oversight. Successful processes take into account not only technical issues and requirements, but business needs as well. A successful software change management strategy combines effective internal processes with clearly defined personnel roles and tools optimized for efficient management. This chapter describes the standard change management processes that need to be followed for the effective execution of a project. It describes overall best practices for a successful software change management process that should be adopted for a project.

In "Project X-1", the following process was adopted to manage the change. All the change requests were tracked and documented. Primarily there were changes in the requirements. All the changes, unless very critical (in terms of impact to the architecture and design) to the project, were taken up after the completion of original scope of work. The change requests amounted to additional effort of 600 person days and were successfully implemented as hot fixes after the "in-scope" product was developed.

PROCESS OVERVIEW

A consistent, repeatable software change management process takes both technical and business issues into account. The goal is to maintain access to software tools and services while minimizing the impact on users, organizational infrastructure, and staff. An effective software change management process consists of three major phases:

- Process foundations
- Preplanning and Change proposal
- Deploying the package and Follow-up

More details on these phases are as below.

Phase 1: Process Foundations

To effectively manage change requests and application deployment across the organization, there needs to be both a technical infrastructure (business analyst, technical lead, project manager) and a process infrastructure to help ensure that sound decisions are made and that all major stakeholders are involved in the process. These infrastructure elements are:

Configuration standards/Software change process
- A well-defined and documented change management process
- Specific to a project's or organization's needs

Technical Advisory Board (TAB)
- A team consisting of business analyst, technical lead, developer, tester, and project manager.
- Receive and collect the change requests from the project team and customer, get the impact analysis done, evaluate the analysis, prepare the estimate for the changes required, get an approval from the Change Control Board (CCB), and manage the changes based on the decision by CCB.

Change Control Board (CCB)
- An administration board consisting of major stakeholders in the project, such as the program manager, sponsor, and other key stakeholders
- Responsible for approving or declining the change requests in a timely manner
- Ensure that the effects of changes are understood and that the interests of each department are taken into account as part of the software release
- Responsible to the business organization and functions as the bridge between technical staff and business staff
- Responsible for the impact on the business needs, in case the change request is not approved

Phase 2: Preplanning and Change Proposal

Before proposing a change to the change control board, a preliminary research and development needs to be done for an initial change proposal that describes the primary technical and business impacts of the update. This is a business proposal that makes the benefits of the update/change clear and gives stakeholders a heads up about possible impacts. The preplanning/change proposal process consists of the following major steps:

Determine the need for change
- Clear business or technical benefit for a change to core, approved baseline (Requirement specifications, source code, documents, etc.).
- Evaluate and prioritize changes.

Perform initial high-level analysis and testing to more clearly identify potential impacts
- Identify major impact to the overall environment so that additional development, testing, and mitigation efforts could be planned.

- Aim to understand and document the software impacts, not solve all potential problems. More complete application impact and regression testing is performed later in the process once CCB has approved the initial change request.

Develop a preliminary assessment of impacts and requirements
- Assess impacts on project team and support staff, business processes, and service availability, and end-users.

- Analyze impact on the scope of the project, schedule, cost and effort impact, priority, feasibility, decision on when it can be done, availability of staff, etc.

- Generate a change proposal with the above details, including the cost needed for the impact analysis activity.

Get approval from CCB for performing the detailed impact analysis on the Change Request (CR) and document the impact analysis
- Based on the approval from CCB, perform a detailed analysis on the CR. Document the findings.

- The purpose of the document is to communicate information to key stakeholders so they can understand why the software change is important and how it will affect them both during and after deployment, so they can plan business and departmental activities accordingly.

- Document should contain all the knowledge gathered during initial impact analysis, test, and preplanning.

- Document to also be refined by the CCB itself, as each stakeholder provides additional information or requirements. The proposal itself may need to be revised and resubmitted in light of new data.

- Document the cost for development effort and schedule details to implement the CR.

- Approval of the change proposal by the CCB means approval to dedicate all needed resource to the project with the intention of completing it, as defined in the final proposal.

Phase 3: Deploying the Package and Follow-Up

Request assignment

- Technical Advisory Board (TAB) to receive the approval and assign the change request to the concerned developer in the team.

Detailed analysis

- Perform a detailed analysis on the change request by taking the approved Change Request (CR) document as the basis.

- Document the detail analysis and design. Update the requirements, and test cases.

- Get an approval from CCB on the implementation of CR, development cost, and schedule.

Implementation/Deployment

- Develop and test the change.

- Change could be fixing of a defect, minor/major enhancement, impacted code/design, etc.

- Perform a regression to see that the impact areas are covered.

Closure

- Incorporate the change in the next planned release.

- Receive an acceptance (sign off) from the customer after the acceptance testing.

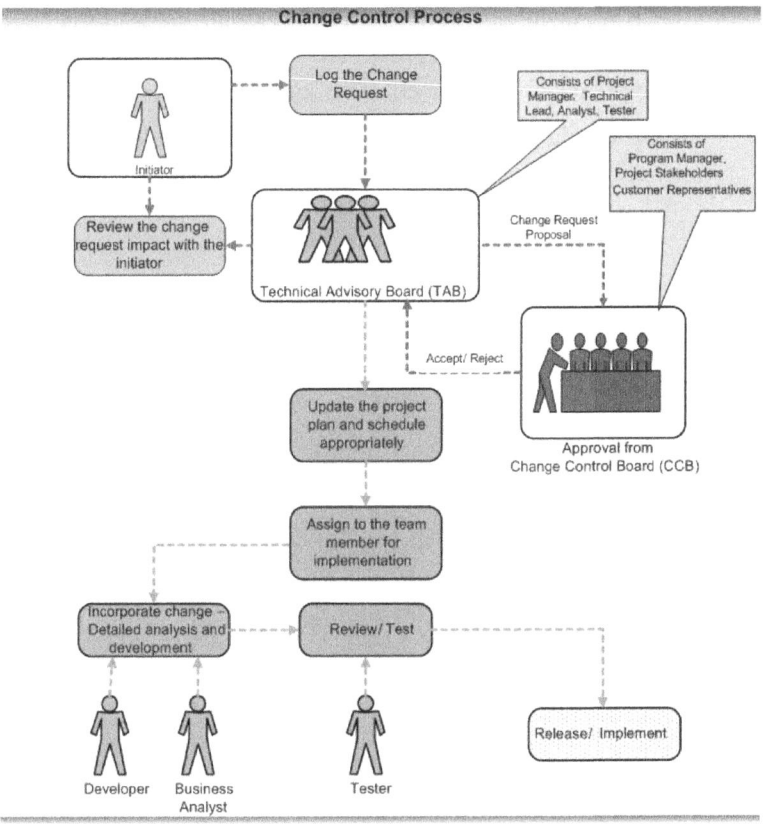

Change Control Process

Log the Change Request

Initiator

Review the change request impact with the initiator

Technical Advisory Board (TAB)

Consists of Project Manager, Technical Lead, Analyst, Tester

Consists of Program Manager, Project Stakeholders Customer Representatives

Change Request Proposal

Accept/ Reject

Update the project plan and schedule appropriately

Approval from Change Control Board (CCB)

Assign to the team member for implementation

Incorporate change – Detailed analysis and development

Review/ Test

Release/ Implement

Developer   Business Analyst

Tester

Dependencies

There are certain dependencies that the project team has when dealing with a CR and in order to take care of these dependencies, project manager plays an active role. The project manager should liaison between the project team and the other relevant groups so that the dependencies could be managed in time to work on the CR successfully.

- Change Control Board should provide the approval/rejection on the CR within the stipulated timeline, as previously agreed upon. This is to avoid any kind of delays in implementing the change request.

- CCB needs to take into account the current status of the projects and consider appropriate time when the change request could be implemented, as suggested by the TAB.

- CCB should also provide details on the urgency and priority of the change request implementation for a given CR.

CHAPTER 10
QUALITY MANAGEMENT

Quality management[17] is the process for ensuring that all project activities necessary to plan, design, and implement a project are effective and efficient with respect to the purpose of the objective and its performance. Project quality management is not a separate, independent process that occurs at the end of an activity to measure the level of quality of the output. It should be a part of every project management process, from the moment the project initiates to the final steps in the project closure phase. It is more about preventing and avoiding than measuring and fixing poor quality outputs.

Quality management focuses on improving stakeholders' satisfaction through continuous and incremental improvements to processes, including removing unnecessary activities, and it achieves that by the continuous improvement of the quality of material and services provided to the beneficiaries. *Quality* has been defined as the totality of characteristics of an entity that bear on its ability to satisfy stated or implied needs. The stated and implied quality needs are the inputs used in defining project requirements from the sponsor and the beneficiaries. It is also defined as the conformance to requirements or fitness for use, which means that the product or services must meet the intended objectives of the project and have a value to the sponsor and beneficiaries and that the beneficiaries can use the material or service as it was originally intended. The central focus of quality management is meeting or exceeding stakeholders' expectations and conforming to the project specifications and design. The ultimate judge for quality is the beneficiary and represents how close the project outputs and deliverables come to meeting the end users' requirements and expectations.

Quality management is not an event; it is a process. A consistently high quality product or service cannot be produced by a defective process. Quality management is a repetitive cycle of measuring quality, updating processes, measuring, and updating processes until the desired quality is achieved.

THE PURPOSE OF QUALITY MANAGEMENT

The main principle of project quality management is to ensure the project will meet or exceed stakeholders' needs and expectations. The project team must develop a good relationship with key stakeholders, especially the sponsor and the beneficiaries of the project, to understand what quality means to them. One of the causes for poor project evaluations is that the project focuses only on meeting the written requirements for the main outputs and ignores other stakeholder needs and expectations for the project. Quality must be viewed on an equal level with scope, schedule, and budget. If a project sponsor is not satisfied with the quality of how the project is delivering the outcomes, the project team will need to make adjustments to scope, schedule, and budget to satisfy the sponsor's needs and expectations. To deliver the project scope on time and on budget is not enough. To achieve stakeholder satisfaction, the project must develop a good working relationship with all stakeholders and understand their stated or implied needs.

Quality management consists of four main processes:

- Quality definition
- Quality assurance
- Quality control
- Quality improvements

QUALITY DEFINITION

The first step on the quality management is to define quality. The project manager and the team must identify what quality standards will be used in the project. The sponsor, the beneficiaries, the organization, and other key stakeholders need to be in concurrence with the definition of quality for the product that is being developed. In some instances, the organization, or the area of specialization of the project (healthcare, telecommunication, etc), may have some standard definitions of quality that can be used by the project. Identifying quality standards is a key component of quality definition that will help identify the key characteristics that will govern project activities and ensure the beneficiaries and sponsor will accept the project outcomes. Quality management implies the ability to anticipate situations and prepare actions that will help bring the desired outcomes. The goal is to prevent defects through actions that will ensure that the project team understands what is defined as quality.

Sources of Quality Definition

One source for definition of quality comes from the sponsor. The project manager must establish conversations with the sponsor to be familiar with and come to a common understanding of what the sponsor defines as quality. The sponsor may have certain standards of what is expected from the project and how the project delivers the expected benefits to the beneficiaries. This is in line with the project's ultimate objective that the project outcomes have the ability to satisfy the stated or implied needs.

Another source for quality definition comes from the beneficiaries or end users. The project manager and team must be able to understand how the beneficiaries define quality from their perspective, a perspective that is more focused on fitness for use. The project outcomes must be relevant to the current needs of the beneficiaries and must result in improvements to their lives. The team can create questions that seek to understand how the beneficiaries define the project will meet their needs as part of the baseline data collection. This will also help in defining what project success looks like from the perspective of a beneficiary.

The development organization may have its own quality standards that can reflect the technical and managerial nature of the project. The organization may require from the project timely and accurate delivery of project information. This may be needed for decision making or compliance to international or locally recognized quality standards that define specific technical areas of the project.

Quality Characteristics

All material or services have characteristics that facilitate the identification of its quality. The characteristics are part of the conditions of how the material, product, and services are able to meet the requirements of the project and are fit for use by the beneficiaries. Quality characteristics relate to the attributes, measures, and methods attached to that particular product or service.

- Functionality is the degree by which product performs its intended function. For example, this is important especially for clinical equipment that deals with human lives.

- Performance is about how well a product or service performs the beneficiaries' intended use. For example, a pharmacy management system should be designed to manage high volume of prescription processing.

- Reliability is the ability of the service or product to perform as intended under normal conditions without unacceptable failures. For example, the software designed to process billing should give accurate details consistently.

- Relevance is the characteristic of how a product or service meets the actual needs of the beneficiaries. It should be pertinent, applicable, and appropriate to its intended use or application.

- Timeliness is how the product or service is delivered in time to solve the problems when it's needed and not after. This is a crucial characteristic for health and emergency relief work.

- Suitability defines the fitness of its use, appropriateness, and correctness.

- Completeness indicates the quality that the service is complete and includes the entire scope of services. For example, training software should be complete and include all the content needed to build a desired skill or knowledge.

- Consistency means services are delivered in the same way for every beneficiary. For example, applications designed to conduct clinical tests need to be done using the same procedure for every patient.

Quality Plan

Part of defining quality involves developing a quality plan and a quality checklist that will be used during the project life cycle phases. This checklist will ensure the project team and other actors are delivering the project outputs according to the quality requirements. Once the project manager has defined the quality standards and quality characteristics, he will create a project quality plan that describes all the quality definitions and standards relevant to the project. It will highlight the standards that must be followed to comply with regulatory requirements set up by the sponsor, the organization, and external agencies, such as the local government and professional organizations.

The quality plan also describes the conditions that the services and materials must possess in order to satisfy the needs and expectations of the project stakeholders. It describes the situations or conditions that make an output fall below quality standards. This information is used to gain a common understanding among the project team to help them identify what is above and what is below a quality standard. The quality plan also includes the procedure to ensure that quality standards are being followed by all project staff. It includes the steps required to monitor and control quality and the approval process to make changes to the quality standards and the quality plan.

For example, as part of "Project X-1" a defect prevention plan was prepared to manage the quality of the product. As part of the plan, one objective was to minimize the number of defects in the product during the development phase. For this, we estimated the maximum number of defects that the product can have during code development phase. This is achieved by multiplying the estimated effort required for product development with defect density. Defect density is defined as number of defects found for completing one unit of work (size), i.e. for one SLOC or WBS unit of work completed, the number of defects found. Defect density value is generally derived from the projects done in the past. Based on our organizational database, the defect density number lies between 0.9 and 1.1. Using the defect density value, the number of defects that can be expected in a product can be determined. This defect count provides the threshold value on the defects that can be found during product development phase. As a manager, my job was to keep the total number of defects found during the development phase below this threshold value. This implied that the development activity is within control and meeting the quality objectives. Once the threshold count was determined, project manager had to define the strategy to keep the number of defects to minimum. This was done by putting controls such as following coding standards, checklists, self and peer reviews, etc around the development process.

QUALITY ASSURANCE

Assurance is the activity of providing evidence to create confidence among all stakeholders that the quality related activities are being performed effectively and that all planned actions are being done to provide adequate confidence that a product or service will satisfy the stated requirements for quality. Quality assurance is a process to provide confirmation, based on evidence, to ensure to the sponsor, beneficiaries, and stakeholders that the product meets needs, expectations, and other requirements. It assures the existence and effectiveness of processes, procedures and tools. In addition, it details the safeguards in place to make sure that the expected levels of quality will be reached to produce quality outputs.

Quality assurance occurs during the implementation phase of the project and includes the evaluation of the overall performance of the project on a regular basis to provide confidence that the project will satisfy the quality standards defined by the project.

One of the purposes of quality assurance is to find errors and defects as early in the project as possible. The goal is to reduce the chances that products or services will be of poor quality after the project has been completed. Quality assurance is done not only to the products and services delivered by the project, but also to the process and procedures used to manage the project. That includes the way the project uses the tools, techniques, and methodologies to manage scope, schedule, budget, and quality.

Quality Audits

Quality audits are structured reviews of the quality management activities that help identify lessons learned that can improve the performance on current or future project activities. Audits are performed by project staff or consultants with expertise in specific areas. The purpose of a quality audit is to review how the project is using its internal processes to produce the products and services it will deliver to the beneficiaries. Its goal is to find ways to improve the tools, techniques, and processes that create the products and services. If problems are detected during the quality audits, corrective action will be necessary to the tools, processes, and procedures used to ensure quality is reestablished. Part of the audit may include a review of the project staff's understanding of the quality parameters or metrics and skills, expertise, and knowledge of the people in charge of producing or delivering the products or services. If corrective actions are needed, these must be approved through the change control processes.

The PDCA Cycle

The most popular tool used to determine quality assurance is the Shewhart cycle. This cycle for quality assurance consists of four steps: Plan, Do, Check, and Act. These steps are commonly abbreviated as PDCA. The four quality assurance steps within this model stand for:

- Plan: Establish objectives and processes required to deliver the desired results.

- Do: Implement the process developed.

- Check: Monitor and evaluate the implemented process by testing the results against the predetermined objectives.

- Act: Apply actions necessary for improvement, if the results require changes.

The PDCA is an effective method for monitoring quality assurance because it analyzes existing conditions and methods used to provide the product or service to beneficiaries. The goal is to ensure that excellence is inherent in every component of the process. Quality assurance also helps determine whether the steps used to provide the product or service is appropriate for the time and conditions.

Quality assurance demands a degree of detail in order to be fully implemented at every step. Planning, for example, could include investigation into the quality of the code written to develop a software product, the actual integration, or the inspection processes used. The checking step could include beneficiary feedback or surveys to determine if beneficiary needs are being met or exceeded and why they are or are not. Acting could mean a total revision in the delivery process in order to correct a technical flaw. The goal to exceed stakeholder expectations in a measurable and accountable process is provided by quality assurance.

Assurance Versus Control

Quality assurance is often confused with quality control. Quality control is done at the end of a process or activity to verify that quality standards have been met. Quality control by itself does not provide quality, although it may identify problems and suggest ways of improving it. In contrast, quality assurance is a systematic approach to obtaining quality standards. Quality assurance is something that must be planned for from the earliest stages of a project, with appropriate measures taken at every stage. Unfortunately, far too many development projects are implemented with no quality assurance plan, and these projects often fail to meet quality expectations of the sponsors and beneficiaries. To avoid problems, the project must be able to demonstrate consistent compliance with the quality requirements for the project.

QUALITY CONTROL

Quality control is the use of techniques and activities that compare actual quality performance with goals and define appropriate action in response to a shortfall. It is the process that monitors specific project results to determine if they comply with relevant standards and identifies different approaches to eliminate the causes for the unsatisfactory performance. The goal of quality control is to improve quality and involves monitoring the project outputs to determine if they meet the quality standards or definitions based on the project stakeholders' expectations. Quality control also includes how the project performs in its efforts to manage scope, budget, and schedule. Some of the activities pertaining to quality control are as below.

- Acceptance is the process by which the beneficiaries, the sponsor, or other key project stakeholders accept or reject the product or service delivered.

- Reworking is the action taken to bring the rejected product or service into compliance with the requirements, quality specifications, or stakeholder expectations. Rework is expensive; that is why the project must make every effort to do a good job in quality planning and quality assurance to avoid the need for rework. Rework and all the costs associated with it may not be refundable by the sponsor, and the organization may end up covering those costs.

- Adjustments deals with correction or taking the necessary steps to prevent further quality problems or defects, based on quality control measurements. Adjustments are identified to the processes that produce the outputs and the decisions that were taken that lead to the defects and errors. Changes are taken to the change control processes of the project.

Quality Control Tools

There are a few tools that can be used to control quality on a project. Some of important tools are cause and effect diagrams, Pareto[18] charts, and control charts.

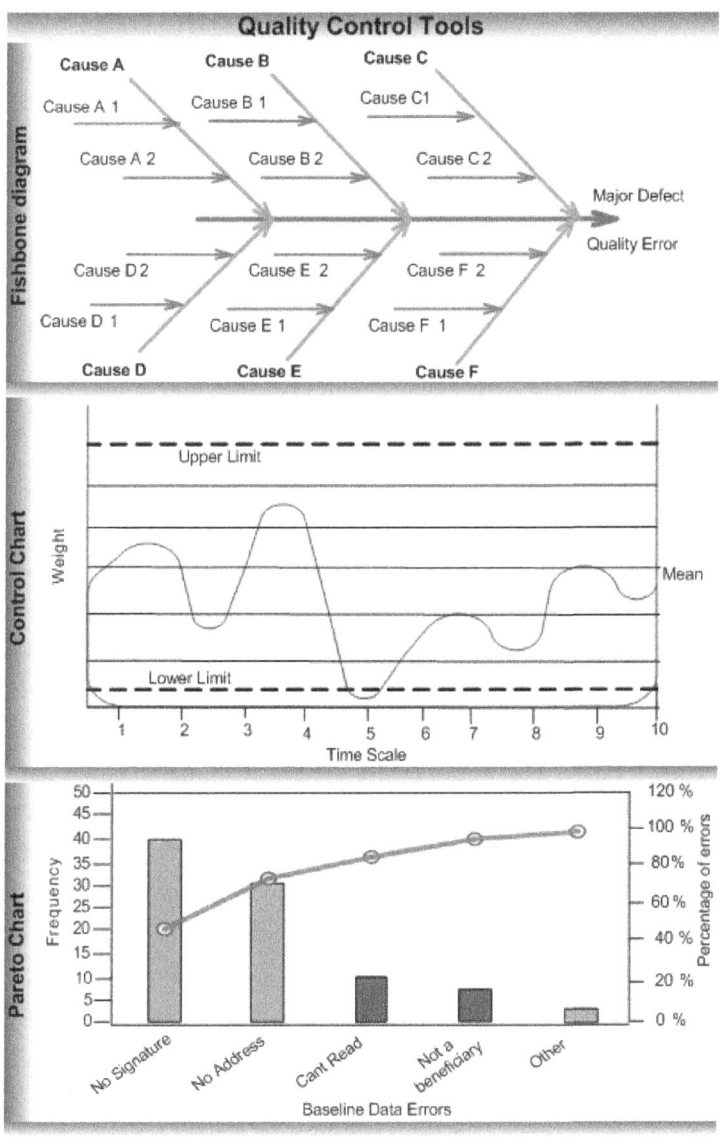

The *Cause and Effect Diagram*, also known as fishbone[19] diagrams or Ishikawa[20] diagrams, is named fishbone diagram because of its fish-like appearance. It is an analysis tool that provides a systematic way of looking at effects and the causes that create or contribute to those effects. The Ishikawa Diagram is employed by a problem-solving team as a tool for assembling all inputs (as to what are the causes of the problem they're addressing) systematically and graphically. The inputs usually come from a brainstorming session. It enables the team to focus on why the problem occurs and not on the history or symptoms of the problem or other topics that digress from the intent of the session. It also displays a real-time snapshot of the collective inputs of the team as it is updated. The possible causes are presented at various levels of detail in connected branches, with the level of detail increasing as the branch goes outward, i.e., an outer branch is a cause of the inner branch it is attached to. Thus, the outermost branches usually indicate the root causes of the problem.

Pareto Charts[21] are based on Pareto's rule, which states that 80 percent of the problems are often due to 20 percent of the causes. The assumption is that most of the results in any situation are determined by a small number of causes and helps identify the vital few contributors that account for most quality problems. The chart is a form of histogram that orders the data by frequency of occurrence. It shows how many defects were generated by a type of category of identified cause. For example, In the Pareto Chart shown above, to determine the "errors" in the collection of beneficiary data, the project team identified five causes ("No Signature", "No Address", "Can't Read", "Not a beneficiary", "Other") and for each cause the "frequency" that contained "errors", the data is plotted. The bars represent each category and the line the cumulative percentage of the errors. The chart allows identifying that 80 percent of the errors could be reduced just by improving the collection of data in two categories, instead of focusing efforts to correct all categories.

Control Charts are graphical displays of data that illustrate the results of a process over time. The purpose of a control chart is to prevent defects, rather than detect them or reject them. The chart allows determining whether a process is in control or out of control over a specified length of time. Control charts are often used to monitor the production of large quantities of products but can also be used to monitor the volume and frequency of errors in documents, cost, and schedule variances, and other items related to project quality management. The figure above illustrates an example of a control chart for the process of controlling the weight of products manufactured for the beneficiaries for sale in international markets. The customer has a limit tolerance for defects; these are the upper and lower control limits in the chart. Random examination of the products reveals data that, once charted on the graph, identifies the times when the production process created items that were outside the control limits. This helps the project determine actions to help the manufacturer improve the quality of their work. Control charts can also be used to the project management areas, such as schedule and budget control, to determine whether the costs variances or schedule variances are outside the acceptable limits set by the sponsor.

QUALITY IMPROVEMENT

It is the systematic approach to the processes of work that looks to remove waste, loss, rework, frustration, and so on in order to make the processes of work more effective, efficient, and appropriate. Quality improvement refers to the application of methods and tools to close the gap between current and expected levels of quality by understanding and addressing system deficiencies and strengths to improve, or in some cases, redesign project processes. A variety of quality improvement approaches exist, ranging from individual performance improvement to redesign of entire project processes.

These approaches differ in terms of time, resources, and complexity, but share the same four steps in quality improvement:

- Identify what has to be improved. This can be done by using the data found in the quality control process, which identifies the areas that need improvement.

- Analyze the problem or system. The team then investigates the causes for the problem and its implications to the project. The causes may be internal or external to the project.

- Develop potential solutions or changes that appear likely to improve the problem or system. The team brainstorms ideas and potential solutions to the problem, taking in consideration its impact to the project schedule and budget. After careful considerations, the team decides and chooses the best alternative.

- Test and implement the solutions. The team may decide to test the solution on a small scale to verify that it is capable of fixing the problem. It tests for the initial assumptions made about the problem and once it confirms that the solution is a viable alternative, the implementation happens on a full scale.

Cost of Quality

The cost of quality is the sum of costs a project will spend to prevent poor quality and any other costs incurred as a result of outputs of poor quality. Poor quality is the waste, errors, or failure to meet stakeholder needs and project requirements. The costs of poor quality can be broken down into the three categories of prevention, appraisal, and failure costs:

- Prevention costs: These are planned costs an organization incurs to ensure that errors are not made at any stage during the delivery process of that product or service to a beneficiary. Examples of prevention costs include quality-planning costs, education and training costs, quality administration staff costs, process control costs, market research costs, field-testing costs, and preventive maintenance costs. The cost of preventing mistakes is always much less than the costs of inspection and correction.

- Appraisal costs: These include the costs of verifying, checking, or evaluating a product or service during the delivery process. Examples of appraisal costs include receiving or incoming inspection costs, internal production audit costs, test and inspection costs, instrument maintenance costs, process measurement and control costs, supplier evaluation costs, and audit report costs.

- Failure costs: A project incurs these costs because the product or service did not meet the requirements and had to be fixed or replaced, or the service had to be repeated.

Leadership

The main cause of quality problems is a lack of leadership. In order to establish and implement effective quality projects, senior management must lead the way. A large percentage of quality problems are associated with management, not technical issues. It is the responsibility of the development organization's senior management to take responsibility for creating, supporting, and promoting quality programs.

Quality problems should be taken as an opportunity for improvement. Problems can help identify more fundamental or systemic root causes and help develop ways to improve the process. Unfortunately, projects do not have a culture that promotes the identification of problems for the fear that making improvements is an admission that the current way of doing things is flawed or that those responsible are poor performers. Improved performance cannot occur unless the members of the project team feel comfortable speaking truthfully and are confident that their suggestions will be taken seriously.

Maturity Models

Another approach to improve quality is the use of maturity models, which are frameworks for helping organizations and projects improve their processes. The model includes a method for assessing the project's maturity levels as a first step to determine the improvements needed to increase the capacity of the project to deliver the project outputs as promised. The use of the word *maturity* implies that capabilities must be grown over time in order to produce repeatable success in project management. Maturity indicates understanding, or visibility, into why success occurs and ways to correct or prevent common problems. Model implies change, a progression, or steps in a process. Project management maturity is the progressive development of an organization's project management approach, methodology, strategy, and decision-making process. The appropriate level of maturity can vary for each organization based on specific goals, strategies, resource capabilities, scope, and needs.

The proper level of maturity to which an organization should strive is determined during a detailed assessment conducted by a professional project management consulting team. The organization has achieved full project management maturity when it has met the requirements and standards for project management effectiveness and it is capable of demonstrating improvements, such as on-time project delivery, cost reductions, organizational efficiency, and quality outcomes.

Project quality maturity usually consists of five levels:

- Level 1. Informal level; there is no defined processes for quality practices or standards. The organization may be in the initial stages of considering how projects should define quality, but most efforts are informal and ad-hoc.

- Level 2. Defined level; the organization has defines some basic quality standards and project quality policies that are being adopted. But not all projects are using it in a consistent manner.

- Level 3. Repeatable level; the quality process is well documented and is an organizational standard. All projects are using it and producing consistent and repeatable results.

- Level 4. Controlled level; all projects are required to use quality planning standard processes. The organization has a unit or roles that coordinate quality standards and assurance and quality audits are done on a regular basis.

- Level 5. Optimized level; the quality process includes guidelines for feeding improvements back into the process. Metrics are used as key criteria for quality decisions, and quality results are predictable. The model helps an organization identify where they stand and where they should strive to reach. It is a simple way to determine the level of maturity required for a project or organization. Some organizations may be comfortable with achieving a level three while others may be encouraged to reach a level four, due to the need to comply with legal or regulatory standards.

Continuous Improvement

Quality is not something that is achieved at the end of a phase or at the end of the project; it is a continuous process to ensure quality is performed in all aspects of the project. The goal is to continuously improve, based on the lessons learned and new insights provided by the project. To be effective, it should happen during all activities of the project. Continuous improvement, in regard to project quality, always focuses on improving stakeholder satisfaction through continuous and incremental improvements to processes, including the removal of any unnecessary activities. Applying a process that continuously improves every element of the project can achieve better results than trying to wait until the end of a phase or a midterm evaluation to start making adjustments and improvements to the work. It requires little effort, and by doing small incremental improvements, the project can reach significant levels of quality.

To implement continuous improvements, it necessary to have a culture of reflection that allows the project team to learn from mistakes and apply the lesson on the next phase or cycle and not spend time and effort trying to put blame; otherwise, the team will fear reporting any problems with quality, and it will be too late to do anything once the sponsor or the beneficiaries find out.

CONCLUSIONS

Quality management activities will vary based on the size and scope of the project at hand. At a minimum, the quality management process must be designed to:

- Identify and set relevant quality specifications as part of the project initiation process.

- Communicate quality specifications through documented acceptance criteria.

- Ensure that all stakeholders understand and accept these quality specifications.

- Ensure that the project is executed with the use of established project management processes.

- Build the deliverables based on quality specifications.

- Review and test deliverables on a periodic basis to ensure adherence to quality specifications.

Measure quality success with the use of the lessons learned analysis (interim or post-project). This lessons learned analysis should be designed to address both process and deliverables quality.

Quality management cannot guarantee project success, but if quality is not a driving force in project planning and execution, success will be a far more elusive goal. As with any other process, quality management is a matter of balance. Quality is achieved when business value is met, customers are satisfied, and all tangible quality defects are resolved as needed.

CHAPTER 11
ISSUE AND CONFLICT MANAGEMENT

ISSUE MANAGEMENT

Within the project life cycle, unforeseen issues often arise that result in a delay of project delivery. There could be various issues in a project, such as suppliers not delivering on time, technology not performing as expected, equipment failing, skilled resources not being available, and so on. There needs to be a process in place for resolving project issues quickly and efficiently. The following section describes the process that can be followed.

STEPS FOR PROJECT ISSUE MANAGEMENT

Issue management is the process of identifying and resolving issues within a project. By quickly and efficiently managing issues, the project manager can:

- limit the effects of unforeseen events on the project

- reduce the time spent in administering project issues

- greatly improve chances of project success

The issue management process is comprised of the following procedures:

Step 1: Identify the issue

Any member of the project team may identify a new project issue. An issue form is completed to describe the issue and rate its current impact on the project. The actions required to resolve the issues are also identified.

Step 2: Review the issue

The issue forms are then forwarded to the project manager, who investigates the issue and determines the overall issue priority. The priority of the issue is determined by its current impact on the project's ability to achieve its stated objectives. If the issue is severely impacting the project, then it is assigned a high priority rating and forwarded to the project board for review. When determining the issue priority, the project manager considers whether the:

- deliverables listed in the project contract are currently being affected by the issue.

- quality targets specified in the quality plan are currently being affected by the issue.

- timeframes specified in the project plan are currently being affected by the issue.

- resources specified in the resource plan are currently being affected by the issue.

- budget specified in the financial plan is currently being affected by the issue.

If the project manager believes this is not a high priority issue but should still be acted on immediately, he or she will implement a suite of actions to resolve the issue quickly and efficiently.

Step 3: Assign issue actions

The project board reviews all high priority issues by considering the current impact of each issue on the project. It may then decide to:

- ignore the issue, as board members believe it is not impacting the project

- validate the issue and request further information that is needed to make a decision
- decide on a suite of actions to resolve the issue

The project manager is then responsible for scheduling and implementing these actions and reviewing the issue on a regular basis to ensure that it has been resolved accordingly. Throughout the issue management process, the project manager can monitor and control issues impacting the project by keeping the issue register or log up-to-date.

By completing these three steps for each issue that arises, the project manager will be able to minimize the effect that issues have on the project and, thereby, increase its chances of success.

CONFLICT MANAGEMENT

Overview

Conflict occurs when individuals or groups are not obtaining what they need or want and are seeking their own self-interest. Sometimes, the individual is not aware of the need and unconsciously starts to act out. Other times, the individual is very aware of what he or she wants and actively works at achieving the goal.

A project manager needs to know certain facts about conflict. Conflict is inevitable. In today's environment, there are various factors that could result in a conflict. Projects involve people's lives, jobs, family, pride, self-concept, ego, and sense of mission or purpose. If any of these factors get affected, it could make them act in a manner that can result in a conflict. There are indicators to let the project manager know about a conflict early in the game. Based on the reason for the conflict, the project manager can adopt strategies to prevent or resolve the conflict. Although inevitable, conflict can be minimized, diverted, and/or resolved.

There are multiple reasons that can bring in conflict. The people involved in a project come from different backgrounds and have different lifestyles, family orientations, and aspirations, and it is possible that when the team comes together, there could be conflict of interests among the individuals. Some of the factors that can bring in conflict are poor communications, aspiration to seek power, dissatisfaction with management style, weak leadership—inability to direct the team toward a common goal, lack of openness, change in leadership, work environment, customer influence, favoritism, and so on.

A project manager should be aware of the possible causes that can bring in the conflicts in the team. It is the experience of the project manager that counts, as handling conflicts is more of a soft skill than having technical knowledge. The manager should be able to sense the possibility of a conflict occurring in a team based on the circumstances and should be prepared to prevent the conflict before it occurs. Some of the indicators, or clues, that can help project manager in predicting the possibility of conflict are body language of the team member, tendency to have disagreement regardless of the issue, withholding bad news and giving unpleasant surprises, tendency to give strong public statements, airing disagreements through media, showing a desire for power, having conflicts in the value system, increasing lack of respect, open disagreement, and lack of clear goals.

Characteristics of Conflict

Conflict is inevitable. As discussed above, when a number of people working together as a team, conflicts are bound to happen. It is the project manager's experience and ability that can make the conflict work toward the common goal of the project or against it.

Conflict is destructive when it takes attention away from important activities. It may sound obvious that conflicts are always destructive, but that is not always the case. A conflict is considered destructive when final goal of the project gets impacted. It can polarize people and groups, resulting in reduced cooperation. The other destructive impact could be irresponsible and harmful behavior of the team member or team, such as fighting, name-calling, etc. This can undermine morale or self-concept of the people, increase or sharpen differences among people, and, as a result, impact the project and its outcome.

Conflict is constructive when it results in solutions to problems. A conflict can bring people together on an issue and result in clarification of important problems and issues. This causes authentic communication, brings people together, helps release emotion, anxiety, and stress, builds cooperation among people through learning more about each other, and helps individual develop understanding and skills.

Techniques for Avoiding and Resolving Conflict

A project manager should take appropriate measures to prevent conflicts from happening, and if they have already occurred, minimize and resolve them in the early stages itself. This can save lot of effort and stress to the project manager and the project teams. The manager should deal with a conflict head on. The team should have clear goals to follow, and the manager has the responsibility to define them and communicate them effectively. The importance of planning and communication is immense here. The manager should be honest about concerns and agree to disagree where necessary, as healthy disagreements would build better decisions.

An effective management style and ability to let go of the ego from the management style also pays a lot in terms of controlling and managing a conflict. Any differences in the values should be discussed openly, and a mutual consensus should be reached. The importance of following the policies should be stressed upon continually, as this brings an order in the team and helps in reducing the chances of conflicts.

Any decision and judgment based on data and appropriate information is more convincing for the team members to understand and accept. Hence, the manager should communicate honestly as needed with appropriate data and information. A sound management system with effective process, role and responsibility definitions, clear goals, and effective communication can reduce the possibility of conflicts occurring in the projects among the team members and teams.

At times, when the conflict has reached the peak, a manager may have to take bold steps to resolve the conflict. The situation may demand changes in the way things have always been done. It could be a change in the process that is being followed, change in the leadership, team member, project organization structure, etc. If a situation arises where the project manager has to act as a mediator, he should be determined and able to articulate advocates for both the sides and bring the parties together to agree on the compromise. In case there are rampant rumors about certain things, he should be able to clarify and put an end to the rumors by providing data-based facts. Threats from the team members, or any parties, should be handled strongly without any fear. The project manager may have to take the harsh decision of letting go the individual from the project and find a suitable replacement for the individual.

In summary, if the project manager understands the reasons for a conflict and has effective strategy to handle it, the management of conflict becomes much easier. Some of the key contributors toward a conflict could be conflict with self; needs or wants of the team not being met; values being tested; perceptions being questioned; assumptions being made; knowledge being minimal; expectations being too high or too low; and the personality, race, or gender difference being present.

Reaching Consensus Through Collaboration

Groups often collaborate closely in order to reach consensus or agreement. The ability to use collaboration requires the recognition of and respect for everyone's ideas, opinions, and suggestions. Consensus requires that each participant must agree on the point being discussed before it becomes a part of the decision. Not every point will meet with everyone's complete approval. Unanimity is not the goal. The goal is to have individuals accept a point of view based on logic. When individuals can understand and accept the logic of a differing point of view, it must be assumed that consensus has been reached. Follow these guidelines for reaching consensus:

- Avoid arguing over individual ranking or position. Present a position as logically as possible.

- Avoid "win-lose" statements. Discard the notion that someone must win.

- Avoid changing minds only in order to avoid conflict and to achieve harmony.

- Avoid majority voting, averaging, bargaining, or coin flipping. These do not lead to consensus. Treat differences of opinion as indicative of incomplete sharing of relevant information; keep asking questions.

- Keep the attitude that holding different views is both natural and healthy to a group.

View initial agreement as suspect. Explore the reasons underlying apparent agreement, and make sure that members have willingly agreed.

CHAPTER 12
COST MANAGEMENT

Project cost[22] management includes the processes required to ensure that the project is completed within an approved budget. Project managers are in a tough spot—they are the liaison between the customer and the project team that will complete the customer's project. Project managers and their stakeholders need to go into any project with a common goal—identify an affordable scope and a plan of how to achieve it. Too often, cost is ignored in project planning. For projects to be successful, cost management is a very crucial aspect. Project managers must make sure their projects are well defined, have accurate time and cost estimates, and have a realistic budget that they are involved in approving.

Regardless of scope or schedule, projects need funds to complete the work. Technically, even projects that use only labor has funds attached to them, as someone, somewhere are paying for that labor. What happens if the correct amount of funds to complete the project scope is not available? The project is doomed.

PROJECT COST MANAGEMENT PROCESSES

There are three steps in project cost process:

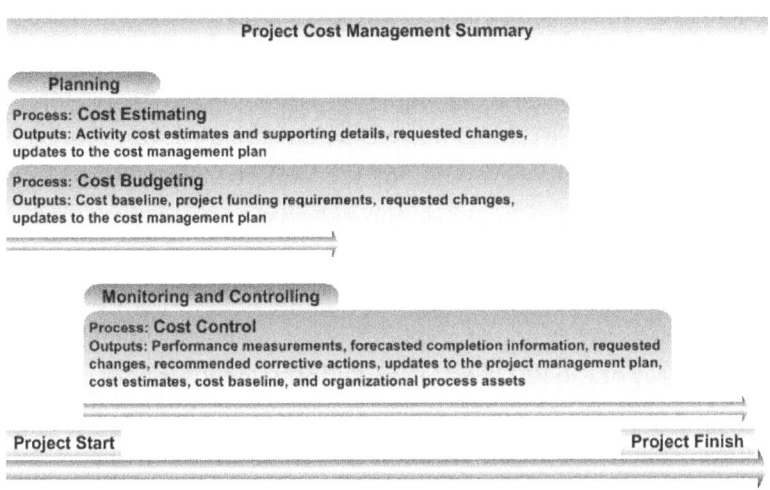

Cost Estimating

It is not possible to know the final project cost of the project until the project is complete because it is difficult to accurately predict the future. What can be done is to create an estimate. An estimate is more than pulling a random number out of the air, and adding 20 percent for good measure (Please refer to the chapters on Estimation for details). A real estimate evolves as project details become available. This is progressive elaboration. Project estimates start out broad, and as the project deliverables come into focus, it is possible to more accurately define the estimates. Each estimate should provide an acceptable range of variance, the conditions of the estimates, and any assumptions made by the estimate provider. A good estimate clearly defines what the project will accomplish, the assumptions made, how long the estimate is valid, and how much the project will cost, based on current information. A good estimate presents to the stakeholder everything relevant to the proposed work, without holding back any secrets. If there's a disagreement in price, assumptions, or range variance, it's better to discuss this issue now, rather than a few weeks into the project execution. There are three major estimate types that project managers should rely on:

The Ballpark Estimate is also known as the rough order of magnitude (ROM). A ROM estimate is based on high-level objectives and provides a bird's-eye view of the project deliverables. Most ROM estimates, depending on the industry, have a range of variance from -25 percent all the way to +75 percent. The project manager shouldn't invest too much time in creating these initial estimates, just as the customer shouldn't place too much confidence in the accuracy of the ROM estimate. Unfortunately, for both parties, there's a consistent breakdown in expectations when it comes to ROM estimates. Typically, the project manager blindly throws out the ROM estimate, and the customer clings to the ROM forever. In reality, ROM estimates are simply for eyeballing the project's initial perceived costs.

The Budget Estimate (or top-down estimate) is a bit more accurate. Formulated fairly early in the project's planning stage, the budget estimate is most often based on analogous estimating, taking budget lessons learned from a similar project and applying them to the current project. In the budget estimate process, the top-down approaches is taken up, where the estimation starts at a high level and then proceeds toward the details by breaking down the high level to more detailed level. Like the ROM, this estimate should include conditions, a range of variance, and any assumptions that went into your calculations. A budget estimate is quick but not very accurate. The range of variance on the budget estimate is from -10 percent to +25 percent.

The Definitive Estimate (or bottom-up estimate) is the most accurate of the estimate types but takes the most time to create. The definitive estimate requires a work breakdown structure (WBS). A

WBS is a deliverables-oriented decomposition of the project scope. A WBS is required in order to create the definitive estimate; this aids in accounting for the cost of each deliverable. Each deliverable in the WBS can have time and costs associated with it. Depending on the size of the project, the project manager needs to create a WBS dictionary to take advantage of the code of accounts for each of the WBS elements: defining each element, the party responsible for the element, time and costs associated with each component, and other notes or relevant facts. Tied to the WBS dictionary are time, costs, and relevant information on each deliverable. A definitive estimate takes lots of time to create, but it's the most accurate estimate one can provide. This is also referred to as a bottom-up estimate because the estimate starts from zero (the bottom) and accounts for everything the project will purchase, create, or deliver. The range of variance on a definitive estimate is relatively low: -5 percent to +10 percent. While definitive estimates are ideal for accuracy, they're not easy to create because so much effort has to go into the project before the project manager can create the definitive estimate.

With any type of estimate, the project manager must provide the range of variance and an explanation of how the estimate was created. Without these explanations, the customer is led to believe that the price quoted is the final price that the customer will see.

Cost Budgeting

Cost budgeting involves allocating the project cost estimate to individual work items over time. The WBS is a required input to the cost budgeting process, since it defines the work items. An important goal is to produce a cost baseline, a time-phased budget that project managers use to measure and monitor cost performance. Estimating costs for each major project activity over time provides management with a foundation for project cost control. Cost budgeting also provides information for project funding require-ments—at what point in time will the money be needed.

Cost Control

Projects suffer from a universal law: the first-time, first-use penalty. The concept of the first-time, first-use penalty is that it's next to impossible to accurately estimate the cost of something that has never been attempted. Information technology is so unique, so multifaceted, and has so many fronts that the constant movement of its variables creates a love-hate relationship for any organization trying to create a software project cost estimate. When it comes to cost and things that can affect cost, the project manager must con-sider the risk and ramifications of the first-time, first-use penalty. This universal law can spell disaster for any software project. The longer a project manager goes without at least nodding in the direc-tion of the first-time, first-use penalty, the bigger the pending fall.

Project cost control includes monitoring cost performance, ensuring that only appropriate project changes are included in a revised cost baseline, and informing project stakeholders of autho-rized changes to the project that will affect costs. Many organiza-tions around the globe have problems with cost control. A perfor-mance review meeting can be a powerful tool to help control project costs. Knowing you have to report on your progress is an incentive for people to perform better. Performance measurement is another important tool for cost control. There are many general accounting approaches for measuring cost performance, but earned value man-agement is a tool unique to project management.

BASIC PRINCIPLES OF COST MANAGEMENT

Cost Management Plan

A cost management plan is a document that describes how the organization will manage cost variance on the project; for example, how to respond to proposals from suppliers that are higher or lower than estimates. A large percentage of total project costs are often labor costs, so project managers must develop and track estimates for labor. Many organizations estimate the number of people or hours they need by department or skill over the life cycle of a project.

Different Types of Costs Involved in Project

Cash flow analysis determines the estimated annual costs and benefits for a project and the resulting annual cash flow. Too many projects with high cash flow needs in the same year may not be able to be supported, which will impact profitability. *Tangible costs or benefits* are those costs or benefits that an organization can easily measure in dollars. A task that was allocated $150,000 but actually costs $100,000 would have a tangible benefit of $50,000, if the assets allocated are used for other projects. *Intangible costs or benefits* are costs or benefits that are difficult to measure in monetary terms.

- Costs—resources used to research related areas of a project but not billed to the project

- Benefits—goodwill, prestige, general statements of improved productivity not easily translated in dollars

Direct costs are costs that can be directly related to producing the products and services of the project. For example, salaries and the cost of hardware and software purchased specifically for the project are part of this category.

Indirect costs are costs that are not directly related to the products or services of the project but are indirectly related to performing the project. Cost of electricity, paper towels, etc., are included in this type of costs.

Sunk cost is money that has been spent in the past on project. When deciding what projects to invest in or continue, the sunk costs should not be included to continue funding a failed project because "a great deal of money has already been spent on it" and it is not a valid way to decide on which projects to fund.

Reserves are dollars included in a cost estimate to mitigate cost risk by allowing for future situations that are difficult to predict.

- Contingency reserves allow for future situations that may be partially planned for (sometimes called known unknowns) and are included in the project cost baseline. Recruiting and training costs for expected personnel turnover during a project.

- Management reserves allow for future situations that are unpredictable (sometimes called unknown unknowns): the extended absence of a manager or the supplier goes out of business.

What Could Change Cost Estimates?

As the project moves toward completion, there will likely be a need to revise the project's price. If the project started with a ROM estimate, the original estimate could be wildly wrong. The customer who reads the ROM estimate should know that the final cost is likely to be much different from that estimate. Poor planning is the major cause of poor estimates. Rushed estimates, bloated estimates, or estimates that are "low-balled" just to get the project moving are bound for budget reviews, unpleasant conversations, and project reassessments.

Sometimes, it's not the project manager's fault when the estimate must change: The cost of materials has changed; the anticipated time to complete the project work was wrong; or the basis for decisions were faulty. In these instances, the project manager still has to communicate the variances, but it's easier than taking the blame when that blame is all yours. Poor estimates can also be the fault of the customer, stakeholders, or even the project sponsor. When the stakeholder is responsible, the increase in cost is usually tied to a change request. Ideally, when the customer and the project sponsor sign off on the scope statement, no changes should ever be made to that scope. Of course, errors and omissions, technological enhancements, and value-added changes all affect the scope's resistance to change.

If the customer demands new deliverables in the project scope, a price tag is usually associated with those demands. Even changes that replace current scope components may have a price; time and effort may already have been invested in these deliverables. When the project scope changes, the budget usually has to change as well.

Typical Problems with Cost Estimates

- Estimates are done too quickly. Many estimates must be done quickly, before clear system requirements have been produced.

- Lack of estimating experience. The people developing the cost estimates often don't have much experience, especially on large projects. There is not enough accurate, reliable project data available, on which to base estimates.

- Human beings are biased toward underestimation. Senior team members make estimates based on their skill level but should take into account the junior people on the project.

- Management desires accuracy but wants to spend less in order to win a bid or internal funding. Top management never forgets the first estimate and rarely, if ever, remembers how approved changes affect the estimate. The project manager must keep the communication lines open at all times.

- The importance of realistic project cost estimates is not emphasized from the outset.

- Many of the original cost estimates for projects are low to begin with and based on very unclear project requirements

- Many professionals think preparing cost estimates is a job for accountants, when in fact, it is a very demanding and important skill that project managers need to acquire

- Many projects involve new technology or business processes that involve untested products and inherent risks.

Cost of Software Defects

It is much more cost effective to spend money on defining user requirements and doing early testing on projects than to wait for problems to appear after implementation. Just to give an idea, if fixing a defect during requirements and analysis phase costs $1000, then for the same defect to be fixed in the post-product release phase would cost $30,000. The following gives an indication on the cost overrun depending on when a defect is found and fixed during the life cycle of the software development. Based on the experience, it is found that the cost to repair defects, based on which phase of the project they were found in, can vary significantly.

- Requirements and Analysis—1X

- Coding and Unit Test—5X

- Integration and System Test—10X

- Beta Test—15X

- Post-Product Release—30X

Note—X is a normalized unit of cost and can be expressed in dollars, person-hours, etc.

Earned Value Management (EVM)

EVM is a project performance measurement technique that integrates scope, time, and cost data. Given a baseline (original plan and approved changes), it can be determined how well the project is meeting its goals. The following actual information is needed on a periodic basis to use EVM.

- Was a WBS item completed, or approximately how much of the work was completed?

- Actual start and end dates

- Actual cost

Earned Value Management Terms

- The Planned Value (PV), formerly called the Budgeted Cost of Work Scheduled (BCWS), also called the budget, is that portion of the approved total cost estimate planned to be spent on an activity during a given period

- Actual Cost (AC), formerly called Actual Cost of Work Performed (ACWP), is the total of direct and indirect costs incurred in accomplishing work on an activity during a given period.

- The earned value (EV), formerly called the Budgeted Cost of Work Performed (BCWP), is an estimate of the value of the physical work actually completed. EV is based on the original planned costs for the project or activity and the rate at which the team is completing work on the project or activity to date.

- Budget at Completion (BAC), is the total budget allocated to the project.

- Rate of Performance (RP) is the ratio of actual work completed to the percentage of work planned to have been completed at any given time during the life of the project or activity.

Earned Value Formulas

The following tables shows the formulas used to calculate the Earn Value for a project:

Term	Formula
Earned Value	EV= PV to date * RP
Cost Variance	CV = EV- AC
Schedule Variance	SV = EV - PV
Cost Performance Index	CPI = EV/AC
Schedule Performance Index	SPI = EV/PV
Estimate at Completion (EAC)	EAC = BAC/CPI
Estimated Time to Complete	Original Time Estimate / SPI

Negative numbers for cost and schedule variance indicate problems in those areas. If the CV is negative, it means that performing the work cost more than planned. A negative SV means that it took longer than planned to perform the work.

CPI can be used to estimate the projected cost of completing the project based on performance to date (EAC). If EAC=1: the planned and actual costs are the same; EAC<1: over budget; EAC>1: under budget.

SPI can be used to estimate the projected time to complete the project. If SPI=1: on schedule; SPI <1 behind schedule; SPI >1 ahead of schedule.

As an example, the following chart helps visualize how a certain project is performing after five months using EV chart.

- If the project goes as planned, it will finish in twelve months at a cost of $100,000.

- The actual cost line is always right on or above the earned value line. Interpretation: This means costs are equal to or more than planned.

- The planned value line is pretty close to the EV line, just slightly higher in the last month. Interpretation: The project has been right on schedule, until last month when the project fell behind schedule.

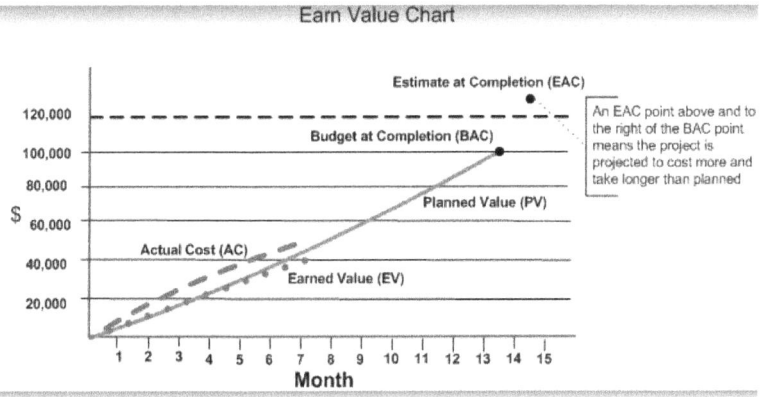

Earn Value Chart

CHAPTER 13
DELIVERABLES, MILESTONES, AND ACCEPTANCE CRITERIA

Deliverables and Milestones

When planning a project, the project manager should establish a series of milestones, where a milestone is an endpoint of a software process activity. At each milestone, there should be a formal output, and a milestone report, which can be represented to management. Milestone reports need not be large documents. They may simply be a short report of achievements in a project activity. Milestones should represent the end of a distinct, logical stage in the project. Indefinite milestones statuses such as "Coding 80 percent complete," which are impossible to validate are useless for management team or stakeholders.

A deliverable is a project result that is delivered to the customer. It is usually delivered at the end of some major project phase, such as completion of requirements specifications, design, etc. Deliverables are usually milestones, but milestones need not to be deliverables. Milestones may be internal project results that are used by the most of the project managers to check project progress but which are not delivered to the customers.

For a project manager, in order to organize his time and work for the project he has, he should set up the milestones and define a deliverable for each major milestone. They enable the progress of the project to be easily measured and controlled.

Significance of Defining a Milestone

A milestone is a sort of deadline inside of the project for a certain task. A project can have many important tasks or steps to do, and the end of each of these important tasks can be set as a milestone in the project plan. These milestones should be checked as per the plan, and reaching a milestone would help the project manager to get an idea on the percentage completion of the project as such. As a milestone is reached, it would mean that one of the important tasks in the project has been accomplished and the next important task can be initiated and worked upon. This also ensures that nothing is skipped and the total project time is very well divided into pieces that are enough to finish the project in the planned time. Basically, tracking the project and its progress becomes easy and meaningful.

Milestones keep projects on track and also provide conditional approvals that enable the management authority to approve the project to proceed, with minor revisions noted. When milestones are set, the changes that appear when least expected can be managed, as they are taken step-by-step, milestone-by-milestone.

Milestones are also good when work has to be divided for the team members. The task assignment and tracking becomes easier and can help the manager in evaluating the performance of the individuals in the team. Each milestone in the project is like a sub-project with in a large project. Completion of all these subprojects as per the plan will ensure that the project is completed successfully in the given budget and timeframe.

In summary, milestones serve three important goals. They provide

- "Measurements," showing that tangible progress has been made.

- "Validation," allowing moving on to the "next step" in the project if the milestone is met or enabling corrective action if the milestone is not met.

- "Short-term work targets," to motivate project team members.

Milestone Management

Milestone management begins with identification. Milestone identification occurs in the initial planning phases, as the project is structured and defined. As the milestone identification process begins, specific levels must be considered:

- Individual Milestones: individual work assignments made to project team members. This serves the purpose of providing the individual staff members with an opportunity to measure and report assigned work progress at an accomplishments level (linking individual tasks to overall project results.).

- Team Milestones: relating to team assignments and responsibilities. The purpose it takes care of is to provide one or more project teams with an opportunity to report on assigned work and accomplishments at an accomplishments level (linking team responsibilities to overall project results).

- Major Milestones: relating to interim results and progress. The purpose is to track project progress, deliverables, and events at the "big picture" level.

Depending on specific circumstances, milestones can be identified and tracked at each of these levels as needed to meet project goals. If a project manager needs to motivate project staff, individual, and/or team, milestone management is essential. Milestones provide an opportunity to track and manage projects according to a timeline of accomplishments, in addition to the necessary, but more mundane, work hour allocations and assignments. Milestone identification and reporting is essential to management support. To maintain appropriate support for the project, the project manager must be able to translate progress from baseline percentages into tangible accomplishments. For that reason, milestones must be described in meaningful terms that meet all of the following elements:

- Milestone Description—To identify and describe the milestone in relevant terms. The description must match milestone purpose as "measurement," "checkpoint," or "work target."

- Milestone Date—To specify the milestone "due date," that is, the specific point in time when milestone must be met.

- Milestone Results—To specify the expected result and meaning, that is, what will happen next once the milestone is met?

- Milestone Risks—To identify any risks involved if and when the milestone is not met as needed and expected.

To identify project milestones, the project must be broken down into a structured timeline of logical checkpoints (major task sets, phases, or other logical phases). These checkpoints determine the flow of the project, and milestones can be inserted into this flow at strategic points, based on needs and purpose. As such, for identification purposes, each potential milestone can be viewed from the following perspectives:

- Timing: Checkpoint Assignment (Milestone Date)

- Level: Individual, Team, or Major Milestone

- Type: Proposal/Recommendation, Approval/Decision, Deliverable, or Event

- Purpose: Measurement, Validation, or Work Target

Once milestones are identified and documented as part of the project plan and schedule, the tracking process will begin. Milestones should be identified and established at sufficient points in the project timeline to allow for effective monitoring. If milestones are set only at the end of a phase, mid-point problems may be missed, and it may be too late to take corrective actions. Individual and team milestones can be used to feed major milestones, acting as pre-cursors to monitor and predict milestone progress. It stands to reason that if individual and/or team milestones are not being met, major milestones will likely share the same fate. If milestones are being met or are ahead of schedule, the project can proceed as planned. If the milestones are not being met, then certain defining questions must be addressed:

- Which milestones are not being met?

- What are the likely reasons for any milestone mishaps?

- What can be done to correct or mitigate these issues and problems?

CONCLUSIONS

Naturally, corrective actions will vary, based on the nature of the problem or delay, but one thing is clear—without milestones, a project manager is left with two options: try to track overall progress based on individual task assignments, or wait until the scheduled project completion date to find out if the project is actually complete. Neither option makes much sense. With milestones, the project manager can manage his projects for results and goals. As each milestone date approaches, he will have a true sense of the project in terms of the schedule, goals, results, and next steps. The project manager will either find himself on the right track, or off target. In either event, he will know where he stands and can react accordingly.

ACCEPTANCE CRITERIA

Acceptance criteria represents a specific and defined list of conditions that must be met before a project has been considered completed and the project deliverables can and will be accepted by the assigning party. The acceptance criteria should be outlined in specific detail before work on the project has commenced, and a very careful timeline should be set forth to make sure that all parties are onboard. Acceptance criteria can represent certain essential requirements that must be met within the final deliverables themselves or specific conditions that must be met during the process, in which those deliverables are assembled and completed. In providing a series of acceptance criteria to the assignee, the assigning party should, when possible, prioritize the acceptance criteria. In the event that a series of acceptance criteria is not met or is met only partially, the final set of deliverables can either be refused for acceptance outright or, in some cases, it may be assigned the status of conditional acceptance, that being, an acceptance pending modification or correction to better meet the acceptance criteria.

Most often, our clients or bosses themselves have not thought through what exactly it is that they want. Somehow, when the project manager and the team fail to read their minds and produce their wants on the first try, the end result is obvious. The project manager and the team are found to be at fault, and they may even be forced into apologizing for their inability to deliver expected results.

Acceptance Criteria Process

A project manager will be considered at fault if he initiates a project without getting a complete understanding of what is the expectation of the sponsor from the project. With an incomplete understanding, the project manager can end up delivering products, services, or results that don't serve the true, root needs of the project sponsors and stakeholders.

An acceptance criterion is one of the processes in the software development world that should not be neglected. As far as defining a process is concerned, one definition comes from PMI, where a process is considered to be a set of interrelated actions and activities performed to achieve a specified set of products, results, or services. Software projects usually involve systems environments, where a system may be described simply as any collection of inputs, processes, and outputs. In such an environment, quality may be built into a product only through repeatable, consistent processes. One way to improve chances of success of a project is by better documenting stakeholder project needs from the beginning. Acceptance criteria need to be specific, measurable, attainable, realistic, time-bound, and motivated. During the planning stage, the project manager needs to make sure he understands what has to be achieved. Documenting acceptance criteria forces the project manager to consciously think of project goals and articulate them clearly. Once articulated, acceptance criteria can then help shape team efforts at execution. It only makes sense to perform work that seems reasonable to achieve the scope of the project as defined in the plans. An acceptance criterion points the project manager and the team in the right direction in the first place and then serves as a landmark to guide any corrective actions needed as the project progresses toward completion.

Toward the end of the project, during the acceptance phase, the actual results are measured against the criteria and determine corrective action needed, if any. It is at this point where acceptance criteria truly determine the success or failure of project efforts. If acceptance criteria are not defined in advance for measuring project performance, then the measurements are meaningless. If the project manager has not gotten advance agreement from the sponsors regarding the relevancy and accuracy of the project acceptance criteria, then the chances of achieving success are limited.

For example, in "Project X-1", one of the acceptance criteria was that the final system tested code can have not more than

- "0" Blocker defects (Blocks development and/or testing work, product cannot run)

- "0" Critical defects (Crashes, loss of data, severe memory leak)

- "3" Major defects (Important element of functionality is affected and the user can proceed with the testing process)

- "7" Minor defects (Important element of functionality is not affected. Mainly cosmetic issues such as: Incorrect or not help test on screens, drop down lists repeat an option, spelling mistakes, incorrect font or color

- "10" Cosmetic defects (Defects unlikely to notice)

It is not an easy task for a project manager to get an agreement on the acceptance criteria in advance of the work. Chances of getting agreement on the acceptance criteria in advance are greatly increased if it is documented based on the understanding with the sponsors and other stakeholders. A few of the challenges with this include:

- It may not be wise to ask business people to sign off on technical acceptance criteria.

- Similarly, it is risky asking technical people to write business-oriented acceptance criteria.

- Beware of politicians that refuse to accept accountability by acknowledging acceptance criteria in advance.

- Avoid including measurable components that do not reflect the intended result properly.

One benefit of having sponsors sign off on the acceptance criteria in advance of the work is their increased willingness to actually use those criteria for measuring the success of the finished work product. Take advantage of the Plan Do Check Act process to *Plan* the acceptance criteria for the project and to work with sponsors to *Check* on the compliance of the work results to those same acceptance criteria.

APPENDIX—A
PROJECT, PRODUCT AND STAKEHOLDER

PROJECT MANAGEMENT LIFE CYCLE

The Project Management Life cycle has four phases: *Initiation, Planning, Execution, and Closure.* Each project life cycle phase is described below, along with the tasks needed to complete it.

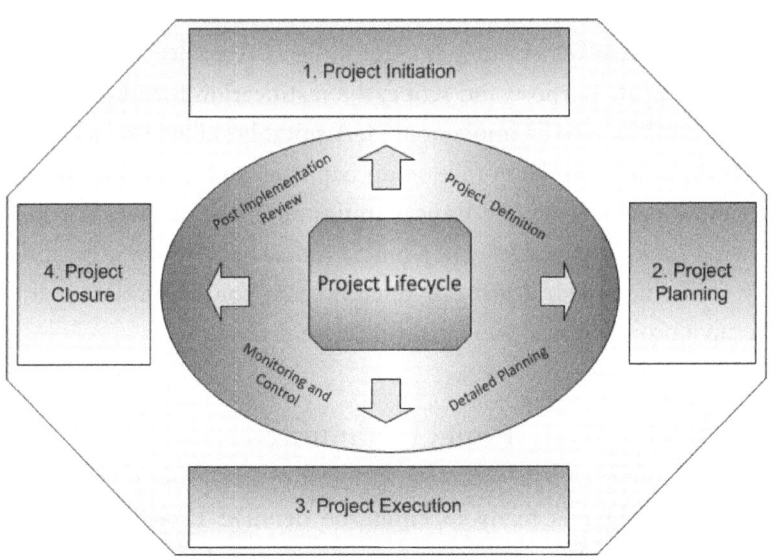

Typically, a project management life cycle comprises four phases:

- Initiation involves starting up the project by documenting a business case, feasibility study, terms of reference, appointing the team, and setting up a project office.

- Planning involves setting out the roadmap for the project by creating the following plans: project plan, resource plan, financial plan, quality plan, acceptance plan, and communications plan.

- Execution involves building the deliverables and controlling the project delivery, scope, costs, quality, risks, and issues.

- Closure involves winding down the project by releasing staff, handing over deliverables to the customer, and completing a post-implementation review.

A more detailed description of the Project Management Methodology and life cycle follows:

Project Initiation

Project Initiation is the first phase in the project life cycle and essentially involves starting up the project. A project is initiated by defining its purpose and scope, the justification for initiating it, and the solution to be implemented. A suitably skilled project team is brought in, a project office setup happens, and an end-of-phase review is performed. The Project Initiation phase involves the following six key steps: Develop a business case, Undertake a feasibility study, Establish a term of reference, Appoint a project team, Setup a project office, and Perform phase review.

Project Planning

After defining the project and appointing the project team, the project manager is ready to enter the detailed Project Planning phase. This involves creating a suite of planning documents to help guide the team throughout the project delivery. The Planning Phase involves completing the ten key steps, as shown in the diagram.

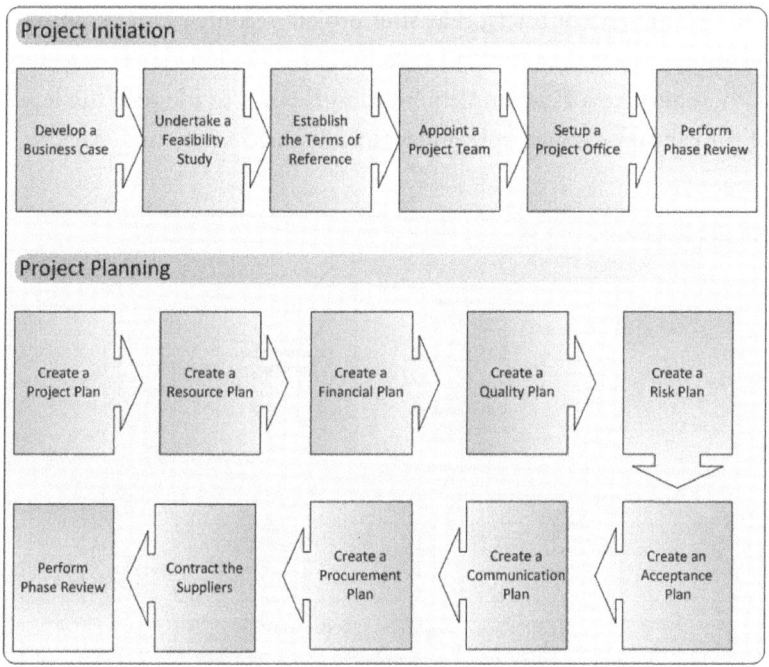

Project Execution

With a clear definition of the project and a suite of detailed project plans, the Execution phase of the project can be started. This is the phase in which the deliverables are physically built and presented to the customer for acceptance. While each deliverable is being constructed, a suite of management processes are undertaken to monitor and control the deliverables being output by the project. These processes include managing time, cost, quality, change, risks, issues, suppliers, customers, and communication.

Once all the deliverables have been produced and the customer has accepted the final solution, the project is ready for closure.

Project Closure

Project Closure involves releasing the final deliverables to the customer, handing over project documentation to the business, terminating supplier contracts, releasing project resources, and communicating project closure to all stakeholders. The last remaining step is to undertake a Post Implementation Review to identify the level of project success and note any lessons learned for future projects.

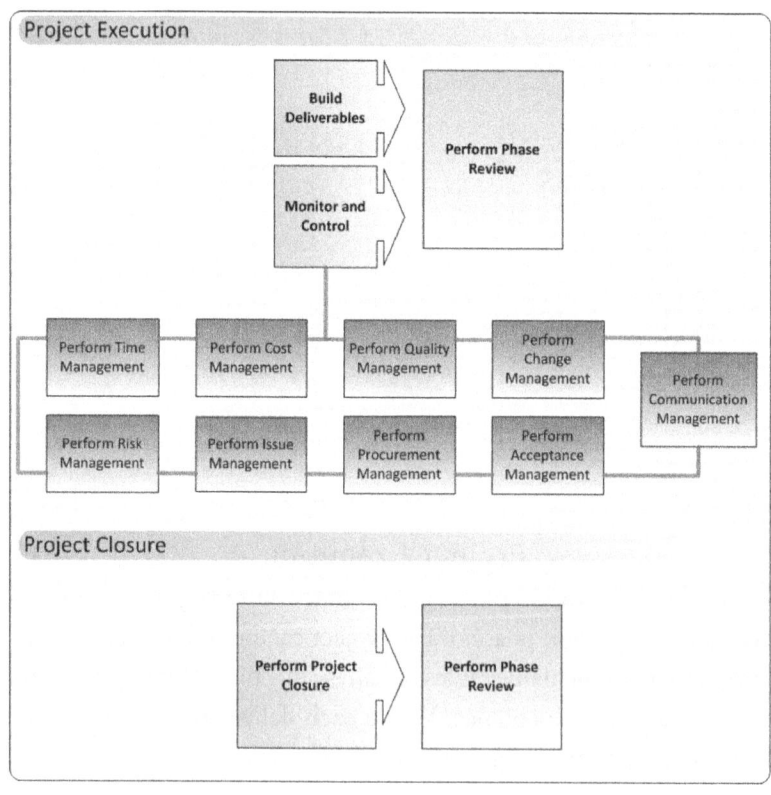

RELATION BETWEEN PROJECT STAKEHOLDERS AND PROJECT LIFE CYCLE

Stakeholder

Project stakeholders are individuals and organizations that are actively involved in the project or whose interests may be affected as a result of project execution or project completion. They may also exert influence over the project's objectives and outcomes. The project management team must identify the stakeholders, determine their requirements and expectations, and to the extent possible, manage their influence in relation to the requirements to ensure a successful project. The figure below illustrates the relationship between stakeholders and the project team.

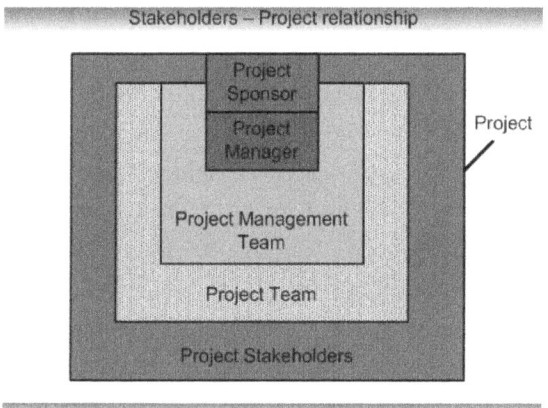

Stakeholders have varying levels of responsibility and authority when participating on a project, and these can change over the course of the project's life cycle. Their responsibility and authority range from occasional contributions in surveys and focus groups to full project sponsorship, which includes providing financial and political support. Stakeholders who ignore this responsibility can have a damaging impact on the project objectives. Likewise, project managers who ignore stakeholders can expect a damaging impact on project outcomes.

Sometimes, stakeholder identification can be difficult. Failure to identify a key stakeholder can cause major problems for a project. Stakeholders may have a positive or negative influence on a project. Positive stakeholders are those who would normally benefit from a successful outcome from the project, while negative stakeholders are those who see negative outcomes from the project's success. For example, business leaders from a community that will benefit from an industrial expansion project may be positive stakeholders because they see economic benefit to the community from the project's success. Conversely, environmental groups could be negative stakeholders if they view the project as doing harm to the environment. In the case of positive stakeholders, their interests are best served by helping the project succeed, for example, helping the project obtains the needed permits to proceed. The negative stakeholders' interest would be better served by impeding the project's progress by demanding more extensive environmental reviews. Negative stakeholders are often overlooked by the project team at the risk of failing to bring their projects to a successful end.

Key stakeholders on every project include:

- Project manager—The person responsible for managing the project.

- Customer/user—The person or organization that will use the project's product. There may be multiple layers of customers. For example, the customers for a new pharmaceutical product can include the doctors who prescribe it, the patients who take it, and the insurers who pay for it. In some application areas, the customer and user are synonymous; while in others, customer refers to the entity acquiring the project's product, and users are those who will directly utilize the project's product.

- Performing organization—The enterprise or vendor whose employees are most directly involved in doing the work of the project.

- Project team members—The group that is performing the work of the project.

- Project management team—The members of the project team who are directly involved in project management activities.

- Sponsor—The person or group that provides the financial resources, in cash or in kind, for the project.

- Influencers—People or groups that are not directly related to the acquisition or use of the project's product but due to an individual's position in the customer organization or performing organization, can influence, positively or negatively, the course of the project.

- Project Management Office (PMO)—If it exists in the performing organization, the PMO can be a stakeholder if it has direct or indirect responsibility for the outcome of the project.

In addition to these key stakeholders, there are many different names and categories of project stakeholders, including internal and external, owners and investors, sellers and contractors, team members and their families, government agencies and media outlets, individual citizens, temporary or permanent lobbying organizations, and society-at-large. The naming or grouping of stakeholders is primarily an aid to identifying which individuals and organizations view themselves as stakeholders. Stakeholder roles and responsibilities can overlap. Project managers must manage stakeholder expectations, which can be difficult because stakeholders often have very different or conflicting objectives. For example, the manager of a department that has requested a new management information system may desire low cost, the system architect may emphasize technical excellence, and the programming contractor may be most interested in maximizing its profit.

Characteristics of the Project Life Cycle

The project life cycle defines the phases that connect the beginning of a project to its end. Depending on the type of project being undertaken, the project life cycle may differ, but in general, it has standard phases, as described in the section above.

The transition from one phase to another within a project's life cycle generally involves, and is usually defined by, some form of technical transfer or handoff. Deliverables from one phase are usually reviewed for completeness and accuracy and approved before work starts on the next phase. However, it is not uncommon for a phase to begin prior to the approval of the previous phase's deliverables, when the risks involved are deemed acceptable. This practice of overlapping phases, normally done in sequence, is an example of the application of the schedule compression technique called fast tracking.

There is no single best way to define an ideal project life cycle. Some organizations have established policies that standardize all projects with a single life cycle, while others allow the project management team to choose the most appropriate life cycle for the team's project. Further, industry common practices will often lead to the use of a preferred life cycle within that industry.

Project life cycles generally define:

- What technical work to do in each phase (for example, in which phase should the architect's work be performed?).

- When the deliverables are to be generated in each phase and how each deliverable is reviewed, verified, and validated.

- Who is involved in each phase (for example, concurrent engineering requires that the implementers be involved with requirements and design).

- How to control and approve each phase.

Project life cycle descriptions can be very general or very detailed. Highly detailed descriptions of life cycles can include forms, charts, and checklists to provide structure and control. Most project life cycles share a number of common characteristics:

- Phases are generally sequential and are usually defined by some form of technical information transfer or technical component handoff.

- Cost and staffing levels are low at the start, peak during the intermediate phases, and drop rapidly as the project draws to a conclusion.

- The level of uncertainty is highest and, hence, risk of failing to achieve the objectives is greatest at the start of the project. The certainty of completion generally gets progressively better as the project continues.

- The ability of the stakeholders to influence the final characteristics of the project's product and the final cost of the project is highest at the start and gets progressively lower as the project continues. A major contributor to this phenomenon is that the cost of changes and correcting errors generally increases as the project continues.

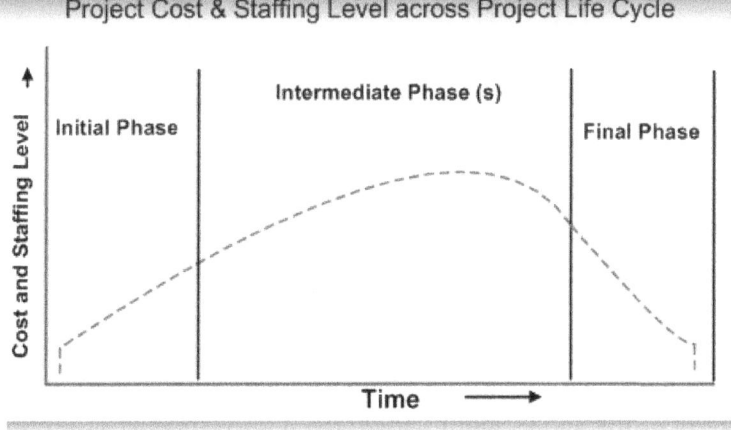

Project Cost & Staffing Level across Project Life Cycle

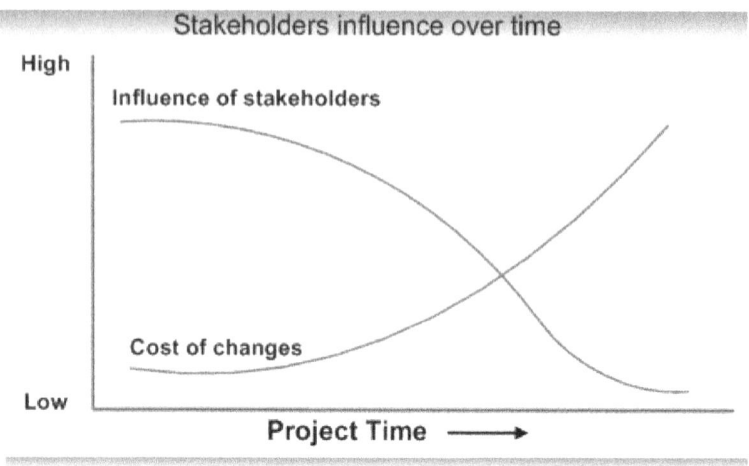

Stakeholders influence over time

Although many project life cycles have similar phase names with similar deliverables, few life cycles are identical. Some can have four or five phases, but others may have nine or more. Single application areas are known to have significant variations. One organization's software development life cycle can have a single design phase, while another can have separate phases for architectural and detailed design.

Characteristics of Project Phases

The completion and approval of one or more deliverables characterizes a project phase. A deliverable is a measurable, verifiable work product, such as a specification, feasibility study report, detailed design document, or working prototype. Some deliverables can correspond to the project management process, whereas others are the end products or components of the end products for which the project was conceived. The deliverables, and hence the phases, are part of a generally sequential process designed to ensure proper control of the project and to attain the desired product or service, which is the objective of the project.

In any specific project, for reasons of size, complexity, level of risk, and cash flow constraints, phases can be further subdivided into sub phases. Each sub-phase is aligned with one or more specific deliverables for monitoring and control. The majority of these sub-phase deliverables are related to the primary phase deliverable, and the phases typically take their names from these phase deliverables: requirements, design, build, test, turnover, and others, as appropriate.

A project phase is generally concluded with a review of the work accomplished and the deliverables to determine acceptance, whether extra work is still required or whether the phase should be considered closed. A management review is often held to reach a decision to start the activities of the next phase without closing the current phase, for example, when the project manager chooses fast tracking as the course of action.

Formal phase completion does not include authorizing the subsequent phase. For effective control, each phase is formally initiated to produce a phase-dependent output of the Initiating Process Group, specifying what is allowed and expected for that phase, as shown in figure below. A phase-end review can be held with the explicit goals of obtaining authorization to close the current phase and to initiate the subsequent one. Sometimes, both authorizations can be gained at one review. Phase-end reviews are also called phase exits or phase gates.

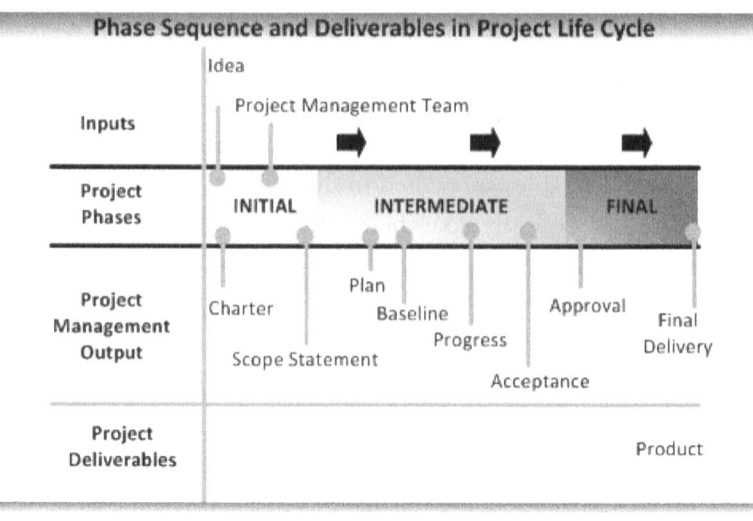

Inputs	Idea	Project Management Team	➡	➡	➡	
Project Phases		INITIAL	INTERMEDIATE		FINAL	
Project Management Output	Charter	Plan Scope Statement	Baseline Progress Acceptance		Approval	Final Delivery
Project Deliverables					Product	

PROJECT LIFE CYCLE AND PRODUCT LIFE CYCLE RELATIONSHIPS

Many projects are linked to the ongoing work of the performing organization. Some organizations formally approve projects only after completion of a feasibility study, a preliminary plan, or some other equivalent form of analysis; in these cases, the preliminary planning or analysis takes the form of a separate project. For example, additional phases could come from developing and testing a prototype prior to initiating the project for the development of the final product.

The driving forces that create the stimuli for a project are typically referred to as problems, opportunities, or business requirements. The effect of these pressures is that management generally must prioritize this request with respect to the needs and resource demands of other potential projects.

The project life cycle definition will also identify which transitional actions at the end of the project are included or not included, in order to link the project to the ongoing operations of the performing organization. Examples would be when a new product is released to manufacturing or a new software program is turned over to marketing. Care should be taken to distinguish the project life cycle from the product life cycle. The following figure illustrates the product life cycle, starting with the business plan, through idea, to product, ongoing operations, and product divestment. The project life cycle goes through a series of phases to create the product. Additional projects can include a performance upgrade to the product. In some application areas, such as new product development or software development, organizations consider the project life cycle as part of the product life cycle.

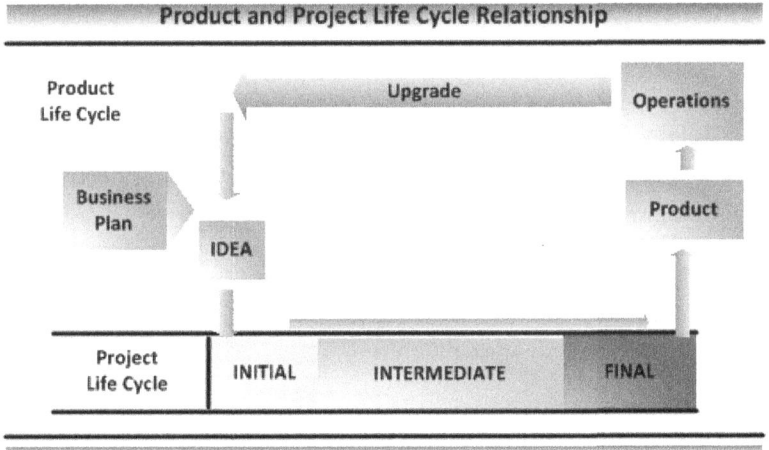

Product and Project Life Cycle Relationship

SAMPLE WORK BREAKDOWN STRUCTURE FOR SOFTWARE

The following Work Breakdown Structure is very detailed and is meant to be tailored to each project's specific tracking needs and requirements.

PROJECT MANAGEMENT ACTIVITIES WBS FORM

Project Management Activities – WBS Form

1. Project Management

• Project Management Plan
  • Define task execution plans
  • Define project schedule/milestones
  • Define prelim software functional requirements
  • Develop project WBS
  • Define Software management metrics process
  • Define/allocate project functions -
    • Hardware engineering
    • Software engineering
    • Configuration Management
    • Software Quality Assurance
    • Project support
    • Software metrics
    • Determine staffing
  • Determine software engineering tool requirements
  • Determine training requirements
  • Plan activities/reviews
• Management Reporting

2. Software Estimation	

1. Preliminary Project Estimate
  • Establish resource estimation method
    • Identify similar old projects
    • Find historical component sizes
    • Develop new function sizes
    • Identify potential risk areas
    • Develop cost/schedule estimation variance
    • Estimate critical computer resources
    • Review/refine with project Personnel
	2. System Requirements Phase Estimate
	  • Establish software estimate file
	  • Develop high-level requirements WBS
	  • Develop baseline software estimates
	  • Peer review of estimate
	  • Refine/record estimates

3. Software Requirements Phase Estimate Update
  • Develop high-level design WBS
  • Develop baseline requirements phase estimates
  • Conduct peer review of estimate
  • Refine/record estimates periodically
	4. Design Phase Estimate Update
	  • Develop detailed CUT WBS
	  • Develop baseline CUT estimates
	  • Peer Review of estimate
	  • Refine/record estimates periodically

5. Code and Unit Test Phase Estimate Update
  • Update detailed WBS
  • Update/revise estimates
	6. Integration Phase Estimate Update
	  • Update detailed WBS
	  • Update/revise estimates
	  • Update/revise risk assessment

• Update/revise risk assessment	• Update/revise O&M estimate
• Develop preliminary O&M estimate	• Formal inspection of estimate
• Peer Review of estimate	
7. Post-Deployment Phase Estimate	
• Close out/report final size, effort, cost estimates and variance	

3. Risk Management	
1. Preliminary Risk Management Plan	**2.** Risk Management Plan Review
• Identify potential risk areas	/Inspection
• Analyze risk areas	• Update Risk Management Plan
• Prioritize risks	• Baseline Risk Management Plan
• Identify risk tracking metrics	• Update/revise risk assessment
• Write Plan	

4. Software Metrics
1. Preliminary Risk Management Plan
• Software Measurement Plan
• Tailor basic metrics process
• Define risk metrics process
• Update Measurement Plan
• Track and analyze cost and schedule variance, progress, code size, critical computer resources, documentation size, requirements testability, Change Requests, build/release content, staffing , computer resource utilization, and defects
• Formal reports
• Report final project analysis

5. System Engineering	
1. Analyze operational requirements	**2.** Define computer resource constraints
• Hardware/software trade-off studies	• Memory
• Sizing/timing studies	• Throughput
• Identify risks	• I/O channel utilization
	• I/O throughput
	• Storage
	• Database overhead
3. Preliminary SSS	**4.** Preliminary IRS
• Define system states	• Identify HWCIs / CSCIs interfaces
• Define modes of operation	• Draw interface diagrams
• Define system capability	• Identify for each interface
• Define external interface requirements	• Timing
• Write external interface descript	• Protocol
• Define physical characteristics	• Priority
• Define system quality requirements	• Unit of measure
• Reliability	• Limits/ranges
• Maintainability	• Data elements
• Availability	• Precision
• Environmental conditions	• SSS/IRS inspection and review

	• System Requirements Review
• Transportability	• Update SSS
• Flexibility and expansion	• Baseline SSS
• Specify design/construct requirements	• Update Preliminary IRS
• Define system workmanship requirements	
• Define system interchange requirements	
• Define system safety requirements	
• Define system security requirements	
• Define system logistics	
• Specify personnel requirements	
• Define training requirements	
• Determine for each System/Segment	
• Purpose	
• Description	
• Identify capabilities	
• Identify requirements precedence	
• QA provisions	
• Inspection responsibility	
• Special Tests and exams	
• Requirements cross reference	

6. Configuration Management	7. Software Quality Assurance
• Preliminary CM Plan	• Preliminary SQA Plan
• CM Plan review/inspection	• Plan software quality metrics process
• Update CM Plan	• SQA plan inspection and review
• Baseline CM Plan	• Update SQA Plan
• Set Up CCB	• Baseline SQA Plan
• Conduct/maintain configuration status accounting	
• Prepare Configuration Status Report	
• Conduct Functional and Physical Configuration Audit	
• Process CR	
• Generate inputs to the software version description	
• Prepare Version Control Reports	

PROJECT DEVELOPMENT CYCLE ACTIVITIES WBS FORM

Development Cycle Activities – WBS form

1. Software Project Plan
• Preliminary SPP
• Define formal review procedures/criteria
• Define Software Development Library procedures
• Define corrective action process
• Define Problem/Change Report Format
• Define design standards
• Define coding standards
• Define testing approach
• Define requirements traceability process
• SPP inspection(s)/review(s)
• Update SPP
• Baseline SPP

2. Interface Requirements	3. Database Requirements
• Analyze Preliminary IRS	• Preliminary Database Design Document
• Interface Design Document	• Analyze database requirements
• Interface (1 – N) define	• Identify data requirements
• Data elements	• Perform database studies
• Message descriptions	• Database Design Document inspection(s)
• Priority	• Participate in High Level Design review
• Communications protocol	• Update Database Design Document
• Interface inspection(s)/walkthrough(s)	• Baseline Database Design Document
• Interface rework	
• Interface Design Document inspection(s)	
• IDD rework	
• Participate in High Level Design review	
• Update Interface Design Document	
• Baseline Interface Design Document	

4. Developmental Software	5. Functional Requirements
• Analyze system requirements	• Analyze CSCI requirements
• Identify software requirements	• Preliminary SRS
• Determine derived software requirements	• Identify internal interfaces
• Identify candidate COTS software	• Identify functional/derived requirements
• Identify candidate reusable software	• Engineering
• Perform feasibility studies	• Data elements

• Select computer language(s) • Allocate functions/identify CSCIs • Determine software requirement testability • CSCI (1 – N)	• Safety • Security • Human engineering • Identify software quality factors • Identify design constraints • Identify qualification methods • Trace requirements to SSS • SRS inspection(s)/review(s) • Software Specification Review • Update SRS • Baseline SRS

6. Preliminary Design	7. Detailed Design

• Preliminary Design analysis
 • Identify SUs or components
 • Identify internal interfaces
 • Identify external interfaces
 • SAD and High Level Design (HLD)
  • Overview
  • Architecture
  • Memory/processing time allocation
  • CSCI design description
 • For SU (1-N)
  • Identify allocated requirements
  • Identify SUs
  • Identify relationships between SUs
  • Data flow and execution control
  • Identify derived requirements
  • Trace requirements to SRS
  • SU inspection(s)/walkthrough(s)
  • SU design rework
 • Preliminary SAD inspection(s)/review(s)
 • Preliminary Design Review
 • Update Preliminary SAD
	• Detailed SAD and Low Level Design
	 • For SU (1-N)
	  • Describe constraints
	  • Describe input/output data elements
	  • Describe local data elements
	  • Describe interrupts and signals
	  • Describe algorithms
	  • Describe data structures
	  • Describe local datafiles / database
	  • Describe limitations
	  • Trace requirements to Preliminary
	   SAD
	  • SU inspection(s)/walkthrough(s)
	  • SU design rework
	 • SAD inspection(s)/review(s)
	 • SAD rework
	 • Critical Design Review
	 • Update SAD
	 • Baseline SAD

8. Code and Unit Test	9. Test Readiness Review

• SU (1 – N)
  • Design/document unit test
  • Code and compile
  • Write comments/header
  • Code inspection(s)/walkthrough(s)
  • Rework
  • Testing and analysis
	• Single Unit integration and testing
	  • Analyze Software Test Report
	  • Perform necessary rework
	  • Perform SU regression testing
	  • Update SDFs
	 • Test readiness review
	 • CSCI integration and testing

• Rework • Maintain SDF • Turn over accepted SU to CM	• Analyze Software Test Report • Perform necessary rework • Perform SU regression testing • Update SDFs

10. Software Integration and Testing	

• Software Test Plan
  • Determine general test requirements
  • Determine test classes
    • Stress
    • Timing
    • Erroneous input
    • Maximum capacity
  • Determine test levels
    • CSCI
    • CSCI to CSCI integration
    • CSCI to HWCI integration
    • System
  • Determine test definitions
  • Test (1 – N)
    • Determine objective
    • Determine special requirements
    • Identify test type/class
    • Determine qualification method
    • Cross reference to SRS requirements
    • Determine type of data to record
    • Identify assumptions/constraints
    • Determine test schedule
    • Identify data analysis techniques
	• Perform Integration & Testing
	  • System
	    • Integrate CSCIs
	    • Write System Test Description
	    • Conduct Test Readiness Review
	    • Perform testing and analysis
	    • Write System Test Report
	    • Rework
	    • Regression testing
	  • CSCI
	    • Integrate SUs
	    • Write Software Test Description
	    • Conduct Test Readiness Review
	    • Perform testing and analysis
	    • Write Software Test Report
	    • Rework
	    • Regression testing
	  • SU
	    • Integrate SUs
	    • Write Software Test Description
	    • Conduct Test Readiness Review
	    • Perform testing and analysis
	    • Write Software Test Report
	    • Testing and analysis
	    • Rework
	    • Regression testing

CMM MATRIX

The following table represents the CMM Matrix cross reference for the software project planning key process area.

Goal/ Key Practice	Sub Key Practice	Description	Relevant Process/ Document description
Goal 1		Software estimates are documented for use in planning and tracking the software project.	
Goal 2		Software project activities and commitments are planned and documented.	
Goal 3		Affected groups and individuals agree to their commitments related to the software project.	
Commitment 1		A project software manager is designated to be responsible for negotiating commitments and developing the project's software development plan.	SPP Process
Commitment 2		The project follows a written organizational policy for planning a software project. This policy typically states that:	SPP Process
	C2.1	The system requirements allocated to software are used as the basis for planning the software project.	
	C2.2	The software project's commitments are negotiated between the project manager, the project software manager and the other software managers.	
	C2.3	Involvement of other engineering groups in the software activities is negotiated with these groups and is documented.	
	C2.4	Affected groups review the software project's software size estimates, effort and cost estimates, schedules, and other commitments.	
	C2.5	Senior management reviews all software project commitments made to individuals and groups external to the organization.	
	C2.6	The project's software development plan is managed and controlled.	
Ability 1		A documented and approved statement of work exists for the software project.	SPP Process
	AB1.1	The statement of work covers scope of the work, technical goals and objectives, identification of customers and end users, imposed standards, assigned responsibilities, cost and schedule constraints and goals, dependencies between the software project and other organizations, resource constraints and goals, and other constraints and goals for development and/or maintenance.	
	AB1.2	The statement of work is reviewed by the project manager, the project software manager, the other software managers, and other affected groups.	
	AB1.3	The statement of work is managed and controlled.	
Ability 2		Responsibilities for developing the software development plan are assigned.	SPP Process/SPP Template
	AB 2.1	The project software manager, directly or by delegation, coordinates the project's software planning.	
	AB2.2	Responsibilities for the software work products and activities are partitioned and assigned to software managers in a traceable accountable manner.	
Ability 3		Adequate resources and funding are provided for planning the software project.	SPP Process/ SPP Template, Org Training Plan
	AB3.1	Where feasible, experienced individuals, who have expertise in the application domain of the software project being planned, are available to develop the software development plan.	
	AB3.2	Tools to support the software project planning activities are made available.	
Ability 4		The software managers, software engineers, and other individuals	Appropriate

		involved in the software project planning are trained in the software estimating and planning procedures applicable to their areas of responsibility.	training courses
Activity 1		The software engineering group participates on the project proposal team.	SPP Process
	AC 1.1	The software engineering group is involved in proposal preparation and submission, clarification discussions and submissions, and negotiations of changes to commitments that affect the software project.	
	AC 1.2	The software engineering group reviews the project's proposed commitments.	
Activity 2		Software project planning is initiated in the early stages of, and in parallel with, overall project planning.	SPP Process
Activity 3		The software engineering group participates with other affected groups in the overall project planning throughout the project's life.	SPP Process
	AC 3.1	The software engineering group reviews the project-level plans.	
Activity 4		Software project commitments made to individuals and groups external to the organization are reviewed with senior management according to a documented procedure.	SPP Process
Activity 5		A software life cycle with predefined stages of manageable size is identified or defined.	SPP Process, Assets doc, SPP Template
Activity 6		The project's software development plan is developed according to a documented procedure. This procedure typically specifies that:	SPP Process, SPP Template
	AC6.1	The software development plan is based on and conforms to the customer's standards, as appropriate; the project's standards; the approved statement of work; and the allocated requirements.	
	AC6.2	Plans for software-related groups and other engineering groups involved in the activities of the software engineering group are negotiated with those groups, the support efforts are budgeted, and the agreements are documented.	
	AC6.3	Plans for involvement of the software engineering group in the activities of other software-related groups and other engineering groups are negotiated with those groups, the support efforts are budgeted, and the agreements are documented.	
	AC6.4	The software development plan is reviewed by the project manager, the project software manager, and other software managers and other affected groups.	
	AC6.5	The software development plan is managed and controlled.	
Activity 7		The plan for the software project is documented. The software development plan covers:	SPP Template
	AC7.1	The software project's purpose, scope, goals, and objectives.	
	AC7.2	Selection of a software life cycle.	
	AC7.3	Identification of the selected procedures, methods, and standards for developing and/or maintaining the software.	
	AC7.4	Identification of software work products to be developed.	
	AC7.5	Size estimates of the software work products and any changes to the software work products.	
	AC7.6	Estimates of the software project's effort and costs.	
	AC7.7	Estimated use of critical computer resources.	
	AC7.8	The software project's schedules, including identification of milestones and reviews.	
	AC7.9	Identification and assessment of the project's software risks.	
	AC7.10	Plans for the project's software engineering facilities and support	

		tools.	
Activity 8		Software work products that are needed to establish and maintain control of the software project are identified.	SPP Template
Activity 9		Estimates for the size of the software work products (or changes to the size of the software work products) are derived according to a documented procedure. This procedure typically states that:	Software Estimation Process
	AC 9.1	Size estimates are made for all major software work products and activities.	
	AC9.2	Software work products are decomposed to the granularity needed to meet the estimating objectives.	
	AC9.3	Historical data are used where available.	
	AC9.4	Size estimating assumptions are documented.	
	AC9.5	Size estimates are documented, reviewed, and agreed to.	
Activity 10		Estimates for the software project's effort and costs are derived according to a documented procedure. This procedure typically specifies that:	Software Estimation Process
	AC10.1	Estimates for the software project's effort and costs are related to the size estimates of the software work products (or the size of the changes)	
	AC10.2	Productivity data (historical and/or current) are used for the estimates when available; sources and rationale for these data are documented.	
	AC10.3	Effort, staffing, and cost estimates are based on past experience.	
	AC10.4	Estimates and the assumptions made in deriving the estimates are documented, reviewed, and agreed to.	
Activity 11		Estimates for the project's critical computer resources are derived according to a documented procedure.	Software Estimation Process
	AC11.1	Critical computer resources for the project are identified.	
	AC11.2	Estimates for the critical computer resources are related to the estimates of the size of the software work products, the operational processing load, and the communications traffic.	
	AC11.3	Estimates of the critical computer resources are documented, reviewed, and agreed to.	
Activity 12		The project's software schedule is derived according to a documented procedure. This procedure typically specifies that:	Software Estimation Process
	AC12.1	The software schedule is related to the size estimate of the software work products (or the size of changes), and the software effort and costs.	
	AC12.2	The software schedule is based on past experience.	
	AC12.3	The software schedule accommodates the imposed milestone dates, critical dependency dates, and other constraints.	
	AC12.4	The software schedule activities are of appropriate duration and the milestones are of appropriate time separation to support accuracy in progress measurement.	
	AC12.5	Assumptions made in deriving the schedule are documented.	
	AC12.6	The software schedule is documented, reviewed, and agreed to.	
Activity 13		The software risks associated with the cost, resource, schedule, and technical aspects of the project are identified, assessed, and documented.	Estimation Process, SPP Template, Risk Mgmt Process, SPP Process
	AC13.1	The risks are analyzed and prioritized based on their potential impact to the project.	
	AC13.2	Contingencies for the risks are identified.	
Activity 14		Plans for the project's software engineering facilities and support	SPP

		tools are prepared.	Template
	AC14.1	Estimates of capacity requirements for these facilities and support tools are based on the size estimates of the software work products and other characteristics.	
	AC14.2	Responsibilities are assigned and commitments are negotiated to procure or develop these facilities and support tools.	
	AC14.3	The plans are reviewed by all affected groups.	
Activity 15		Software planning data are recorded.	Software Estimation Process; SPP Template; SPP Process
	AC 15.1	Information recorded includes the estimates and the associated information needed to reconstruct the estimates and assess their reasonableness.	
	AC15.2	The software planning data are managed and controlled.	
Measurement 1		Measurements are made and used to determine the status of the software planning activities.	Practical Software Measurement
Verification 1		The activities for software project planning are reviewed with senior management on a periodic basis.	SPP Process
	V1.1	The technical, cost, staffing, and schedule performance is reviewed.	
	V1.2	Conflicts and issues not resolvable at lower levels are addressed.	
	V1.3	Software project risks are addressed.	
	V1.4	Action items are assigned, reviewed, and tracked to closure.	
	V1.5	A summary report from each meeting is prepared and distributed to the affected groups and individuals.	
Verification 2		The activities for software project planning are reviewed with the project manager on both a periodic and event-driven basis.	SPP Process
	V2.1	Affected groups are represented.	
	V2.2	Status and current results of the software project planning activities are reviewed against the software project's statement of work and allocated requirements.	
	V2.3	Dependencies between groups are addressed.	
	V2.4	Conflicts and issues not resolvable at lower levels are addressed.	
	V2.5	Software project risks are reviewed.	
	V2.6	Action items are assigned, reviewed, and tracked to closure.	
	V2.7	A summary report from each meeting is prepared and distributed to the affected groups and individuals.	
Verification 3		The software quality assurance group reviews and/or audits the activities and work products for software project planning and report the results. At a minimum, these reviews and/or audits verify:	SQA Process
	V3.1	The activities for software estimating and planning.	
	V3.2	The activities for reviewing and making project commitments.	
	V3.3	The activities for preparing the software development plan.	
	V3.4	The standards used for preparing the software development plan.	
	V3.5	The content of the software development plan.	

SOFTWARE PROJECT PLAN TEMPLATE

Project Management Plan for <Project>
Version 1.0 draft 1
Prepared by <Author>
<Organization>
<Date created>
<Change the footer and header text to reflect the correct copyright information, company name, and project name.>

<TABLE OF CONTENTS>

<Note: This template contains primarily guidance text, shown with in "< >." When creating a project management plan from this template, replace the guidance text with your own specific information for the project. If a section of this template is not applicable to your project, leave the section heading in the plan and briefly state why it does not apply. Feel free to tailor this comprehensive template to best meet the needs of your organization's projects.>

OVERVIEW

<This section provides an overview of the project's motivation, objectives, success criteria, major deliverables, and constraints. You might include a top-level summary of major milestones, required resources, schedule, and budget. >

Project Purpose, Objectives, and Success Criteria

<Define the purpose, scope, and objectives of the project and its delivered products. This information might already appear in the Vision and Scope Document. If so, avoid duplicating information in both places. Briefly state the business needs to be satisfied and the methods by which satisfaction of those needs will be determined. Define quantitative and measurable business objectives. Define the criteria by which key stakeholders will judge how successful the project is. State the relationship of this project to other projects and the integration of this product with other products. Other specific issues to address might include:

- Shared resources and their availability.
- Shared designs, code, and hardware components.
- Feature dependencies.
- Schedule dependencies.

Project Deliverables

<List the major items to be delivered to the customers, subcontractors, integrators, or other parties. As appropriate, list the deliverables, their recipients, interim and final delivery dates, and delivery method.>

Assumptions, Dependencies, and Constraints

<This subsection describes known assumptions upon which the project is based (facts that are known to be true are not assumptions), any external events or externally supplied items upon which the project depends, and the constraints under which the project will be conducted. Of the five project dimensions of features, quality, schedule, cost, and staff, determine and document which are constraints, which are project success drivers, and which are degrees of freedom. Give each assumption, dependency, and constraint a unique identifier, such as AS-1, DE-2, and CO-3, to facilitate referring to them elsewhere.>

References

<List all documents and any other materials used as sources of information for this plan. For online documents, provide hyperlinks wherever possible.>

Definitions and Acronyms

<Define any acronyms or project-specific terms. For each acronym, give both the meaning of the abbreviation and a definition of the item.>

Evolution of the Plan

<Describe the method for producing both scheduled and unscheduled updates to this plan and how the new information will be disseminated. For example, you could state that you will review the plan every time the product requirements specification or certain other major project artifacts are updated or when project constraints or resources change. Alternatively or additionally, you could schedule periodic project reviews at specified milestones and update the plan as needed following each review. Describe mechanisms for

placing the baseline version and future revisions of the plan under configuration control.>

PROJECT ORGANIZATION

<This section describes interfaces to entities outside of the project, identifies the internal project structure, and defines roles and responsibilities for the project.>

External Interfaces

<Describe the organizational boundaries between the project and external entities. Define and describe communication with senior management, customers, subcontractors, purchasing, sales, marketing, legal, finance, procurement, installation and support organizations, standards or certification bodies, auditors, manufacturing, and the like.>

Internal Structure

<Describe the internal structure of the project organization, including interfaces between the units of the software team. It might be helpful to include organization charts or matrix diagrams to illustrate lines of authority, responsibility, and communication. Identify representatives of key units, such as senior management, engineering support functions (configuration management, quality assurance, verification, and validation), and process improvement.>

Roles and Responsibilities

<List the major project team roles and the individuals who will fill these roles, along with the specific responsibilities those individuals will have. Identify the organizational units or project team roles that are responsible for all major work activities and support-

ing processes. Consider the following list of potential project roles, adapted to your organization's local terminology

- project manager
- Product Manager
- Technical Lead
- Software Lead
- Hardware Lead
- Architect
- Systems Engineer
- Requirements Analyst
- Software Engineer
- Hardware Engineer
- Test Engineer
- Configuration Control Board
- Configuration Management Manager or Coordinator
- Quality Assurance Manager, Coordinator, or Engineer
- Technical Applications Support
- Subject Matter Expert

Identify other internal and external project stakeholders who are not specifically members of the project team. Describe their relevance to the project and their degree of interaction for specific project activities. Potential topics to address regarding stakeholders include:

- A list of all relevant stakeholders and the rationale for each stakeholder's involvement
- Project roles and responsibilities of stakeholders during each life cycle phase
- Relationships between stakeholders
- Relative importance of each stakeholder to project success by project phase

- Resources (such as training, materials, time, or funding) needed to ensure adequate stakeholder participation

- Schedule for phasing of stakeholder participation>

MANAGERIAL PROCESS PLANS

<This section defines the various project management plans and activities for the project. >

Startup Plans

<This section specifies plans that will lay a solid foundation for a successful project. Depending on the size and scope of the project, you may incorporate these plans directly in this section, or each section may simply contain a reference or hyperlink to a separate document.>

Estimation Plan

<This section describes how project estimates will be prepared, including:

- The methods, tools, and techniques that will be used to estimate project size, effort, cost, schedule, and critical computer resource requirements.

- The timing of the estimates.

- Who will participate in the estimation process.

- How the estimates will be documented, reviewed, and reported.>

You can include the actual estimates in this section, or they can be stored elsewhere. For each estimate made, document the estimation method used, the assumptions made, and the confidence level for the estimate. Describe the rationale behind contingency buffers incorporated into estimates. Specify the methods to be used periodically to re-estimate the cost, time, and resources needed to complete the project. >

Staffing Plan

<Specify the number of staff needed by skill area or project role (see section 2.3), along with required skill levels, and the duration for which each staff member is needed. Describe the anticipated staffing profile (the mix of skills and effort levels needed at various times in the project), when people will be added to the project or depart from it, and how new team members will be brought up to speed. Specify the sources of the staff: internal from your department, internal from another department within your organization, hiring of a new employee, or hiring of contractors. Document the following information in this section:

- Available internal candidates, their skill sets, and dates of availability
- Requirements for external candidates, including job classifications and descriptions
- Selection of candidates and assignments to tasks
- Availability and duration of assignment for all candidates>

Staff Training Plan

<This section specifies any training that will be needed to ensure the necessary skill levels needed for the project. The types of training, number of people to be trained, and the training methods should be specified. The project manager's responsibilities include identifying training requirements and working with local sources to provide training.>

Resource Acquisition Plan

<This section specifies the plan for acquiring the resources, other than personnel, needed to successfully complete the project. Describe the resource acquisition process. Specify the points in the project schedule when the various acquisition activities will be needed. List any constraints, such as contention for shared resources (e.g., test facilities). Address any known resource issues. Nonhuman resource categories are:

- Development resources: the software and hardware tools required to execute the project (number and size of computers, operating systems, databases, software tools needed, network connectivity needed, CM, and other support tools)

- Test resources: the software and hardware tools required to test the software and integrated products (number and size of computers, operating systems, software products, tools for test case management and test automation, test equipment, and network connectivity); details could appear in the Test Plan

- Product resources: memory, disk, and other resources required by the final product. At the end of development and engineering testing, this product will have its operating environment resources identified, so they can be included in the user documentation that will be part of the product distribution.>

Project Commitments

<Record commitments that the project as a whole is making to external parties, as well as major commitments that one individual or group within the project team is making to another. This gives those involved a clear, shared understanding of their commitments and allows project participants to track whether or not commitments are being fulfilled. A table is a convenient way to record these

commitments. Describe how project commitment changes will be communicated to the affected parties.>

Work Plan

<Specify the various work activities required to produce the project's major deliverables, including contents and timing of the activities. Use a work breakdown structure or a table to depict the work activities, corresponding deliverables, and the relationships among the activities. If the work breakdown structure is stored in a separate location, such as a project-tracking tool, provide a reference or link to that location here. For each work package, specify factors such as staff, budget, and other resources needed, estimated duration, work products to be produced, and predecessor tasks. Decompose tasks to a degree that will permit accurate estimation and will reveal risks and complexity.

Identify major progress milestones at sufficient granularity that tracking against these milestones will indicate whether significant deviations are taking place from the planned objectives. Early milestones provide visibility to see if the project is straying off course.>

Control Plan

<This section describes how the project will control and report on the project status and activities. Specify the frequency at which the various project status indicators are to be monitored and specific events that could trigger a status evaluation.>

Data Control Plan
<Describe how the project will manage its data, including deliverable and non-deliverable documents, project status metrics, reports, specifications, and so on. Address the following:
- Types of data to be managed

- Content and format description where pertinent (such as templates to be used)
- Data requirements lists for suppliers
- Privacy requirements
- Security requirements and procedures
- Mechanisms for data collection, retrieval, distribution, and archiving>

Requirements Control Plan
<Specify the mechanisms for measuring, reporting, and controlling changes to the product requirements. Describe how to assess the impact of requirement changes on product scope and quality, and on project schedule, budget, resources, and risk factors. If a separate change control process is being followed, refer to that here. If changes in requirements affect project schedule or other commitments, update this Project Management Plan, other plans, estimates, and commitments to reflect the changes. Incorporate the tasks and effort to perform the requirements control steps into the project's work breakdown structure and schedule.>

Schedule Control Plan
<Specify the control mechanisms used to measure the progress of the work completed at milestones. Specify the methods and tools used to compare actual schedule performance to planned performance and to implement corrective action when actual performance deviates from planned or required performance. A project schedule in the form of a Gantt chart should be created, preferably in a project-tracking tool. Describe how contingency buffers will be tapped and revised when actual performance falls behind estimates. Describe how and when schedules will be modified and how agreement and commitment to the revised schedules will be achieved.>

Budget Control Plan

<Specify the control mechanisms used to measure the cost of work completed, compare actual to budgeted cost, and implement corrective actions when actual cost deviates excessively from budgeted cost. Specify the intervals or points at which cost reporting is needed and the methods and tools that will be used to manage the budget. For example, you might say that the Department Manager is responsible for forecasting and controlling budgets and expenses on an annual basis, and the project manager is responsible for tracking actual hours and for reporting actual and estimated project hours by milestone to the Department Manager.>

Communication, Tracking, and Reporting Plan

<Identify the regular reports and communications expected of the project, such as weekly status reports, regular reviews, and as-needed communication. The exact types of communication vary between groups, but it is useful to identify the planned means at the start of the project. Specify the reporting mechanisms, report contents, and information flows used to communicate the status of requirements, schedule, budget, quality, risks, and other status indicators both within the project and to external stakeholders. Special communication issues, such as offshore outsourcing, require particular attention. A table is a convenient way to describe the communication expectations.>

Metrics Collection Plan

<Specify the methods, tools, and techniques used to collect and retain project metrics. The metrics to be collected, the collection frequency, and how the metrics will be validated, analyzed, reported, stored, and used should all be addressed.>

Risk Management Plan

<This section specifies the plan for identifying, analyzing, prioritizing, and controlling project risks. It should describe the procedures for contingency planning and the methods used in tracking risks, evaluating changes in individual risk exposures, and responding to those changes. Include a plan for ongoing risk identification throughout the project's life cycle. Document the risks in a separate risk list (possibly an appendix to this plan), not in this section. A large project should create a separate risk management plan. Identify the risk management tasks to be performed, who is responsible for each, and the target date for completion of each task. Estimate the percentage of project effort or the number of hours planned for risk management activities. Incorporate risk management tasks into the project schedule and budget. >

Issue Resolution Plan

<Describe how problems, issues, and action items that arise on the project will be documented, resolved, and tracked to closure. Identify the project's decision makers for issues such as requirements baselining, requirements changes, resource contention, priority conflicts, etc.>

Project Closeout Plan

<This section describes the actions necessary to ensure an orderly closeout of the project. Address staff reassignment, archiving of project materials, recording of metrics, holding a project retrospective, and preparation of a final report to include lessons learned and analysis of project objectives achieved.>

Technical Process Plans

<This section describes the technical approaches to be used on the project. Depending on the size and scope of the project, these plans may be incorporated directly in this section, or each section may simply contain a reference or hyperlink to an external plan. For example, nearly every project should create separate Configuration Management and Quality Assurance Plans.>

Process Model

<Describe the product development life cycle that the project will use. Examples include waterfall, iterative, and incremental (e.g., evolutionary, spiral, or agile). If an iterative or incremental model is used, identify clear milestones and provide the planned iteration number for each task in the work breakdown structure. The project's Gantt chart should reflect the model used. Identify checkpoints at which management reviews are needed.>

Methods, Tools, and Techniques

<This section describes the design and development methodologies, programming languages, software and hardware tools, and operating environments to be used, as well as pertinent technical and management standards and procedures. Describe the following:

- The hardware, OS, and network environments for development, test, and operation

- Software tools, including those for requirements management, design modeling, source code and document version control, compiler or IDE, build automation, and so on

- Development methodologies, including requirements development practices, design methodologies and notations, programming languages, coding standards, documentation standards, and system integration procedure

- Quality assurance practices, including methods of technical peer review, unit testing, debugging tools, defect tracking, integration and system testing, and test automation. The details of these approaches will appear in a separate QA Plan or Test Plan.>

Configuration Management Plan

<This section could contain the configuration management plan for this project. For medium to large projects, this section should refer to a separate document. The CM plan should describe the activities and methods used for configuration identification, control, status accounting, auditing, and release management. The configuration management plan should address the initial baselining of work products, logging and analysis of change requests, change control board procedures, tracking of changes in progress, and procedures for notifying concerned parties when baselines are established and changed. Estimate the percentage of project effort or the number of hours planned for configuration management activities. Incorporate CM tasks into the project schedule and budget. List the personnel responsible for establishing the baselines, maintaining the configuration management system, and conducting CM reviews and audits.>

Quality Assurance Plan

<This section could contain the quality assurance plan for this project. For any but very small projects, this section should refer to a separate document. The QA plan should describe the activities and methods used to build a high-quality product by the sensible application of an appropriate process. The plan should indicate the relationships among the quality assurance, testing (or verification and validation), peer review, audit, and configuration management activities. Identify the quality-related tasks to be performed, who is

responsible for each, and the target date for completion. Estimate the percentage of project effort or the number of hours planned for quality assurance activities. Incorporate QA tasks into the project schedule and budget. List the personnel responsible for performing identified QA tasks.>

Documentation Plan

<Describe the plans for creating system documentation deliverables, including installation and maintenance guides, user guides, reference manuals, online help systems, release notes, and so forth. List the documents to be created. For each type of documentation, describe: any pertinent template, standard, or conventions to be followed; who will prepare it; who will review it; target dates for initial delivery and baselining; and information about recipients, distribution, or storage. A table is a convenient way to record this information.>

Process Improvement Plan

<This section describes plans for assessing the project and its processes, determining areas for process improvement, and implementing improvement plans without seriously disrupting an ongoing project. Each project should address at least one process improvement activity, selected from the following list:

- New procedure or a new example of how to implement an existing procedure or process
- Improved procedure or template based on lessons learned
- New tool or improved use of a current tool

List the specific new process approaches to be tried and the anticipated impacts on the project. As the project progresses, track how the new approaches are being used, how they are affecting the project, and whether they had to be modified. Capture lessons learned from these experiences during the project retrospective.

ABBREVIATIONS AND ACRONYMS

- AC- Actual Cost: formerly called Actual Cost of Work Performed (ACWP), is the total of direct and indirect costs incurred in accomplishing work on an activity during a given period.

- ACT - Annual Change Traffic: The fraction of the software product's source code which changes during a year, either through addition or modification. The ACT can be used to determine the product size in order to estimate software maintenance effort.

- ACWP - Actual Cost of Work Performed: is total costs actually incurred and recorded in accomplishing work performed during a given time period for a schedule activity or work breakdown structure component or a project. Actual cost can sometimes be direct labor hours alone, direct costs alone, or all costs including indirect costs.

- ASP - Application Service Provider: is a business that provides computer-based services to customers over a network.

- BAC - Budget at Completion: is the total planned value (PV or BCWS) at the end of the project.

- BCWP - Budgeted Cost of Work Performed: is commonly known as Earned Value (EV).

- BCWS - Budgeted Cost of Work Scheduled: is also referred to as Planned Value (PV).

- CCB - Change Control Board: is a committee that makes decisions regarding whether or not proposed changes to a software project should be implemented. The change control board is constituted of project stakeholders or their representatives.

- CCM–Configuration Change Management: This refers to the process that is followed to manage the changes that may occur in the configuration management process and is described in the configuration management plan document or software project plan document of a project.

- CI- Configuration Item: refers to the fundamental structural unit of a configuration management system. Examples of CIs include individual requirements documents, software, models, plans, etc.

- CM- Configuration Management: is a field of project management that focuses on establishing and maintaining consistency of a system or product's performance and its functional and physical attributes with its requirements, design, and operational information throughout its life.

- CMM- Capability Maturity Model: describes the principles and practices underlying software process maturity. It is intended to help software organizations improve the maturity of their software processes in terms of an evolutionary path from ad hoc, chaotic processes to mature, disciplined software processes. The focus is on identifying key process areas and the exemplary practices that may comprise a discipliCMP- Configuration Management Plan: is a document that defines how the project office will maintain control of project baselines and items that must be tracked and managed in a formal and systematic fashion.

- COCOMO -The COnstructive COst Model: is an algorithmic software cost estimation model developed by Barry Boehm. The model uses a basic regression formula, with parameters that are derived from historical project data and current project characteristics.

- COTS - Commercial, off-the-shelf: is a term defining technology which is ready-made and available for sale, lease, or license to the general public. The term often refers to computer software or hardware systems and may also include free software with commercial support.

- CPI - Cost Performance Index: provides the actual cost efficiency of a project. The CPI is determined by measuring the ratio of Earned Value to Actual Costs. A CPI value equal to or greater than 1 represents a favorable condition, whereas a value less than 1 indicates that the cost performance is not good.

- CR - Change Request: is a document containing a call for an adjustment of a system. It is of great importance in the change management process.

- CSA - Configuration Status Accounting: is the process of creating and organizing the knowledge base necessary for the performance of configuration management. In addition to facilitating configuration management, the purpose of CSA is to provide a highly reliable source of configuration information to support all program/project activities including program management, systems engineering, software development and maintenance, logistic support, modification, and maintenance.

- CSCI - Configuration Software Configuration Item: This specifically refers to a software configuration item such as source code, process documents, requirements, test scripts, and so on.

- CUT - Code and Unit Testing: refers to one of the phases of project life cycle in which code development and unit level testing is carried out.

- CV - Cost Variance: indicates how much over or under budget the project is. It is calculated as a difference between the Earned Value (EV) and Actual Cost (AC). Positive cost variance indicated the project is under budged and a negative cost variance indicates the project is over budget.

- EAC - Estimate At Completion: is the project manager's projection of total cost of the project at completion.

- ETVX - Entry Criteria, Task, Validation, Exit criteria.

- EV- Earned Value: The earned value (EV), formerly called the Budgeted Cost of Work Performed (BCWP), is an estimate of the value of the physical work actually completed. EV is based on the original planned costs for the project or activity and the rate at which the team is completing work on the project or activity to date.

- EVM- Earn Value Management: is a project management technique for measuring project performance and progress in an objective manner. EVM has the ability to combine measurements of scope, schedule, and cost in a single integrated system. Earned Value Management is notable for its ability to provide accurate forecasts of project performance problems.

- FCA - Functional Configuration Audit: The FCA is the formal examination of the "as-tested" functional characteristics of a configuration item (CI). The audit is to verify that the item has achieved the requirements specified in its functional baseline documentation, and to identify and record any discrepancies. Functional configuration audits are conducted on both hardware and software configuration items to assure that the technical documentation accurately reflects the functional characteristics of each

- FMEA - Failure Mode and Effect Analysis: is a procedure in product development and operations management for analysis of potential failure modes within a system for classification by the severity and likelihood of the failures.

- FSD - Functional Specification Document: is the documentation used in systems engineering and software development that describes the requested behavior of an engineering system. The documentation typically describes what is needed by the system user as well as requested properties of inputs and outputs of the system being developed.

- GUI - Graphical User Interface: is a type of user interface that allows users to interact with electronic devices with images rather than text commands. A GUI represents the information and actions available to a user through graphical icons and visual indicators such as secondary notation, as opposed to text-based interfaces, typed command labels or text navigation. The actions are usually performed through direct manipulation of the graphical elements.

- HLD- High Level Design: provides an overview of a solution, platform, system, product, service, or process. It briefly describes all platforms, systems, products, services and processes that it depends upon and includes any important changes that need to be made to them. A high-level design document will usually include a high-level architecture diagram depicting the components, interfaces and networks that need to be further specified or developed. The document may also depict or otherwise refer to work flows and/or data flows between component systems. In addition, there should be brief consideration of all significant commercial, legal, environmental, security, safety and technical risks, issues and assumptions.

- HWCI - Hardware Configuration Item: This specifically refers to a hardware configuration item such as computer systems, input output devices, printers, and so on.

- IEEE - Institute of Electrical and Electronics Engineers: It is World's largest professional association for the advancement of technology.

- IDD - Interface Design Description: describes the interface characteristics of one or more systems, subsystems, Configuration Items (CIs), manual operations, or other system components. An IDD may describe any number of interfaces. These are generally documented in Software Architecture Document (SAD).

- IRS - Interface Requirements Specification: specifies the requirements imposed on one or more systems, subsystems, Configuration Items (CIs), manual operations, or other system components to achieve one or more interfaces among these entities. This can be documented in requirement specification document.

- IT - Information Technology: the study, design, development, implementation, support or management of computer-based information systems, particularly software applications and computer hardware.

- KSLOC - Thousands of Source Line Of Code

- LAN - Local Area Network: is a computer network that connects computers and devices in a limited geographical area such as home, school, computer laboratory or office building.

- LCC - Life Cycle Cost: is sum of all recurring and one-time (non-recurring) costs over the full life span or a specified period of a good, service, structure, or system. In includes purchase price, installation cost, operating costs, maintenance and upgrade costs, and remaining (residual or salvage) value at the end of ownership or its useful life.

- LLD- Low Level Design: provides a complete and detailed specification of the design for the software that will be developed in the project, including the classes, member and non-member functions, and associations between classes that are involved.

- O&M - Operations & Maintenance

- PCA - Physical Configuration Audit: is the formal examination of the "as-built" configuration of a configuration item against its technical documentation to establish or verify the configuration item's product baseline. The PCA is used to examine the actual configuration of the Configuration Item (CI) that is representative of the product configuration in order to verify that the related design documentation matches the design of the deliverable CI. It is also used to validate many of the supporting processes that the contractor uses in the production of the CI.

- PDCA - Plan Do Check Act: is an iterative four-step problem-solving process typically used in business process improvement. It is also known as the Deming circle/cycle/wheel, Shewhart cycle, control circle/cycle, or plan–do–study–act (PDSA).

- PERT - Program Evaluation and Review Technique: is a model for project management designed to analyze and represent the tasks involved in completing a given project.

- PM - Project Manager

- PMBOK - Project Management Body Of Knowledge: is a term that describes knowledge in the profession of project management.

- PMI - Project Management Institute: is World's leading professional association for project management.

- PMO - Project Management Office: is the department or group that defines and maintains the standards of process, generally related to project management, within the organization. The PMO strives to standardize and introduce economies of repetition in the execution of projects.

- PoC - Proof of Concept: is realization of a certain method or idea(s) to demonstrate its feasibility, or a demonstration in principle, whose purpose is to verify that some concept or theory is probably capable of being useful.

- PV- Planned Value: formerly called the Budgeted Cost of Work Scheduled (BCWS), also called the budget, is that portion of the approved total cost estimate planned to be spent on an activity during a given period.

- QA - Quality Assurance: is the systematic monitoring and evaluation of the various aspects of a project, service or facility to maximize the probability that minimum standards of quality are being attained by the production process. Two principles included in QA are: "Fit for purpose" - the product should be suitable for the intended purpose; and "Right first time" - mistakes should be eliminated. QA includes regulation of the quality of raw materials, assemblies, products and components, services related to production, and management, production and inspection processes.

- RAD- Rapid Application Development: refers to a type of software development methodology that uses minimal planning in favor of rapid prototyping. The "planning" of software developed using RAD is interleaved with writing the software itself. The lack of extensive pre-planning generally allows software to be written much faster, and makes it easier to change requirements.

- REVIC- Revised Enhanced Version of Intermediate COCOMO

- ROM - Rough Order of Magnitude: is also called ball park estimate and provides a high level effort and cost effort required to complete a work item or project.

- RP-Rate of Performance: is the ratio of actual work completed to the percentage of work planned to have been completed at any given time during the life of the project or activity.

- RPN - Risk Priority Number: is a technique for analyzing the risk associated with potential problems identified during a Failure Mode and Effects Analysis (FMEA). The

RPN value for a risk determines the priority with which the risk should be handled.

- RUP- Rational Unified Process: is a comprehensive process framework that provides industry-tested practices for software and systems delivery and implementation and for effective project management.

- SAD- Software Architecture Document: provides a comprehensive architectural overview of the system, using a number of different architectural views to depict different aspects of the system.

- SDF- Software Development Folder: Is a computer system folder in which all the relevant artifacts with respect to the project development activity are stored.

- SEF- Software Estimation Folder: is the folder which contains all the relevant information with respect to project estimation.

- SLOC- Source Line Of Code: is a software metric used to measure the size of a software program by counting the number of lines in the text of the program's source code. SLOC is typically used to predict the amount of effort that will be required to develop a program, as well as to estimate programming productivity or effort once the software is produced.

- SPI- Schedule Performance Index: It is a measure of project efficiency. A SPI score of 1 or greater is an optimum goal as it shows that the project is on track and has favorable conditions of meeting the required goals. However, a SPI value less than 1 should be avoided as it indicates that the project is not on track.

- SPP- Software Project Plan: is a comprehensive document that contains the processes, methods, and execution strategy that is required for the development of a product.

- SQA- Software Quality Assurance: consists of a means of monitoring the software engineering processes and methods used to ensure quality. The methods by which this is accomplished are many and varied, and may include ensuring conformance to one or more standards, such as ISO 9000 or a model such as CMMI.

- SRS- Software Requirement Specification: a requirements specification for a software system - is a complete description of the behavior of a system to be developed. It includes a set of use cases that describe all the interactions the users will have with the software. Use cases are also known as functional requirements. In addition to use cases, the SRS also contains non-functional (or supplementary) requirements. Non-functional requirements are requirements which impose constraints on the design or implementation (such as performance engineering requirements, quality standards, or design constraints).

- SSS- System and Subsystem Specification: specifies the requirements for a system or subsystem and the methods to be used to ensure that each requirement has been met. Requirements pertaining to system or subsystem's external interfaces may be presented in the SSS or in one or more IRS referenced from the SSS.

- SU- Software Unit: is the lowest group of software code created to perform a specified function or functions. It is an element of a computer software component that is separately testable.

- SV- Schedule Variance: Schedule Variance indicates how much ahead or behind schedule the project is. It is calculated as the difference between Earned value (EV) and Planned Value (PV). Positive variance indicates that the project is ahead of schedule and negative variance indicates that the project is behind schedule.

- TAB- Technical Advisory Board: is a group of technical experts that provides technical advice to the project team. This kind of group can be created for managing software change request or any other activity where technical support is required.

- WBS- Work Breakdown Structure: is a tool used to define and group a project's discrete work elements in a way that helps organize and define the total work scope of the project. A work breakdown structure element may be a product, data, a service, or any combination. A WBS also provides the necessary framework for detailed cost estimating and control along with providing guidance for schedule development and control. Additionally the WBS is a dynamic tool and can be revised and updated as needed by the project manager.

ENDNOTES

1   James Lewis, "Mastering Project Management," New York: McGraw Hill, 1998.

2   Matt Klein, "Powerful Project Management: A Balanced Blend of Art and Science," last modified January 26, 2006, http://www.allpm.com/modules.php?op=modload&name= News&file=article&sid=1476.

3   Kate Belzer, "Project Management: Still more art than science," accessed April 19, 2008, http://www.pmforum. org/library/papers/2001/ArtthanScience.pdf.

4   "Project Management–Wikipedia, the free encyclopedia," accessed June 09, 2010, http://en.wikipedia.org/wiki/ Project_management.

5   "All about project management," accessed September 15, 2008, http://managementhelp.org/plan_dec/project/project.htm.

6   John Katzenbach, "Wisdom of Teams: Creating the high-performance organization," Harvard Business School press, 1994.

7   Francis Fukuyama, " Trust," Penguin Books, 1995

8   Project Management Institute, "A guide to project the project management body of knowledge," in *Project Scope Management,* ed. PMI Standards Committee, (North Carolina: PMI Publication Division, 2000), 47–50.

9   Max Wideman, "Max's project management wisdom," accessed August 12, 2010, http://www.maxwideman.com/guests/scope/definition.htm.

10 William Pinkerton, "Project Management," McGraw Hill, 2003.

11 Flavio Roberto and Sandro Cabral, "FEMA and PMBOK applied to project risk management," *Journal of Information Systems and Technology Management*, V01.5, No. 2, 2008: 347–364.

12 James P. Lewis, "The world class project manager," Boston: Perseus, 2000.

13 "Critical Path Analysis and PERT Charts," accessed on June 08, 2009, http://www.mindtools.com/critpath.html.

14 Capers Jones, "Applied Software Measurements, 2nd edition," McGraw Hills,1997.

15 Eric Matson, "The Seven Sins of Deadly Meetings," accessed June 09, 2008, http://www.fastcompany.com/magazine/02/meetings.html#.

16 IEEE, "IEEE standard for software verification and validation plan," accessed on Jul 31, 2009, http://ieeexplore.ieee.org/ie15/2487/1028/00026585.pdf.

17 Tom Peters and Bob Waterman, "In search of excellence" New York: Warner, 1984.

18 "Pareto chart," accessed August 10, 2008, http://en.wikipedia.org/wiki/Pareto_chart.

19 "Fishbone diagram–A problem analysis tool," accessed July 10, 2009, http://quality.enr.state.nc.us/tools/fishbone.htm.

20 "Ishikawa diagram–One of the basic tools of quality," accessed August 10, 2009, http://en.wikipedia.org/wiki/Ishikawa_diagram.

21 "Pareto chart," accessed August 10, 2008, http://www.isixsigma.com/index.php?option=com_k2&view=item&id=1268:pareto-chart-bar-chart-histogram-and-the-pareto-principle-80/20-rule&Itemid=209.

22 Parviz F. Rad, "Project Estimating and Cost Management," Project Management Institute, 2001.

Lightning Source UK Ltd.
Milton Keynes UK
UKOW07f1114090215

245928UK00001B/298/P